1938

1938
American Historical Panorama

Sheldon Spear

ARCHWAY
PUBLISHING

Archway Publishing books may be ordered
through booksellers or by contacting:

Archway Publishing
1663 Liberty Drive
Bloomington, IN 47403
www.archwaypublishing.com
844-669-3957

ISBN: 978-1-6657-4027-2 (sc)
ISBN: 978-1-6657-4028-9 (e)

Library of Congress Control Number: 2023904661

Print information available on the last page.

Archway Publishing rev. date: 05/03/2023

CONTENTS

DEDICATION

To the future generation, my granddaughters Erin and Paige Greenfield, Zoe and Cora Spear, and Miriam and Ruth Lemberg-Spear. And in memory of Marilyn Spear, my sister, Robert "Sandy" Sanjour, my brother-in-law, Matt Kruger, my friend, and Bob Mittrick, my colleague.

INTRODUCTION

Books on history take a variety of forms. They can be biographical or autobiographical, short or lengthy monographs, or highly analytical studies sometimes influenced by other social sciences, especially economics.

Included too are books that focus on short, or relatively short time periods. The late Barbara Tuchman wrote a number of these, the best known of which are *The Guns of August* (on the weeks leading to the outbreak of the First World War), *The Proud Tower* (on Europe at the turn of the twentieth century), and *A Distant Mirror* (on the curious resemblance of the fourteenth century to the twentieth). American journalist Otto Friedrich authored *Before the Deluge,* a portrait of Berlin in the decade before the ascent of Nazism. Another genre consists of books that concentrate on a single year or less. One excellent example is British scholar Giles MacDonogh's *1938. Hitler's Gamble,* which details the Nazi leader's overcoming the still formidable opposition to him within the army's leadership ranks and his cowing of Britain and France in the months before the Munich Agreement.

Public historian Jay Winik has produced two fine books of this type on American history: *April 1865: The Month that Saved America* and *1944: FDR and the Year that Changed History.* Nineteen twenty and nineteen twenty-seven have drawn the talents of three writers: Eric Burns' *1920: The Year that Made the Decade Roar;* Gerald Leinwand's *1927: High*

Tide of the Twenties; and Bill Bryson's *One Summer: America, 1927.*

With a bit of trepidation, I followed the coverage pattern of the last three studies, which eventually resulted in *1938: American Historical Panorama.* As an historically knowledgeable cousin of mine reminded me, other years in our country's past were equally characterized by innovation and/or chaos. I agreed. But perhaps 1938, a year of general peace – with the exception of major wars in Spain and China – is at least near the top of the innovation-chaos continuum.

Autumn of 1938 brought one of the worst hurricanes to ravage American soil since the beginning of European colonization. The storm of September 21st killed approximately 680 people, and that was more than the 1871 Chicago Fire and the 1906 San Francisco Earthquake combined. Eastern Long Island and most of New England were devastated. The storm's destructiveness can perhaps best be grasped by its felling of 275,000,000 trees!

Although the world was still generally at peace in 1938, the prospects of the U. S. being drawn into a future war were increasing. Germany seemed to be pushing Europe into another general conflict, and its espionage agents were already active here. Just as ominous was Japan's vicious aggression against China, some of which touched Americans. For example, in December 1937 Japanese aircraft sank the U. S. Navy gunboat *Panay.* It had been cruising the Yangtze River in case it was needed to safeguard the lives of Americans during the assault on Nanking. Later, in the summer of 1938, while flying over Chinese soil, an American civilian plane suffered a similar fate. Meanwhile, across the world in Spain, approximately two thousand volunteers from the U. S. eventually joined the conflict against General Franco's rebels who were heavily supported by Germany and Italy. More than eight hundred Americans died in the Spanish Civil War.

Members of the Abraham Lincoln Battalion and their compatriots fighting in Spain were genuine heroes, though not always recognized as such at home. There was little if any discord, however, about the heroic qualities of pioneer aviators. Charles A. Lindbergh had long led the field due to his 1927 solo transatlantic flight. But by the late thirties, his status had declined because of his obvious admiration for Hitler's Germany. Howard Hughes, a one-time and future movie producer, had broken several speed records in flights over U. S. territory. In 1938, with a small crew and an ultra-modern plane he himself had partly designed, Hughes became the nation's new top aviator by breaking the record for circumnavigating the globe.

Nineteen thirty-eight also saw the advent of the superhero. Two young men from a Jewish immigrant neighborhood of Cleveland, writer Jerry Siegel and artist Joe Shuster, sold Superman to a comic book company. He became popular immediately and, in time, there was a Superman comic strip, a radio show, a movie serial, and several TV shows and feature films. This superhero also inspired others, such as Batman, Captain Marvel, and Wonder Woman. Unfortunately for Jerry and Joe, corporate interests kept them from making the huge profits they thought they deserved for their creative efforts.

Franklin D. Roosevelt was a bit of a superhero himself – certainly among the most popular of U. S presidents. His New Deal clearly dominated the country's politics. Yet the miseries associated with the Great Depression, before and during 1938, stimulated the growth of radical groups of both the left and the right.

Membership in the Communist Party of the United States rose from 7,000 in 1930 to 75,000 in 1938, not counting "fellow travelers." Massive unemployment certainly aided recruitment, but so did the party's embrace of idealistic causes. That strategy drew many intellectuals and young people. At least half the

Americans fighting fascism in Spain, for instance, were party members.

Extremism of the right was also part of the country's political life by 1938. There were numerous right-wing organizations, though many of them were small. They differed from conservatives by their focus on white supremacy, anti-Semitism, and fulsome praise for European fascism. The two largest groups were probably the German-American Bund and the followers of Father Charles E. Coughlin.

The Bund was outwardly more akin to Germany's Nazis than any other neo-fascist group in the U. S. Most of its members were German-born aliens whose uniforms included Swastika arm bands and military-style gray shirts similar to those worn by Hitler's Brown Shirts. Father Coughlin evolved from an ordinary Catholic priest in a Detroit-area parish to an enthusiastic supporter of the New Deal and, by 1938, to a fervent acolyte of Hitler and Mussolini. His success largely stemmed from skillful radio broadcasts that attracted millions.

Nineteen thirty-eight was not a good year economically for America. A modest recovery had been visible from 1933 to the spring of 1937, but by the fall of the latter year there was "a recession within a recession," (also called "the Roosevelt recession" by his political foes). The situation improved somewhat by the summer of 1938, although a really strong economy did not become apparent before the rearmament drive of 1940-41.

Still, for many people, life had its positive side. The "Kings of Swing" – bandleaders Benny Goodman, Tommy Dorsey, Artie Shaw, and many others – brought the variety of Jazz known as Swing to the height of its popularity. The wild dancing, or jitterbugging, of teenagers often accompanied the frenetic rhythms. And even at home residents could engage in listening or even dancing to the lively songs emanating from their radios or phonographs.

Radio was one of the two mass entertainment media of 1938. It provided millions with varied programming, including adventure shows, comedy, music of all kinds, and news programs. Movies were the other form of mass entertainment. A lack of realism characterized both media. The cinematic world was largely devoid of poverty, conflicts of interest, ideological ferment, and realistic sexuality. Yet it was by no means lacking in entertainment value, and at very reasonable prices.

For people who liked to read, there was no shortage of material and plenty of diversity. Novelists and mystery writers active in 1938 included Daphne du Maurier, Agatha Christie, James T. Farrell, Richard Wright, Margaret Mitchell, Dashiell Hammett, Raymond Chandler, and numerous others. Excellent plays, such as John Steinbeck's *Of Mice and Men*, Thornton Wilder's *Our Town*, and Robert Sherwood's *Abe Lincoln in Illinois* were available to those who could afford Broadway prices.

Yet despite the excitement surrounding novels and plays, newspaper and magazine readers far outnumbered bookworms and playgoers. In the absence of television and online programming, newspapers – far more numerous than today's counterparts – provided most of the information reaching the general public.

Americans were also sports enthusiasts, with baseball as their "national pastime." Nineteen thirty-eight was clearly an exciting major league season. Its most memorable moments involved Detroit Tigers' first baseman Hank Greenberg's quest to surpass Babe Ruth's record of sixty homeruns set in 1927. Greenberg had to confront not only the tensions on the field but the continued popularity of the retired Babe and the stimulus to anti-Semitism provoked by the challenger's Jewish ethnicity. For these reasons and others, Hank fell two homers short of tying and three short of breaking the Babe's record.

Acknowledgements are due to the many authors whose works assisted me in writing this book. Accessibility was made possible through inter-library loan, particularly through the cooperation of the staff of the Back Mountain Public Library in Dallas, Pennsylvania. The assistance of the Osterhout Public Library in Wilkes-Barre, Pennsylvania was also useful. With respect to Chapter Eight, *Dealing with Nazi Anti-Semitism*, the services of the Franklin D. Roosevelt Presidential Library in Hyde Park, N. Y. and the New York Public Library were crucial. Good friend Marybeth Goll provided me with a copy of the September 19th, 1938 issue of LIFE magazine.

Technically I owe a lot to Maryanne Sadowski, librarian at King's College in Wilkes-Barre who helped me gain access to articles from the *New York Times*, available through the college's data base. I was also assisted in this effort by my late friend Matthew Kruger. Had he lived, the electronically knowledgeable Matt also would have written a chapter for this book about the important advances in the field of television during the year 1938. Cousin Rafael Chaiken furnished me with useful information on publishing possibilities. His father, Dr. Seth Chaiken, contributed a chapter on Philo T. Farnsworth, a major inventor of television. And my friend Harvey Rappaport provided guidance in the selection of photographic illustrations.

My children – Jennifer, Geoffrey, and Eric Spear – were extremely helpful in assisting me with issues that sometimes bedeviled this computer semi-literate. In fact, Jennifer could be deemed the book's loving technical adviser. Finally, my wife Marsha Spear suggested a title, related information about her late uncle Milton Cooper, a Spanish Civil War veteran, and cheered me with her usual encouragement and love.

CHAPTER 1

The Great Long Island/New England Hurricane of September 21, 1938

The periodic hurricane seasons are a reminder that such storms constitute the most powerful natural force affecting Planet Earth. One of the most devastating was the Great Long Island/New England hurricane of September 21st, 1938, which killed more people – 680 – than the 1906 San Francisco Earthquake and the 1871 Chicago Fire combined.

Atlantic hurricanes form near the Cape Verde Islands off the coast of West Africa. Aram Goudsouzian, a recent historian of the 1938 storm, succinctly describes the genesis and development of such storms:

> In this belt, the equatorial sun heats the ocean's surface, causing evaporation. The column of hot, humid air then ascends and cools. Water vapor condenses into water drops, releasing energy and generating heat, which keeps the air rising. The air pressure at the surface plunges – the signature of a developing hurricane. Strong winds form when air rushes in to fill the void left by the column of ascending air. Because the earth rotates, these winds follow a circular

> pattern … Given proper conditions – humid air,
> constant winds, warm surface water – these
> spiraling winds can accelerate, and the system
> can become a hurricane…[1]

By September 10th, 1938 a system, such as the one described by Goudsouzian, had evolved into a tropical storm which the prevailing easterly winds pushed westward across the Atlantic. A Brazilian freighter located it on September 16th about ten degrees west of the Caribbean islands. Pulling in more water vapor, its wind speeds now approached one hundred miles per hour, causing the U. S. Weather Bureau to upgrade the tropical storm to a hurricane.

By September 20th the hurricane was centered a few miles east of the Bahamas. But instead of ravaging these islands, the state of Florida, and the mid-Atlantic coast, it moved northward in response to a high-pressure movement from the west. At the same time another high-pressure system, north of Bermuda, prevented movement out to sea. Between noon and two in the afternoon the New Jersey coast and parts of New York City suffered what in retrospect turned out to be moderate damage. However, landfall on eastern Long Island's southern coast – for thirty minutes beginning at ten minutes past two in the afternoon – revealed the storm's full potential.

Many elements contributed to what became a huge weather-related disaster. First, ordinary people as well as "experts" simply did not expect a devastating hurricane to hit Long Island and most of New England. There was at least some justification for this view since the last similar storm had occurred in 1815 – far beyond the memory of the living. Much more remote in time was the super New England storm of 1635. In either case, however, far fewer people had resided in vulnerable coastal areas than was the case in 1938.

Collateral weather conditions also contributed appreciably to the hurricane's ferocity. The summer of 1938 had been abnormally rainy in the northeast so that the ground was saturated. This would enable the September storm to feed off rising warm water vapor far longer than if the summer had been drier. Simultaneously the heavy rainfall had pushed rivers and creeks to levels not far below their respective flood stages. High tides also happened to be at their peak by September 21st.

Moreover, human defenses were very much weaker than they would become in subsequent decades. Missing were radar and current television weather reports employing on-the-scene observers, all of which would lead to timely evacuation orders. Weather forecasters on 1938 relied heavily on reports of data from private ships, which usually took several hours to process. Not until a future generation would the U. S. Weather Bureau possess the tools of modern meteorology: radar, jet aircraft, and satellites equipped with TV cameras. According to one sarcastic chronicler, 1938-vintage technological devices were "the 16th century thermometer, the 17th century mercurial barometer, and the medieval weather vane."[2] It was not until *1958* that the National Hurricane Center was created.

Given these limitations, forecasters did not usually announce a storm until its impact was imminent. The Jacksonville office of the U. S. Weather Bureau had predicted a hurricane event for Florida; but for reasons already discussed, it never occurred. Only a very junior employee in the Washington, D. C. Bureau office accurately forecast the storm's direction, speed, and intensity, but he was overruled by his superior and the entire senior staff. The Bureau's ineptitude guaranteed that the element of surprise would be a deadly one.

Eastern Long Island's Suffolk County was the first area to receive the hurricane's full wrath. The first wave accompanying the storm crashed upon the shore with such force that it was recorded on a seismograph in Alaska! The Bellport, Long Island Coast Guard Station later reported that its barometer had fallen to 27.94, the lowest reading ever recorded on land in the northeast. Of the 179 houses in Westhampton, 153 either collapsed or were swept out to sea. Southampton, East Hampton, and other upscale communities suffered similar damage. The county's death total was in the neighborhood of fifty. (Given the racist outlook of the day, a *New York Times account* could not refrain from reporting that "two Negro women were listed as missing at Southampton ...."[3]

Author Barrington Boardman recounts a bit of black humor concerning the "Long Island Express." A Suffolk County resident had ordered a barometer through the mail from a Manhattan store. It arrived on the morning of September 21st. The needle pointed below twenty-eight, where the dial indicated "Hurricanes and Tornados." When banging the instrument against the wall did not budge the needle, the owner assumed a malfunction and drove to the local post office to return the item. While he was gone, his house blew away.[4]

Traveling at sixty miles per hour, the fastest moving speed ever recorded for a hurricane, the storm crossed Long Island Sound to ravage the coast of eastern Connecticut and Rhode Island. Residents there were not forewarned because of the outage of electric, telephone, and telegraph service on Long Island. The storm's power intensified when it combined with a frontal system along the Connecticut River Valley. Up to seventeen inches of rainfall would result over several hours. Casualties and destruction of property were extraordinarily high throughout much of New England. For example, the storm surge swept a number of unwary beach strollers to their deaths while others, seeking refuge on the top floors of their beach-front cottages, found none. Others drowned in their cars or were killed by falling trees or telephone poles.

Among the houses destroyed was that of actress Katharine Hepburn's family on the Connecticut coast. The dislodged structure floated one-third of a mile downstream before getting stuck on a stone bridge near the mouth of the Connecticut

River.[5] River flooding caused serious damage to towns and farms along or near their banks.

The hurricane was disastrous to the little state of Rhode Island and particularly to its state capital, Providence – situated on the Providence River and the northern shore of Narragansett Bay. A one-hundred-foot wave rolling over the city left thirteen feet of water in downtown streets. It would be two weeks before central city was reopened to traffic and (somewhat) normal business life resumed. Providence and other devastated towns also experienced looting, which unfortunately is a common post-disaster occurrence. State governments responded by imposing martial law.[6]

The hurricane continued through New England on a north-northwest path, producing flooding and winds averaging 121 miles per hour. Employees at the Blue Hill Observatory near Boston measured one gust at 186 miles per hour. Sea water killed vegetation twenty miles inland, and tides rose to seventeen feet above the mean high-water level. Ocean salt sprayed windows as far north as Montpelier, Vermont, which is located 120 miles from the New England coast. A survivor in New Hampshire's White Mountains characterized the destruction in that area as nearly as bad as what he had witnessed on World War I's Western Front.

Finally, in the morning hours of September 22nd, the storm faded away in Canada's Province of Quebec. Losses were enormous. As indicated, 680 people died and 63,000 were left homeless. Nine thousand buildings were destroyed and 15,000 damaged. Five hundred thousand electricity customers lost their service, as did a comparable number of telephone users. An estimated 26,000 autos were smashed or otherwise rendered useless, while regional rail service was disrupted for weeks. Fishing fleets and maritime communities were nearly wiped out; and hundreds of New England's landmark church steeples lay toppled. But perhaps most dramatic of all, the storm felled the staggering total of 275,000,000 trees!

Though less catastrophic, destruction along the hurricane's western fringes was not inconsequential. Winds and high waves along the New Jersey coast damaged boardwalks and pavilions. Further north, grateful officials at the state's Palisades Park credited dam-building beavers with keeping flooding to a minimum.[7] Across the Hudson River, New York City suffered what one of its newspapers termed a "near-hurricane." Specifically, this included the uprooting of numerous trees, especially in Central Park and in the Boroughs of Brooklyn and Queens. Flooding closed many streets, highways, bridges, tunnels, and portions of the subway system. The city's initial casualty count found ten dead, five injured, and two missing. Even as far west as Middletown and Port Jervis, New York, there were downed trees and power outages.[8]

The Great Hurricane of 1938 brought permanent changes, such as the shape of the New England coastline. But probably the long-term consequences could have been worse if not for the prevailing spirit of the New Deal, which accepted a major role for the Federal government in providing post-disaster relief. On September 26th, Harry Hopkins, head of the Works Progress Administration (WPA) and a confidant of President Franklin D. Roosevelt, began a five-day visit to the afflicted area. In one of his first statements, he offered work to any able-bodied man at two-to-three times the prevailing WPA wage rates. Other New Deal agencies – the Civilian Conservation Corps, the National Youth Administration, and the Federal Power Commission – followed WPA's lead. Even the Federal Writers' Project, a subsidiary of WPA, commissioned a pictorial history of the disaster.[9]

Of great importance was the intervention of the U. S. Forest Service and the Reconstruction Finance Corporation (RFC). The former established the New England Forest Emergency Project, and the RFC set up the Northeastern Timber Salvage Corporation. These organizations salvaged fallen timber, cleared debris, and opened nurseries to nourish newly planted forests. They also bought timber at prices above market value levels. The timber industry consequently rebounded sharply, even before the enormous stimulation arising from World War II mobilization.[10]

Although modern weather forecasting technology certainly has reduced human casualties, the destructive impact of hurricanes remains formidable. Hurricane "Katrina" (2005) is a case in point. Forecasters knew the storm's likely strength one week before it arrived, but it still wreaked havoc on New Orleans. An ominous reality is that more people than ever before live on America's Atlantic and Gulf coasts.[11]

Notes: Chapter 1

1   Aram Goudsouzian, *The Hurricane of 1938*. Beverly, MA: Commonwealth Editions, 2004, 9.

2   *Ibid.*

3   *NYT.* Sept. 22, 1938, 1.

4   Barrington Boardman, *Isaac Asimov Presents: From Harding to Hiroshima. An Anecdotal History of the United States from 1923 to 1945 based on Little-known Facts and the Lives of People who made History – and Some Who Didn't.* NY: Dembaer Books, 1988, 209.

5   Cherie Burns, *The Great Hurricane: 1938*. NY: Atlantic Monthly Press, 2005, 184. The actress was not in residence at the time.

6   Goudsouzian, *op. cit.*, 66. Assaults on women were another manifestation of the partial breakdown of law and order.

7   Boardman, *op. cit.*, 210.

8   *NYT*, Nov. 22, 1938, 1, 16, 19; Nov. 23, 1938, 1.

9   Goudsouzian, *op. cit.*, 67; Burns, *op. cit.*, 204.

10 Goudsouzian, *op. cit.*, 70.

11 Lourdes B. Aviles, *Taken By Storm 1938. A Social and Meteorological History of the Great New England Hurricane.* Boston: American Meteorological Society, 2013, IX.

CHAPTER 2

Drifting Toward War

T he New England hurricane was not the only catastrophic event that touched parts of the world in 1938. Adolf Hitler's Germany took two significant steps toward fulfillment of its expansionist ambitions. First, in March, Nazi troops occupied neighboring Austria; shortly thereafter other nations, including the U. S., accepted this step as a *fait accompli*. A second and potentially more explosive crisis involved Czechoslovakia, which was the only genuinely democratic nation in East Central Europe. Destroying this republic and incorporating its territory into the Third Reich could also further the achievement of a German-dominated *Mitteleuropa*. Exploitation of German nationalism in the Sudetenland region along the Czech-German border could serve as a pretext for this aggression. But the Czechs had an army of 400,000 ensconced in mountain fortifications facing Germany. They also had defensive alliances with France and the Soviet Union, with Britain a potential ally of France. A German assault, therefore, could ignite another European war less than twenty years since the last one ended.

In the words of one historian, President Franklin D. Roosevelt was "a powerless witness" to events in Europe.[1] He wavered between collective security inclinations and a detestation of fascism on the one hand and the clear isolationism of the

American electorate on the other. New- fangled public opinion polls reflected this desire to avoid involvement in European affairs. So had the extremely narrow loss back in January of the Ludlow Amendment in the House of Representatives – the margin of defeat was only twenty-one votes. This proposed constitutional amendment would have required a national plebiscite to authorize a declaration of war (except in the case of an undisputable aggression against the United States).

Early in 1938 FDR had envisioned a "peace initiative," which would have taken the form of an on-going conference of nations authorized to combat aggression. Essentially this would replace the ineffectual League of Nations, with a U. S.-British partnership assuming a de facto leadership role. But British Prime Minister Neville Chamberlain, already considering the appeasement of Germany and Italy, rejected the scheme.

Roosevelt remained unclear about what to do as the European crisis edged closer to war. On September 26th, 1938 he sent a message to Hitler asking him not to break off negotiations with Britain over Czechoslovakia. Although this message was not the cause, Hitler cabled Chamberlain to suggest a resumption of Anglo-German talks, which were set for Munich on September 29th. The conference also would include France and Italy. After Chamberlain gratefully accepted the German initiative during a speech to Parliament, Roosevelt sent this brief expression of gratitude to the British leader: "Good man."[2] Soon this "good man" and his French ally would sell out Czechoslovakia by acceding to Hitler's demand for cession of the Sudetenland to Germany. This "last demand for territorial revision in Europe" turned out not to be final, however: in March 1939 German troops marched into Prague and eliminated what remained of Czech independence.

The U. S. itself did not come close to hostilities as a result of the crisis that ended at Munich. But hindsight, which in reality is a reflection of documentary evidence, clearly indicates that the country's erstwhile foes would be Germany or Japan, or both. With respect to the former power, the volume of anti-Nazi rhetoric in America was frequent and loud. Former ambassador to Germany William E. Dodd was one notable worrier. He had recently been dismissed from his post because his detestation of the Nazi regime was not entirely shared by his State Department superiors. Unless democratic states acted soon to check fascism, he told a dinner in his honor at New York's Waldorf Astoria, civilization itself would be in grave danger. Hans Dieckhoff, Germany's ambassador to the U. S., protested Dodd's remarks as insulting to his country and *Fuhrer*. But Secretary of State Cordell Hull reminded him that Dodd was no longer employed by the U. S. government and that freedom of speech was an old and cherished American tradition.[3]

German espionage activities in the U. S. were another sign of growing mutual hostility. On January 2nd, 1942 a federal court would sentence thirty-three members of a German spy ring to a total of three hundred years imprisonment. However, their activities dated back to the mid-thirties and had been partially revealed in the spring of 1938. The spy ring had shrewdly placed its members in positions from which they could acquire much sensitive information. The Severasky Aircraft Corporation of Farmingdale, Long Island, N. Y. was the target in this instance. It had developed and was building a pursuit plane, or fighter, for the Army Air Corps, one capable of surpassing speeds of three hundred miles per hour – a very impressive speed for the time. Otto Voss, a naturalized German-born mechanic, worked in the company's assembly division at intervals for several years dating back to January 1936. He spent at least one of his "vacations" on an extended visit to Germany. The FBI arrested him in early March 1938.

In another case, which came to light a month later, the FBI arrested four other men with German backgrounds. Two members of this group were active in the pro-Nazi

German-American Bund. Their haul included Air Corps military codes and defense plans. Army officers assisted the FBI in securing important evidence against the suspects.[4]

By the end of 1938, America's relations with Japan had also deteriorated. Yet the period from the mid-nineteenth century to the early 1930s showed no clear pattern of mutual hostility. The visit of a heavily armed U. S. naval squadron under Commodore Matthew Perry in 1854 forced the isolated nation to open its trade doors. And subsequent contact with the outside world helped to create an intense interest in Japanese culture. The Centennial Exhibition in Philadelphia in 1876 offered a striking example of this fascination. The Japanese bazaar (at the Exhibition) attracted thousands of visitors who often purchased paintings, silks, and other *objets d'art*. The Japanese dwelling, built on the site by workmen brought over specifically for this purpose, was even more popular.[5]

The monstrous earthquake and the ensuing tsunami of September 1923, which killed approximately 140,000 and largely obliterated Tokyo and Yokohama, elicited much sympathy in the outside world, especially among Americans. Huge quantities of aid arrived from the U. S. as well as a relief fund of sixty million dollars (then a sizable sum), which was raised largely by the American Red Cross.

Earlier in the century, many Americans had sympathized with Japan as the underdog in the early stages of the Russo-Japanese War of 1904-05. But with the astonishing success of a supposedly backward Asian country against a European great power, the mood changed. For example, President Theodore Roosevelt's mediation of a peace settlement at Portsmouth, New Hampshire was motivated in part by a desire to limit the scope of a Japanese victory.[6] Two years later Roosevelt dispatched a powerful fleet on a goodwill world tour. Whatever else it signified (and TR was known for the quotation about speaking softly and carrying a big stick), the fleet was a warning to

Japan to moderate its expansionist ambitions and especially not to threaten American interests in east Asia and the western Pacific. Meanwhile, at home, racists in California and other west coast states were increasingly targeting Japanese immigrants. Congressional legislation passed in the early 1920s essentially ended immigration from Asia (as well as drastically curtailing the influx of eastern and southern Europeans).

Japanese imperialism took off in 1895 with a victory in the Sino-Japanese War, which resulted in the acquisition of Taiwan and the supplanting of Chinese influence in Korea. After the Russo-Japanese War, Japan replaced much of Russia's influence in the Chinese region of Manchuria.

An alliance with Britain propelled Japan into the First World War. The Japanese had little interest in European developments; but they used their involvement to seize Germany's bases in China and the western Pacific. Their military succeeded easily against light German resistance. They also aspired to transform China into a de facto Japanese client state. The Twenty-one Demands proposed to China in a draft treaty in early 1915 would be the instrumentality for the achievement of this goal. Besides territorial acquisitions, the Demands required the Chinese government to use Japanese advisers in its military, police, and financial administrations. Fortunately for China, when the United States protested the Demands as an infringement of Chinese sovereignty, Japan felt compelled to retreat from the most radical of them.

At the heart of America's concern was the Open-Door policy, which supported China's territorial integrity and its right to trade with all foreign countries. But Japan's retreat was only partial. In 1918, taking advantage of the involvement of western nations in the European war, she concluded a joint defense treaty with China allegedly designed to stop Communism from spreading from Russia to the Far East. Under its rubric, Japanese troops moved freely throughout much of China.

Japan's thrust for hegemony over China failed to survive the end of the First World War for very long. The U. S. and Britain imposed a settlement that amounted to a major Japanese setback, most of it during the Washington Conference of 1921-22. Japan accepted a naval arms limitation treaty that left its fleet inferior to those of the Anglo-Saxon powers. She was also required to return Shantung, a former German concession, to Chinese sovereignty. Of great symbolic significance, the Nine Power Pact of 1922 liquidated all existing treaties between China and the powers and replaced them with the principles of the Open Door.[7]

Japan's leaders during the 1920s, most of whom could be described as liberals, accepted these terms. They were influenced in part by Woodrow Wilson's idealism and an international framework centering on the League of Nations. The western nations, moreover, recognized Japanese interests in Manchuria, which included leased territory in Liaotung (Kwantung) and the South Manchurian Railway Company.

For those Japanese unable to satisfy their ambitions in the home islands, Manchuria was a new frontier where they could fulfill their dreams. After immigrant problems arose in California, Foreign Minister Komura exclaimed (in effect): "Go west, young man." He meant Manchuria where the number of Japanese residents rose from 68,000 in 1909 to 219,000 in 1930. But this was dwarfed by an *annual* migration of 300,000 to 500,000 Chinese during the same period.[8]

In 1931 rising Chinese numbers and pressure created by the world-wide Depression led plotters in the Kwantung Army (Japanese forces in Manchuria) to take over all of Manchuria. U. S. Secretary of State Henry Stimson proclaimed the "Non-recognition Doctrine," a refusal to accept the Japanese conquest; and the Hoover Administration concentrated the Pacific Fleet at Hawaii. But neither America nor any other power was able to intervene effectively because of their own obsession with the crippling Depression.

The so-called Manchurian Incident was not only a complete military victory but a successful army challenge to political party rule at home. The civilian government tacitly but quickly approved the aggression and proclaimed the birth of a Japanese satellite state called Manchukuo. When a League of Nations commission rejected these moves, Japan simply quit the League. The Japanese economy benefitted from increased access to Manchuria's mineral wealth and the continued military buildup.

Between 1931 and 1937, the Japanese not only consolidated their control of Manchuria but struck periodically at other parts of northern China. Establishing harsh puppet regimes and living off the land intensified the suffering of an already impoverished population. Japan's rationale for these actions almost certainly was a desire to stifle the emergence of a strong and unified China.

An exchange of gunfire between Japanese and Chinese forces on July 7th, 1937 at the Marco Polo Bridge outside of Peking (Beijing) was the start of a war that lasted eight years. Neither side seemed to have planned the incident. But the dispatch of Chinese troops to the north provoked the Japanese to send in three divisions. Peking fell after only one day's fighting, and by mid-August the Japanese had fought their way south to the outskirts of Shanghai. Unexpected ferocious resistance lasting into November infuriated the attackers, whose next target was Nanking (Nanjing), the capital. That city's defenders and its civilian population would become the victims of a barbarous vengeance. It became known as the Rape of Nanking, a record of atrocities among the worst of the pre-World War II era (see also Chapter 3 on the Spanish Civil War).

The Japanese slaughtered perhaps as many as 90,000 POWs, often in the most savage ways imaginable – these included beheading, bayonet stabbing, target practice, disembowelment, burning, and burying alive. Females of all ages and conditions were also murdered, usually after being raped. Estimates of non-military deaths vary greatly, but possibly there were as many as 300,000 of them (out of a total population of approximately 600,000). The slaughter lasted from mid-December 1937 to early February 1938.[9]

Among those caught up in the ravages accompanying the capture of Nanking were American military personnel and civilians. Very few foreigners remained in the city. But Americans and Europeans formed the International Committee for the Nanking Safety Zone, which probably saved thousands of Chinese lives. Meanwhile, a U. S. Navy gunboat, the *Panay*, was off shore patrolling the Yangtze River as part of its mission to save American lives and secure intelligence data. On December 11th, 1937 the *Panay* evacuated diplomatic personnel and journalists, which brought the number of people aboard to five officers, fifty-four enlisted men, and fourteen civilians.

A day later, on December 12th, Japanese aircraft sank the gunboat, killing two crew members and wounding thirty others. The Japanese foreign minister countered the U. S. protest by insisting that the *Panay* and three nearby Standard Oil tankers, also attacked, had been mistakenly identified as Chinese. The pilots, he claimed, had been flying too high to see two freshly painted American flags, each fourteen by eighteen feet, on the vessel's deck. The U. S. government knew this explanation to be untrue because of film footage that showed the planes attacking at low altitudes. Even more incriminating, Navy cryptographers had intercepted radio traffic revealing that the pilots were operating under orders (the Navy kept this information secret in order to conceal its intelligence capability).

U. S. Ambassador to Japan Joseph C. Grew remembered the 1898 sinking of the U. S. S. *Maine*, which had led to the Spanish-American War, and he hoped that the *Panay* incident would not have a similar outcome. This attack was almost certainly the work of fanatical officers rather than orders from Tokyo. A Japanese apology on December 24th included the promise of an indemnity, and payment of $2,214,000 arrived in Washington on April 22nd, 1938.

Although the crisis atmosphere cooled somewhat, it continued because of subsequent Japanese actions. Looting of American property, which was particularly frequent in January 1938, was a major irritant. On January 14th, for example, John M. Allison, the U. S. Consul in Nanking, protested to the Japanese Embassy there against continued looting by soldiers. These acts, Allison declared, could no longer be attributed to the lack of discipline evident during the Army's entry into the city. The looting included all kinds of items, even a piano belonging to the United Christian Missions. A more heinous sort of looting occurred when ten Chinese women, who had taken refuge in an American-owned building, were forcibly removed.[10]

Later that year, on August 24th, fourteen people died when Japanese aircraft shot down a transport plane belonging to the Chinese and American-owned China National Aviation Corporation. The pilot was American. Other planes belonging to neutrals were also shot down. Rejecting a U. S. protest, Japan asserted that the planes had been engaged in "suspicious" activity.[11]

Earlier in the year, in March 1938, a gathering in Washington had discussed the issue of how to deal with Japan's aggressive actions in China. T. A. Bisson, a spokesperson for the Foreign Policy Association who had just returned from one year's stay in the Far East, argued that Japan was wholly responsible for the murderous conflict. Speaking on the opposite side of the issue was Senator William E. Borah, an Idaho Republican and one of the most outspoken isolationists in the country. He condemned the idea of an economic boycott of Japan, which he believed would only worsen American-Japanese relations and probably lead to war.[12]

With renewed recession and ominous war rumblings in Europe, most Americans in 1938 were not deeply interested in the war in China. But readers of the *New York Times*, *TIME*, *Readers' Digest*, and a few other publications could follow events there and sense the war's ferocity. A segment of the Christian population was undoubtedly influenced ty the reports of missionaries on the ground, whose reports were not favorable to Japan. And despite his preoccupation with other problems, President Roosevelt was alarmed by the extension of Japan's power and war crimes committed by its military. His so-called Quarantine speech of October 5th, 1937, in which peace-loving nations were exhorted to quarantine aggressors, was targeted as much against Japan as against Germany and Italy.

In fact, by a quarantine the president probably meant an embargo and/or a blockade. After the *Panay* incident, he actually considered a blockade, which he specifically termed a quarantine. This would have extended from the Aleutian Islands off Alaska all the way to Guam in the South Pacific.[13]

The blockade idea was not implemented, but ill will toward Japan would intensify by the end of 1938. One reason was that nation's growing entente with Nazi Germany, a possible future enemy of the U. S. Another was the announcement of what Prime Minister Konoe Fuminaro deemed the New Order in East Asia. This would be a union of the economies of the region for the sake of building a common defense against the West. Japan would furnish industrial and management skills, financial expertise, and political coordination, while Korea, Manchuria, and North China would provide raw materials. Beyond this, the rest of China would serve as a captive market for Japanese goods and thereby earn the foreign currency to pay for indispensable imports from abroad. Obviously, the American concept of the Open Door in China could not survive such a scheme.[14]

Notes: Chapter 2

1   Frank Freidel, *Franklin D. Roosevelt. A Rendezvous with Destiny.* Boston, Toronto, London: Little Brown and Co., 1990, 289.

2   Kenneth S. Davis, *FDR. Into the Storm 1937-1940.* N. Y.: Random House, 1993, 192 313, 338, 342.

3   *NYT*, Jan. 14, 1938, 1; Jan. 15, 1938, 1.

4   *Ibid.*, Mar. 1, 1938, 9; Mar. 12, 1938, 1; Apr. 7, 1938, 1; June 1, 1938, 12.

5   Sheldon Spear, *Pennsylvania Histories. Two Hundred Years of Personalities and Events, 1750-1950.* Bethlehem, PA.: Lehigh University Press, 2015, 107.

6   Under the Portsmouth Treaty, Japan obtained territorial control over southern Karafuto (Sakhalin), a paramount position in Korea, a leasehold in China's Liaotung peninsula, and the South Manchuria Railway concession. There was no indemnity and, outside of southern Karafuto, no outright annexation. See Peter Duus, ed., *The Cambridge History of Japan.* Vol. 6. *The Twentieth Century.* Cambridge, N. Y., New Rochelle, Melbourne: Cambridge University Press, 1988, 274.

7   *Ibid.*, 283.

8   *Ibid.*, 291.

9   W. G. Beasley, *The Japanese Experience. A Short History of Japan.* Berkeley, Los Angeles, London: University of California Press, 1999, 244; Haruko Cook and Theodore F. Cook, *Japan at War. An Oral History.* N. Y.: The New Press, 1992, 25-26, 44ff. Japanese atrocities in the so-called Second Sino-Japanese War included the use of poison gas (185 times in 1938 alone) and medical experiments on healthy POWs. After the end of World War II, a number of Japanese experimenters found employment with U. S. research projects on biological warfare.

10   *NYT*, Jan. 7, 1938. 1; Jan. 15, 1938. 6; Jan. 23, 1938, 35. On Jan. 26 Consul Allison himself was struck in the face by a Japanese soldier. After the U. S. demanded an apology, Consul-General Katsue Okazaki delivered one on January 30. Interestingly, in 1953 Allison, U. S. Ambassador to Japan and Okazuki, Japanese Foreign Minister, jointly signed the U. S.-Japan Mutual Defense Assistance Agreement.

11   *NYT*, Sept. 1, 1938, 1; Sept. 7, 1938, 13.

12   *Ibid.*, Mar. 7, 1938, 3.

13   Freidel, *op. cit.*, 291-292.

14   Beasley, *op. cit.*, 244-245.

CHAPTER 3

Americans and the Spanish Civil War

A lthough involvement in World War II was delayed until 1941, another war a few years earlier captured the attention and, to a lesser degree, the participation of Americans. This was the Spanish Civil War, which lasted nearly three years – from July 1936 to March 1939. Approximately 410,000 people died in this savage conflict. In addition to the combat deaths and thousands of POWs executed after capture, ideological and class hatreds generated a slaughter of civilians not seen in Europe since the seventeenth century.

With a population of twenty-nine million, Spain was the poorest and most backward country in Western Europe. It had been a feudal monarchy until 1931, when popular riots drove out the king. Huge inequities remained under the newly created republic, however. The major centers of power were landowners with holdings sometimes larger than 75,000 acres, wealthy industrialists, and the Catholic Church which dominated religious, educational, and cultural life. Frequently violent instability was the rule between 1931 and 1936. Outbreaks included general strikes and peasant revolts, political killings by both the left and the right, bank robberies by revolutionaries, and police and paramilitary forces beating hungry farm workers who had the audacity to raid pigs' troughs.

In February 1936 a coalition of liberal, Socialist, and

Communist parties known as the Popular Front narrowly defeated right wing opponents to win a majority in the country's parliament. The new government promised dramatic changes, which greatly alarmed supporters of the defeated right.

A coterie of army generals, most of whom were stationed in North Africa – specifically in Spanish Morocco and the Canary Islands – plotted a revolt that would destroy the new leftist regime. Soon emerging as its leader was General Francisco Franco, who helped put together a force consisting partly of Spanish Foreign Legion troops (a large proportion of Legionnaires were men whose criminal records had been forgiven). The Legion had extensive combat experience against Berber rebels. A larger component of what would soon be called the Nationalist forces were, ironically, Berber or Arab Muslims, called Moors in Spain. Spanish officers had recruited them with false tales of "infidels and Jews" plotting to abolish Islam.

The Nationalist uprising might have been abortive if not for timely logistical support from Europe's leading fascist dictatorships. Especially crucial in light of the Spanish air force's loyalty to the Republic was Adolf Hitler's dispatch of planes to Morocco that were used to transport rebels to the mainland. Benito Mussolini also sent a squadron of bombers, but Hitler sent more planes – twenty of them – which German pilots would use to ferry 15,000 troops to Seville, the jumping-off point for a Nationalist drive to the north. Portugal, a right-wing dictatorship on Spain's western border, was another helpmate. The country served as the launching point for a second Nationalist offensive. It also allowed eight thousand Portuguese to volunteer for service in Franco's Foreign Legion and, more regrettably, handed over pro-Republican refugees to be shot.[1]

Early in the war the Nationalists initiated a wave of terror that often made no sense, except to terrorize real and potential enemies. For example, in the town of Huesca they shot one hundred alleged Freemasons in a community where the order consisted of fewer than a dozen members (Masons were targeted because they had long been anticlerical). In Cordova Nationalist guards forced an imprisoned diabetic to ingest sugar until he died. These killings far exceeded anything German Nazis and Italian fascists had done in the immediate aftermath of their advent to power. Yet by no means was all of the killing the work of rebels. Loyalist sympathizers, for instance, murdered hundreds of Catholic clergy. Equally brutal was the civil war within a civil war, as Communists murdered many of their erstwhile comrades in the Anarchist and Trotskyite movements.[2]

Hitler and Mussolini sent huge quantities of arms and ammunition to Franco, their kindred spirit. These shipments, particularly artillery, tanks, and aircraft – along with thousands of "volunteer" Italian infantry and German air force personnel – proved to be a decisive element in the Nationalists' ultimate victory. Western democracies, on the other hand, refused arms' sales to the Loyalist government despite the latter's ample possession of gold bullion (most of which had resulted from Spain's profitable neutrality during the First World War). Motives behind this behavior varied but certainly included a deep reluctance to be drawn into the conflict or to antagonize their own citizens of a conservative bent. The U. S. Neutrality Acts of 1935, which included an arms embargo placed on belligerents, were based largely on the questionable view that the country had entered World War I in order to protect profits derived from arms sales to the Allies.

The Soviet Union was the only major nation that shipped arms to Republican Spain, though the quantities were never sufficient. Communists consequently became a key component of the Republican coalition. Of perhaps equal importance was the formation by Communist front organizations of five International Brigades, which were comprised of volunteers from countries throughout the world. At their peak, Brigade numbers stood at between 35,000 and 40,000. Medical personnel also joined them, including seventy-five American nurses. Volunteers from the U. S. began filtering into Spain in the later months of 1936. Their total number, though never close to that at any given time, was approximately 2,800, of whom an estimated 750 died in the war.

The law prohibited U. S. citizens from enlisting to fight in foreign wars. But since enforcement could only be carried out on American soil, the volunteers sailed to France where they were enrolled in the ranks of the Republic by personnel recruited for that purpose. The French railway system took the recruits to the Spanish border, which they crossed either by train or by a difficult hike over the Pyrenees. Smaller numbers took boats from the French Mediterranean coast to the Spanish Mediterranean coast. French coastal police intercepted some of these passengers, but most of them were eventually freed and found their way to the fighting front of the war-torn nation.[3]

By the end of January 1937, three hundred Americans had crossed into Spain. Officially they were enrolled in the 17th Battalion of the 15th International Brigade, but unofficially they called themselves the Abraham Lincoln Battalion or, for short, the Lincolns. The American Communist Party (CPUSA) played a key role in supporting the Lincolns and another unit founded a bit later – the George Washington Battalion.

CPUSA propagandists insisted on using the term Brigade for the Lincolns because a Battalion implied something smaller and therefore was a less significant designation. The war in Spain was a *cause celebre* for liberals and leftists in the U. S. and elsewhere, but Communist influence was never hard to find. For example, the North American Committee to Aid Democratic Spain was run by liberals, but Communists took the lead in handling the money raised at events such as rallies, bazaars, dances, auctions, and speaking events.[4]

Eventually the more openly Communist Friends of the Abraham Lincoln Brigade (FALB) became the key supportive organization. It took charge of the recruitment, transportation, and rehabilitation of American volunteers. Under its auspices, returned volunteers toured the country to speak at union halls, universities, or anywhere an audience was willing to listen and donate to the cause. Local and federal law enforcement officers sometimes arrested FALB operatives, often on weak evidence of illegalities. Not to be outdone, the American Socialist Party called for the formation of the Eugene V. Debs Column (after the party's longtime leader), but this effort soon floundered. In the words of historian Cecil Eby: "Only the Communist Party knew how to assess, engage, and mobilize public opinion in the U. S. *vis-à-vis* the Spanish question …."[5]

Three quarters of the American volunteers had Communist connections. Yet there was considerable educational, ethnic, religious, racial, and even regional diversity within the Lincoln Battalion (forty-six states were represented in its ranks). Some of the roughly ninety black volunteers had hoped to fight against Mussolini's conquest of Ethiopia, yet as one of them commented: "This ain't Ethiopia but it'll do."[6] Other Lincolns included a vaudeville acrobat, two FBI fingerprint technicians, a rabbi, and the son of a former Ohio governor. Labor members were numerous, especially unemployed longshoremen, merchant seamen, and clothing workers. One third of the volunteers were from the New York City area, including sixty students, faculty, staff, and graduates of City College alone. Jews constituted close to half of the Lincolns, and in Spain, therefore, they were able to speak Yiddish to Jewish volunteers from European countries. As one recruit remarked about Jewish motivation: "For us it wasn't Franco, it was always Hitler." If there was a prototypical volunteer, he was a New Yorker, a Communist, an immigrant or the son of an immigrant, a trade unionist, or a working-class Jew.[7]

American newspapers soon discovered that the country's volunteers in Spain made sensational copy. Correspondents on the ground were overwhelmingly supportive of the Republic, although their bosses, the owners and editors, were often neutral or pro-Nationalist. One horrific event illustrates this point. Jay Allen of the *Chicago Tribune* reported that after the Nationalists had seized the town of Badajoz near the Portuguese border they executed 1,800 men and a number of women in a bull ring during the course of twelve hours. Allen's coverage of this atrocity prompted Robert McCormack, the archconservative owner of the *Tribune*, to fire him. [8]

A journalistic civil war characterized coverage at the *New York Times*, probably America's most prestigious newspaper. Herbert Matthews, the *Times* correspondent in Loyalist-controlled territory, became a fervent supporter of the Republic in spite of his earlier favorable coverage of Italy's campaign in Ethiopia. It was the bombing and shelling of Madrid that transformed him, although his dispatches were more restrained than his emotions.

Times editors of a strong Catholic religious bent were instrumental in pushing coverage and headlines in a more conservative direction. But the real civil war at the newspaper was not mainly between Matthews and his editors in New York but with the *Times* correspondent covering the war from the Nationalist side – William P Carney – a Texan, devout Catholic, and candid Franco enthusiast. While Matthews emphasized the civilian casualties and the intervention of Germany and Italy, Carney wrote about the contentment of the population in Nationalist-controlled territory and the Republican murder of Catholic priests. [9]

A number of journalists actually abandoned their profession to take up arms for the Republic. One notable example of this was James P. Lardner, the son of well-known columnist Ring Lardner. After three years at Harvard, the younger Lardner became a reporter for the *New York Herald Tribune*. Three years later he got assigned to the paper's Paris bureau from where he traveled to Spain. Deeply sympathetic to the plight of defeated Loyalist forces, he resigned his job and enlisted in the Lincoln Battalion. He was killed on September 24th, 1938 in an area overrun by the Nationalists, who never returned his body.[10]

Well-known individuals from a number of countries visited Spain during its agony. The glamour associated with the International Brigades seemed to be what drew most of them. A most welcome visitor was Paul Robeson, the African American singer who performed *Old Man River* and other hits in barracks, hospital wards, and other humble settings. American writers included Theodore Dreiser, Archibald MacLeish, and Langston Hughes, among many others. But the most celebrated and controversial of all the notables was probably the most popular author of his time.

In his late thirties, Ernest Hemingway had won praise for his novels, *A Farewell to Arms* and *The Sun Also Rises*, and for numerous short stories. Augmenting these literary achievements was the persona he had created for himself, which included big game hunting, carousing with bull fighters, and reeling in sharks and other huge sea creatures. He genuinely loved Spain, as was evident in *The Sun Also Rises* and in *Death in the Afternoon*, a non-fiction work about bull fighting. Viewing the Nationalist revolt as a blow against his Spain, he naturally identified with those Americans who had volunteered for the International Brigades. Their actions seemed similar to his enlistment as an ambulance driver for Italian forces during the First World War.[11]

Hemingway had signed a contract with the North American Newspaper Alliance, a consortium comprising fifty dailies. They paid him $1,000 for each dispatch, which was the equivalent of $15,000 in today's currency. He passed four lengthy sojourns in Spain, two of them in 1938. His companion during much of this time was the rising journalist Martha Gellhorn, whose reports appeared in the weekly magazine *Colliers*. She later became his third wife.

The intensely egotistical Hemingway was always performing before a rapidly changing audience that included other writers, as well as generals, foot soldiers, diplomats, and sundry others. Unlike most of his fellow correspondents, he always had a car at his disposal and plenty of fuel. His girlfriend was among those at his tutorials, often based on his alleged expertise on combat tactics. Interestingly, in the opinion of Gellhorn's biographer Caroline Moorehead, her subject's articles were better than Hemingway's, which she described as frequently contrived and self-centered. On the other hand, she asserted, Gellhorn wrote realistically and sympathetically about civilian suffering under bombardment, especially in Madrid and Barcelona. Still, Hemingway's name is inextricably linked to the Spanish Civil War, a large part of which is due to his 1940 novel *For Whom the Bell Tolls*. The author based the book's hero, Robert Jordan, very much on Major Robert Merriman, who was a prominent figure in the Lincoln Battalion.[12]

Scientific polling was in its infancy in 1938, but it seemed to indicate that a majority of the American people who followed the conflict in Spain supported the Republic. Yet though they distrusted fascism, their isolationist tendencies militated against abandonment of the arms embargo. And, to be sure, the Nationalists had their sympathizers too, the most influential of whom were found among the nation's Catholics. Radicals in Spain and abroad, and especially their Soviet patrons, were anathema to a large majority of the Church's clergy as well as to a significant proportion of its laity. The well-reported violence in Spain against Church personnel and property fueled this hatred. Conservatives of all political stripes backed Franco. Even more enthusiastic were American imitators of Hitler and Mussolini, such as the Detroit-based radio priest Charles E. Coughlin who had a weekly audience estimated at sixteen million.[13]

However, Franco's most useful American supporters were corporate leaders, and nobody more so than Norwegian-born

Torkild Rieber, the CEO of Texaco. Rieber spent his early years as a merchant seaman before joining Texaco and working his way up. By the mid-1930s he had developed strong political views, including a warm admiration for Hitler, Mussolini, and other autocrats. After the outbreak of fighting in Spain, he added Franco to the list.

Rieber broke a contract to sell petroleum products to the Republic, replacing it with a credit arrangement with the Nationalists. He accepted the almost worthless Nationalist currency as legitimate payment. Rieber got away with this because under the embargo regulations of America's neutrality legislation petroleum was not listed as contraband. Texaco was not the only U. S. company supplying Franco. Shell, Atlantic Refining, and Standard Oil of New Jersey followed Rieber's lead, although Texaco continued to be the principal supplier. In fact, Texaco alone would supply the Nationalists with more than twice as much oil as the Republic was able to buy from all sources.[14]

Trucks were another item not banned under the U. S. embargo. Franco's army received 12,000 of them, which were purchased from General Motors, Studebaker, and Ford. Firestone Tires was yet another supplier; and beginning in January 1938 Du Pont sold at least 40,000 bombs to Germany. The latter transaction was not a violation of the Neutrality Acts since Germany was not officially at war with anyone. Yet German aircraft dropped these Du Pont-made bombs in numerous raids on Loyalist military and civilian targets.[15]

Texaco's actual deliveries of oil to Spain were, in fact, technically illegal under the embargo because *American-owned* ships were prohibited from carrying supplies to areas involved in war. But the tankers' manifests were falsified by listing destinations such as Antwerp, Rotterdam, or Amsterdam. Later, at sea, their captains would open sealed instructions redirecting them to ports in Nationalist Spain. The U. S. Department of

Justice eventually found evidence of the fake manifests, but Texaco suffered only a $22,000 fine that was a pittance for a company worth hundreds of millions.[16]

Almost no American newspapers reported on Texaco's credit line to Franco, whether they knew about it or not (most apparently did not). But neither newspapers, nor the U. S. government, nor even Texaco's board of directors had knowledge of Rieber's gift of the *free* transport of petroleum products on the company's tankers. A Spanish scholar doing research in the country's archives decades later made the discovery of what, in practice, was a hidden subsidy to the Nationalists.

The same scholar made an even more remarkable discovery, namely, that Texaco's facilities and personnel amounted to a maritime intelligence network. Rieber and a few of his subordinates placed information they acquired about oil shipments to Loyalist Spain at the disposal of Nationalist, German, and Italian warship commanders and bomber pilots. Tankers carrying oil to the Republic experienced destruction, damage, or capture partly due to this information provided by Texaco.[17]

The Roosevelt Administration scrupulously enforced the embargo on arms sales to Spain, even though the legislation was not supposed to apply to civil wars. And because other democracies also enforced the ban, while Germany and Italy heavily supported Franco, the Loyalists were at a huge disadvantage. President Roosevelt's calculations were straightforward. He knew that the attention of the American people was concentrated on problems relate to the Depression. As the congressional elections of 1938 grew nearer, he also sensed that he could not afford to ignore the influence of the pro-Nationalist Catholic clergy, especially because powerful Catholic politicians often backed their Church's leadership. Nor could FDR and other Democrats ignore the feelings of a sizable bloc consisting of pro-Mussolini Italian-Americans.[18]

In the opinion of historian Cecil Eby, the pressure from American Catholic quarters against lifting the embargo may have influenced the outcome of the war more than any other single event.[19]

By the spring of 1938, the Nationalists had won a series of major victories, including a drive to the Mediterranean that cut Loyalist Spain in two. Simply stated, the latter was now vastly outgunned and outnumbered; and casualties were heavier than ever in the Lincoln Battalion. The Lincolns and their fellow American unit, the George Washington Battalion, suffered so many losses that they had to be merged.[20]

With the likelihood of a total Loyalist defeat, which almost certainly would shift the European balance of power toward fascism, many liberals in and out of the Roosevelt Administration called for ending the embargo. The list included Claude Bowers, a journalist and writer of popular histories who was U. S. Ambassador to the Republic; Secretary of the Interior Harold Ickes; Undersecretary of State Sumner Welles; leading scientist Albert Einstein; Henry L. Stimson, Secretary of State under President Hoover; former Ambassador to Germany William E. Dodd; and Senator Gerald P. Nye, Republican from North Dakota. Though an isolationist, Nye was an Anglophobe who attributed the embargo to British influence.[21]

First Lady Eleanor Roosevelt was a potentially powerful sympathizer of the Republic. In 1937 she had lent her name to a drive that raised funds to buy milk for Spanish children, and she continued to mention their suffering in her newspaper column. She also had established a friendship with the pro-Loyalist journalist Martha Gellhorn, first through Gellhorn's mother who was an old friend of hers. Then Mrs. Roosevelt had enlisted the young woman to tour the South to report on the region's overwhelming poverty and ill health. Over the course of a long correspondence, Gellhorn made sure to inform the First Lady about conditions in Spain. This resulted in a special

White House showing of *The Spanish Earth,* a film by the Dutch director and Communist Joris Ivens on which Gellhorn and Hemingway had collaborated.[22]

In March 1938, on a return trip to Spain, Gellhorn wrote a depressing letter to Mrs. Roosevelt against the backdrop of deadly German and Italian bombing raids on Barcelona and Valencia. "It makes me helpless and crazy with anger," she lamented, "to watch the next Great War hurtling towards us ... Why don't we lift our embargo to Spain ...."[23]

Mrs. Roosevelt did enjoy a modest advisory role with her husband but never to the point where she could openly criticize his actions. As much as he hated fascism, FDR could not allow this sentiment to influence the adoption of specific policies. A *New York Times* article of May 2nd, 1938, under the byline of Arthur Krock stating that the president favored elimination of the embargo on arms sales to Republican Spain, proved to be false. It may have been planted by the White House itself to stir up Catholics and provide Roosevelt with an excuse for inaction when besieged by liberals. Similarly, he told Secretary of the Interior Ickes, probably the strongest Loyalist supporter in the Administration, that Democratic leaders in Congress were jittery over the likely impact of repeal on the Catholic vote. To placate liberals FDR sent his brother-in-law, Hall Roosevelt, to Europe, supposedly to facilitate the shipment of fifty aircraft to the Loyalists. Probably to his relief, the scheme came to naught when the French government closed its border with Spain (which had been open briefly)[24]

Overall, it seems likely that Roosevelt never intended to change course on this issue. He essentially followed the State Department's leadership, and Secretary of State Cordell Hull believed that ending the embargo would only prolong the war and possibly draw the U. S. into a general European conflict. Yet surprisingly, at a cabinet meeting on January 27th, 1939, with the Nationalists on the brink of winning the war, the president conceded that the embargo on arms to Republican Spain had been "a grave mistake."[25]

In the last days of the war the U. S., through the American Red Cross, joined several other countries in shipping flour to Spain. The purpose was to provide food for hungry children (so Eleanor's influence may have been at work here). Unfortunately delays in delivery made the measure less effective than it might have been.[26]

On September 21st, 1938 Loyalist Prime Minister Juan Negrin informed the League of Nations in Geneva that international volunteers would be withdrawn from the front and eventually repatriated to their countries of origin. The return of American volunteers did not always proceed smoothly. Prisoners of war held by the Nationalists constituted one problem, which could have become a political nightmare if the Justice Department decided to prosecute them for military service with a foreign power. But the government could not ignore the problem because of the humanitarian efforts of *New York Times* correspondent William Carney. Despite his pro-Franco sympathies, Carney visited the eighty Americans held at an abandoned monastery near the Nationalist capital of Burgos. Conditions there were what one historian described as a preview of World War II concentration camps.[27]

Carney's *Times* report of July 11th, 1938 helped create sympathy for the captured men, not as bomb-throwing Reds but as homesick and stranded fellow Americans. Prodded by Carney's revelations, the State Department announced that negotiations were under way to obtain the POWs' release. The negotiations were slow and plagued by difficulties, but they proceeded. Eventually the Nationalist released all the remaining American POWs (unfortunately many of their comrades-in-arms had been executed immediately after capture).[28]

In the aftermath of the massive Loyalist defeat in the spring of 1938, at least one hundred American volunteers deserted.

Their experience revealed that they had been outnumbered, outgunned, and outgeneraled. Upon returning home, most of them kept quiet, not wishing to give comfort to Franco apologists and fervent anti-Communists. Yet some of them were so infuriated by Communist actions in Spain, most of all by the violence against fellow leftists, that they spoke out strongly.[29]

The majority of American volunteers were back home by late 1938 or early 1939. The Friends of the Abraham Lincoln Brigade extended considerable help to the men it viewed as politically sound (that is, pro-Communist). FALB was the rough equivalent of a governmental veterans' agency. Its programs included medical treatment, free temporary housing, night courses, arranging job interviews with union leaders, and parties to facilitate contact with women. Many veterans abandoned the FALB after August 1939 in disgust over the Hitler-Stalin Non-aggression Pact. The Veterans of the Abraham Lincoln Brigade (VALB) succeeded FALB later that year. It was a much smaller organization but equally Stalinist in orientation.

Enlistment and repatriation of young Americans in the International Brigades frequently caused major family disturbances. For example, this writer's uncle by marriage, Milton Cooper, had his younger brother Mike inform their anxious mother that Milton had enlisted -- long after he was already overseas. With the return of volunteers this Milton was confused with a dead veteran who had the same first and last names. The family was in deep mourning when their son and brother turned up unharmed.[30]

About six hundred Spanish Civil War veterans joined the U. S. armed forces during World War II. They were not entirely welcome due to their leftist backgrounds; or, as Martin Dies, chairman of the House Committee on Un-American Activities phrased it, because of their "premature anti-fascism." The Army, at first, refused to send them overseas. But this policy was later reversed, and a number of the men fought in the European or Pacific Theaters; several of them won combat medals.[31]

During the years of the Cold War, anti-Communist hysteria focused the attention of the FBI and various congressional committees on former members of the Abraham Lincoln Battalion. Often hounded in mean-spirited ways, such as enduring the unwarranted suspension of medical and other licenses, a few of the veterans spent time in jail for refusing to testify against former comrades. In 1953 the Subversive Activities Control Board, under the McCarran Act, required the VALB to register as a Communist front organization. Twelve years later, however, the U. S. Supreme Court vacated this order on the grounds that the original evidence had become too old to be valid.[32]

An interesting statistic reveals that there was a far higher death *rate* among Americans in the Spanish Civil War than among those who fought in any U.S. wars of the twentieth century. Moreover, as Adam Hochschild points out in his marvelous recent book, American volunteers seldom doubted that they were fighting the first battles of a future world war. As Hochschild notes: "Where else, after all, were Americans being bombed by Nazi pilots more than four years before the United States declared war on Germany and Japan?"[33]

Notes: Chapter 3

1   Adam Hochschild, *Spain in Our Hearts. Americans in the Spanish Civil War, 1936-1939*. Boston, New York: Houghton Mifflin Harcourt, 2016, 30-31.

2   *Ibid.*, 32-33.

3   Steve Nelson, *The Volunteers*. New York: Masses and Mainstream, 1952, *passim*. Nelson was a major figure in the American volunteer force.

4   Cecil Eby, *Between the Bullet and the Lie. American Volunteers in the Spanish Civil War*. New York, Chicago, San Francisco: Holt, Rinehart and Winston, 1969, 3, 23, 99-100.

5   *Ibid.*, 104-105.

6   Hochschild, *op. cit.*, 99.

7   *Ibid.*, 100.

8   *Ibid.*, 36-37.

9   *Ibid.*, 153-155.

10 Eby, *op. cit.*, 299; *NYT*, Apr. 25, 6; Sept. 29, 1938, 4; Oct. 4, 1938, 10.

11 Hochschild, *op. cit.*, 141-142.

12 Caroline Moorehead, *Gellhorn. A Twentieth Century Life*. New York: Henry Holt and Co., 2003, 113, 119, 122.

13 Charles J. Tull, *Father Coughlin and the New Deal*. Syracuse: Syracuse University Press, 1963, 206. Coughlin termed Franco "a rebel for Christ.

14 Hochschild, *op. cit.*, 173.

15 *Ibid.*, 281.

16 *Ibid.*, 173-174.

17 *Ibid.*, 248-250.

18 Davis, *op. cit.*, 249; Freidel, *op. cit.*, *270*.

19 Eby, *op. cit.*, 104.

20 *Ibid.*, 205, 212, 235.

21 Hugh Thomas, *The Spanish Civil War*. New York: Modern Library Paper Edition, 2001, 349.

22 *Ibid.*, 590; Hochschild, *op. cit.*, 205-206.

23 Cited in Hochschild, *op. cit.*, 282. See also Moorehead, *op. cit.*, 142.

24 Davis, *op. cit.*, 249; Hochschild, *op. cit.*, 315.

25 Hochschild, *op. cit.*, 353.

26 Thomas, *op. cit.*, 869.

27 Eby, *op. cit.*, 254.

28 *Ibid.*, 253, 256, 264-265.

29 *Ibid.*, 266-267.

30 *Ibid.*, 311-313. The stories about Milton Cooper were related by his niece Marsha Spear (nee Cooper).

31 Nelson, *op. cit.*, 192.

32 Eby, *op. cit.*, 315, 317.

33 Hochschild, *op. cit.*, XVII.

CHAPTER 4

Another "War":
Radio's War of the Worlds

The Civil War in Spain was certainly real. So was the Sino-Japanese War, while the near-conflict arising from the Czech crisis frightened millions. But for a brief period in late 1938, a fake war on American radio gave rise to a panic of its own. George Orson Welles, an innovative actor, director, writer, and producer, was primarily responsible for creating a show that upset millions and propelled him to notoriety.

Welles was born on May 6th, 1915 in Kenosha, Wisconsin and spent much of his childhood in Chicago and smaller Illinois towns. However, his early years did not adhere to anything resembling a "typical" Midwesterner's. His parents separated when Orson was only four (he rarely used his given first name). After his mother's death when he was nine, the boy lived in Chicago with his father and Maurice Bernstein, a physician and close family friend. When his father died in 1930, Orson chose Dr. Bernstein as his guardian (Mr. Welles's will allowed this freedom of choice).

At age eleven Welles began attending the Todd Seminary for Boys, an elite private institution in Woodstock, Illinois. He thrived there because faculty members gave him the encouragement he needed to develop a theatrical talent that had already become apparent. He subsequently turned down a scholarship to Harvard in order to travel overseas, spending much of his time in Ireland. In 1932, claiming to be an experienced Broadway actor, he persuaded a Dublin theater director to hire him for a number of stage roles. Eventually returning to the Todd Seminary, he directed a writing project entitled *Everybody's Shakespeare* – it was published and remained in print for many years.

In 1933, at the age of eighteen, Welles appeared in a number of plays on the New York stage. Contacts with drama critic Alexander Woollcott and actress Katharine Cornell was responsible for these opportunities. His first job in broadcasting – on *The American School of the Air* – followed shortly thereafter. On November 14th, 1934 Welles married Chicago native and fellow actor Virginia Nicolson, who was the first of three wives (his second wife was the movie star Rita Hayworth).

Over the years 1934-38 Welles's career blossomed as a stage and radio actor, director, and writer. His earnings were excellent, but his work schedule was often overwhelming. It included stage plays, which he directed, or acted in, or both. The earlier plays were part of the New Deal's Federal Theatre Project, a program intended to provide work for unemployed theater people and quality entertainment for those who otherwise had little contact with it. One of these performances was a production of *Macbeth* that was staged at a theater in Harlem with an entirely African American cast. In 1937 Welles and fellow actor John Houseman founded the Mercury Theatre, which performed on Broadway. One production was Shakespeare's *Julius Caesar*, featuring cast members in modern military garb who would march briskly amid glaring spotlights. This modern milieu was a none-too-subtle critique of European fascism.[1]

In the summer of 1938, Welles and Houseman signed a deal with the CBS Radio Network to do a show entitled *Mercury Theatre on the Air*. Its objective would be to present quality programs, the selection of which would be left to Welles. The Network did arrange the scheduling, which was set for Sunday evenings from eight to nine. This was prime time, but unfortunately it faced competition from one of the most popular programs of the day. NBC's *Chase and Sanborn Hour* featured ventriloquist Edgar Bergen and his collection of dummies led by the wise-cracking Charlie McCarthy. Today ventriloquism on the radio may seem absurd, but apparently not to audiences in 1938 and for years to come. The show also hosted various show business guests.

Welles selected an 1890s science fiction thriller – *War of the Worlds*, by British author H. G. Wells – for the October 30th (Halloween eve) time slot. Welles, Houseman, and others collaborated on the script, although the former was so busy directing rehearsals of *Danton's Death*, a Mercury Theatre stage production, that he could not focus on *War...* until two days before air time. Howard Koch, a former lawyer, wrote what was supposed to be the final script. Welles's last-minute revisions were so numerous, however, that Koch had to work from early morning to late at night to integrate them.

Welles was the true creative force behind the dramatic techniques that made *War...* so memorable. His debt to real news coverage and to imitative news shows was considerable. The Lindbergh baby kidnapping, murder, and the subsequent trial constituted a landmark in radio reporting of a deeply moving national experience. Events such as the Spanish Civil War, Japanese aggression and atrocities in China, and the Czech crisis added to the impact of live broadcasting.

But instant coverage of news events was more pertinent to Welles's production techniques. *The March of Time*, on the air from 1932 to 1939, used actors, announcers, and written dialogue to reproduce news stories from *TIME Magazine*. It was at least a partial forerunner of *War...* because it blurred the difference between live and re-created action. For example,

Kenny Delmar, an actor on *The March of Time,* had a voice almost indistinguishable from that of President Roosevelt, whom he played. In *War...* Delmar played the Secretary of the Interior, but the voice was FDR's. One of Welles's first radio parts in New York had been in *The March of Time.* Probably even more influential were two shows written by poet-playwright Archibald MacLeish – *Fall of the City* and its follow-up, *Air Raid.* They used actors, "news reports," and realistic sound effects to describe "attacks" on European cities. Welles had sat in on the first show's rehearsals and listened to a broadcast of the second one.[2]

Welles was a showman whose likely motive was not to scare people but to produce a thriller capable of building an audience more competitive with *The Chase and Sanborn Hour.* He used the technique of a gradual intensification of the action – from insipid music at a (fictitious) New York hotel to "on-location reporters" whose pseudo-interruptions of the hotel music became increasingly longer, dramatic, and ultimately hysterical.

New Jersey was the principal locale of the "action," and real names of towns and roads were used in part. Writer Howard Koch dropped a pencil on a road map of the state. The pencil landed with its point of the tiny town of Grover's Mills, which consequently became the site of the "Martian invasion." But several days before air time, the CBS legal department imposed a number of name changes to ensure that there would be no mistaking the show for reality. So Langley Field became Langhorne Field, the Hotel Biltmore was the Hotel Park Place, and so on. Network lawyers also deleted the cries of advancing Martians – "utia, utia, utia" – as too terrifying. Moreover, there were announcements at the program's beginning, forty-minute mark, and ending that *War...* was absolute fiction. Nor apparently could there have been any doubt about the distinctive radio voice of Welles himself, who played a Princeton University professor (Welles had previously played the Shadow in an extremely popular show of that name). [3]

Yet despite all these precautions, many listeners came to believe that something horrendous was happening, not necessarily a Martian invasion but possibly the impact of a comet or meteor or an invasion by foreign forces, perhaps Germans or Japanese. Remote control devices were in the future, but radio listeners frequently changed stations to avoid commercials or other portions of a program in which they had no interest. Many of those listening to Bergen and McCarthy switched to *War...* when guest Nelson Eddy began singing. Among them were those who had missed the initial announcement about the show's fictional character, and now they missed its repetition at the forty-minute mark. They were drawn in by the suspenseful realism (or even by the "hotel" music).

The best analysis of public reaction to War... was a relatively recent book by A. Brad Schwartz, *Broadcast Hysteria. Orson Welles's* <u>*War of the Worlds*</u> *and the Art of Fake News* (2015). Schwartz's research found that the show inspired a noticeable amount of fear but little general panic. Some listeners spread the word and scared others. Panic was most common when a lot of people lived close together, as in apartment buildings or college dormitories. Telephone communication frequently played a role as, for example, in the small neighboring towns of Meckling and Gaynesville, South Dakota. Listeners sometimes phoned the police or CBS's New York location or those of its affiliates. But the cross-continental flood of calls suggests that, far from losing their heads, many people stopped to think before fleeing. There were no mass flights or abnormally high numbers of auto accidents, suicides, or miscarriages.[4]

It was press coverage, Schwartz asserts, that blew everything out of proportion. Stories of panic, backed by little evidence, spread across the newspaper world in identical or similar language. The *New York Daily News* was particularly irresponsible in its approach, but others were not much better. In Schwartz's view, the newspapers took a complex, multifaceted event and drastically oversimplified it, in the process creating a false narrative of mass panic.[5]

A number of publishers, including those of the prestigious *New York Times*, raised the cry of irresponsible broadcasting, probably attempting to punish their media rivals. Yet news broadcasting and newspaper coverage were more or less coexisting well by 1938. People still depended on the written word for detailed coverage. Lurking in the background was another and certainly less honorable news reporting practice: the sensationalistic journalism that dated back to the "yellow press" of the late nineteenth century.[8]

Welles at first had no inkling of the uproar caused by *War...*, which he almost certainly had not intended to cause. But after a sleepless night, and the insistence of CBS, he did a press interview at the studio. He apologized but insisted that the fictional nature of the broadcast should have been evident. First of all, the story was set in 1939, not in the present (though there was only a fleeting reference to this). Second, listeners should have recognized the program as *Mercury Theatre on the Air* (though it had low ratings and a relatively new time slot). And third, the subject matter, "Martians," should have been a clue (but more people were concerned with falling meteors or poison gas).

Letters to the Federal Communication Commission (FCC) urged it to take punitive action. Even H. G. Wells complained that his story had been distorted and that prospects for his new novel, *Apropos of Dolores*, were ruined. Yet interest in his old novel, and in his new one as well, actually soared.[7] In spite of cries for censorship, and particularly for the creation of a code similar to that of the motion picture studios, the FCC failed to act. The law establishing the agency gave it the right to silence radio stations not acting in the public interest but only if doing so did not constitute censorship or interference with free speech.

Many pro-Welles letter writers supported this approach

and warned that increasing public control over radio would lead to government propaganda, as in Nazi Germany and other authoritarian states. The FCC took no action on *War...* and left it to individual stations to control shows with "indecent" content. One exception was that news terms, such as "flash" and "bulletin," could not be used in fictional programs. The stations themselves proceeded to ban re-enactment of real events and the impersonation of real people.[8]

Within hours of the broadcast, there were rumors that Welles and CBS would be hit by numerous and crippling law suits. However, Welles's lawyer had negotiated a contract with the network that made him responsible only for libel and plagiarism. Nor did any of the $750,000 worth of suits against CBS ever get to court, although a few of them were settled privately.[9]

Comment on *War...* from abroad was negative and tinged with sarcasm. The *London Times*, for instance, mocked Americans for not planning for air raids and then getting scared by improbable nonsense. And in Germany the *Volkischer Beobachter*, the Nazi Party's official newspaper, claimed that the hysterical reaction in the U. S. to *War...*was due to the equally hysterical, and anti-German reports on the Czech crisis. Back in America, a number of members of the intellectual elite attributed the radio episode to the lack of public intelligence. One such individual was drama critic and contributor to the *New Yorker*, Alexander Woollcott, a good friend of Welles, to whom he sent the following telegram: "This only goes to show ... that the intelligent people were all listening to a dummy, and all the dummies were listening to you."[10]

War... continued to have an impact years after the broadcast. It seems to have encouraged young people and others to read more science fiction in book or comic book form. There also were radio versions of *War...* in three foreign countries. Two of them, Chile and Ecuador, had experienced recent traumatic events. Chile's broadcast in 1944 took place against the backdrop of a terrible earthquake that killed approximately 30,000 people and devastated 40,000 square miles. In Quito, Ecuador on February 12th, 1948 a *War...*broadcast inspired a mob to attack and burn the radio station, which caused the death of six people. Ecuador was in a depressed economic condition and had not recovered psychologically from a 1941-42 military defeat at the hands of Peru. Across the Atlantic a Portuguese broadcast of *War...* on June 25th, 1958 caused a good deal of panic.[11]

In the immediate aftermath of the controversial *Mercury Theatre on the Air* program, Welles hoped that the publicity would translate into a favorable run for *Danton's Death* on Broadway. Unfortunately for him, the show received terrible reviews and closed after only twenty-one performances. *Mercury Theatre* consequently expired, but *Mercury Theatre on the Air* continued, albeit with a sponsor – Campbell Soup – a new name – Campbell Playhouse – and a new time slot – Fridays, from nine to ten in the evening. The plays, which were not controversial, received mostly favorable reviews. The program continued until its contract expired in March 1940.[12]

Historians of the motion picture industry often rate *Citizen Kane* (1941) as the best film ever made. Whether or not this opinion is valid Welles, who was co-writer (with Herman Mankiewicz), director, and leading man (playing Kane) saw his youthful career blossom still further (he was only twenty-six in 1941). But despite many critical successes over the next four decades, he never came close to measuring up to early expectations. This is probably why, in radio and television interviews during his twilight years (he died in 1985), Welles insisted that *War...* was an effort to warn the American public about the danger of accepting everything on radio as true. In other words, he took credit for deliberately instigating the furor rather than admitting that it was something wholly unexpected. It was probably too galling for him to concede that one of his greatest achievements was a fluke.[13]

Notes: Chapter 4

1   Frank Brady, *Citizen Welles. A Biography of Orson Welles.* New York: Charles Scribner's Sons, 1989, *passim*; Barbara Leaming, *Orson Welles. A Biography.* New York: Viking Press, Inc., 1985, *passim.*

2   A. Brad Schwartz, *Broadcast Hysteria. Orson Welles's "War of the Worlds" and the Art of Fake News.* New York: Hill and Wang, 2015, 14, 20-21, 24, 31, 52, 78; Brady, *op. cit.*, 166.

3   Leaming, *op. cit.*, 167; Schwartz, *op. cit.*, 49, 60; Simon Callow, *Orson Welles. The Road to Xanadu.* New York: Viking, 1995, 491; *N. Y. Times*, Aug. 14, 1938, X, p. 10.

4   Schwartz, *op. cit.*, 69, 82, 84-86, 89-90

5   *Ibid.*, 100-103.

6   *Ibid.*, 103, 107. See also *NYT* editorial, entitled "Terror By Radio," Nov. 1, 1938, 22.

7   Schwartz, *op. cit.*, 118, 120.

8   *Ibid.*, 133, 142-143, 150.

9   Brady, *op. cit.*, 176.

10   Callow, *op. cit.*, 407; quoted in John Gosling, *"The War of the Worlds." A History of the 1938 Radio Broadcast and Resulting Panic, Including the Original Radio Script by Howard Koch.* Jefferson, North Carolina and London: McFarland & Co., Publishers, 2009, 85, 96.

11   Gosling, *op. cit.*, 99, 110, 125.

12   Callow, *op. cit.*, 411-413; Brady, *op. cit.*, 221-226.

13   Gosling, *op. cit.*, 82, 84.

CHAPTER 5

Aviation Heroes

O rson Welles was either a creative genius or an unfeeling practical joker, or perhaps both. But when it came to the flock of aviators active in the 1930s, the American public overwhelmingly praised them as heroic. Wiley Post, who died with his passenger – humorist Will Rogers – in a crash in Alaska, and Amelia Earhart, the female Lindbergh look-alike, who disappeared forever in the South Pacific, were already legends by 1938. In that year Howard Hughes, also a successful movie producer, was exceeding the exploits of fellow aviators, living or dead.

Howard Hughes, Jr. was born on December 24th, 1905 in Houston, Texas, the son of Howard Hughes, Sr. and Alene Ganos Hughes. The senior Hughes invented a machine that greatly facilitated drilling for oil, an invention that made him, and later his only child, extremely wealthy. The young Hughes attended several prestigious prep schools and briefly Rice University. He was an average student but had already demonstrated a strong mechanical bent. When he was fourteen, his father paid five dollars for the boy's brief ride in a Curtis seaplane, an experience that marked the beginning of a lifelong love affair with flying.

The death of his mother (in 1922) and father (in 1924) made him a young millionaire. By the age of nineteen he had dropped out of Rice, persuaded a Texas judge to free him from a minor's disabilities, and married his first wife, Ella Rice. Later that year he moved to southern California where part of his father's business empire was located and where he spent much of his time furthering his flying ability. At the same time his uncle, Rupert Hughes, a successful film writer and director, convinced him to enter the movie business as a producer.

Hughes enjoyed modest success in films when he was only in his early twenties. A real breakthrough was *Hell's Angels* (1929), which dramatized the experiences of First World War pilots. At a cost of $3.8 million, it was the most extravagant film made in Hollywood up to that point. Hughes closely oversaw the scenes of aerial combat and successfully transformed what had begun as a silent film into one of the earliest "talkies." Among other things, this involved replacing members of the original cast, most of whom lacked English language fluency, with native-born and sometimes glamorous newcomers such as Jean Harlow. Amidst much publicity *Hell's Angels* opened on June 30th, 1930. Dazzling critics and audiences alike, it launched the legend of Hughes as daring, independent, and willing to gamble.[1]

After *Hell's Angels* Hughes left the directing of his productions to talented men, including Lewis Milestone (*The Front Page*) and Howard Hawks (*Scarface*). By 1932, moreover, he had become more interested in flying than moviemaking. He came to own what early biographers characterized as a "small airforce."[2] He was especially interested in his racer, which had been built by Boeing for the U. S. Army Air Corps – he had arranged to buy this plane through the Department of Commerce. Leasing a corner of a Lockheed Aircraft Corporation hangar in Burbank, he hired designers and mechanics whose efforts increased the racer's speed. As expenses rose, he created the Hughes Aircraft Company as a division of the Hughes Tool company.[3]

In 1934 Hughes suspended his Hollywood career (aside from

romantic interludes with screen actresses such as Ida Lupino, Katharine Hepburn, and others). He took his redesigned racer to the Miami area where he easily won a major regional race. His team subsequently built a land plane, called the H-1, that would fly higher and faster than earlier models. Retractable landing gear was one of its unique features.

On September 13th, 1935, with Hughes at the controls, the H-1 set a new speed record of 352 miles per hour over a course in California. He broke additional records in 1936 by flying from Miami to New York City in four hours and twenty-one minutes and cross-country from Burbank to Newark, New Jersey in seven hours and twenty-eight minutes. At the White House on March 3rd, 1937 President Roosevelt presented him with the Harman International Trophy for Best Aviator of the Year. Hughes was only the third individual to win this award – previous recipients were Charles Lindbergh and Wiley Post.[4]

Wiley Post held the record for flying around the world: in 1933 he had accomplished this in seven days and nineteen hours. Hughes was determined to break this record and to do so in a far more scientifically sophisticated manner than his predecessor. He first considered the DC-1 and the Sikorsky S-43 but later abandoned them in favor of the faster Lockheed Model 14 (L-14). The L-14 was a twelve-passenger transport plane that could be readily modified. Hughes's improvements included two more powerful engines and expansion of the plane's fuel capacity. For its time the L-14 was very advanced. Part of its equipment, for example, was an automatic pilot that could fly on a predetermined course for hours at a time. The plane also had an elaborate radio system, and Hughes would arrange for spare parts to be stored in cities and towns where landings might be necessary.[5]

A number of problems held up progress well into 1938. The Department of Commerce twice denied Hughes permission to undertake his flight, first because the project supposedly lacked scientific merit and, second because a similar plane had recently crashed. As late as July 3rd, 1938 Hughes was apparently so uncertain about his ultimate destination that he told the *New York Times* that his plans after reaching Paris were "indefinite."[6]

Government approval finally arrived on July 8th, as the crew of five kept busy at Floyd Bennett Field in Brooklyn by fixing a number of mechanical problems. The L-14 got a new name, which was "New York World's Fair 1939." This had resulted from a request by Grover Whalen, the Fair's chief, to publicize the coming event. Finally, on July 10th, after a very brief speech by Hughes, the crowd of roughly 5,000 assembled at Floyd Bennett watched the plane take off at nineteen minutes past seven in the evening. Loaded with 1,500 gallons of fuel and other necessities, none of the airport's runways were long enough to effect lift-off. Hughes consequently chose the south runway where the paved surface gave way to a flat, smooth stretch of earth.

At the controls as he would be for the entire journey, Hughes flew north toward Old Saybrook, Connecticut, tipping his wings as he passed over current girlfriend Katharine Hepburn's family home. Then he turned northeast toward Boston to take the same route to the Atlantic that Lindbergh had followed – the Great Circle Course – flying over Nova Scotia, Cape Breton Island, and Newfoundland, from where it was 1,800 miles to Ireland.

Hughes flew at an altitude of 7,500 feet and at an average speed of 192 mph. A problem arose when rough weather over Newfoundland led him to turn the engines up to maintain speed. He soon realized that so much fuel was being consumed that the plane might not make it to Paris, the first scheduled stop, without refueling, which would consume precious time. But, fortunately, clearing skies and a tail wind soon provided optimum flying conditions. The plane landed at Le Bourget Field outside of Paris at four in the afternoon. The flight had taken sixteen hours and thirty-eight minutes and, at an average speed of 220 mph, it had cut Lindbergh's 1927 time roughly in half. Thousands of people, and William Bullitt, U. S. Ambassador to France, were waiting to greet the crew.[7]

After a delay of four hours – to fix the tail wheel strut that Hughes discovered had been damaged at Floyd Bennett – the L-14 left Paris at Midnight. Severe cross-winds made the take-off hazardous. Turbulence continued over Germany, but adjustments could not be made because the German government ordered the plane to fly at 12,000 feet in order to prevent observation of military preparations on the ground.

At a quarter past eleven the next morning, Hughes made a perfect landing in Moscow. Friendly crowds, the need to replenish supplies of fuel, food, and water, and a luncheon in their honor did not deter the crew from taking off after two and a half hours on the ground.[8] In the middle of that night, the plane landed at Omsk in western Siberia, 1,380 miles from Moscow. Rain had turned the runway into a sea of mud, no one spoke English, and the preferred high-octane fuel was unavailable. The last Old-World leg of the flight – ten and a half hours and 2,177 miles – took them to Yakutsk in northeastern Siberia, where there was a quick refueling.

Fairbanks, Alaska was the next scheduled destination. The route across Siberia over rugged mountainous terrain may well have been the most dangerous experience yet. According to what turned out to be an inaccurate map supplied by the U. S. Hydrographic Survey, the highest peaks in the area were 6,500 feet. Instead, some of them were actually 10,000 feet, and the plane, its wings coated with ice, barely rose high enough to clear them.[9]

At two minutes past three in the afternoon on July 13th, Hughes landed at Fairbanks. The big crowd included the widow of Wiley Post, who offered the crew a tearful encouragement. After jettisoning just about every item that could possibly reduce flying speed (including ping pong balls), the L-14 headed for home. The next morning there was a thirty-four-minute refueling stop in Minneapolis and then a flight through successive cloud banks across the Great Lakes. Passing over Scranton, Hughes began the descent to New York. At thirty-three minutes past two in the afternoon the plane broke through the clouds near Floyd Bennett Field where a crowd of 25,000 was waiting – landing four minutes later on July 14th, 1938. The "New York World's Fair 1939" had set a record for flying around the world (14,716 miles): three days, nineteen hours, and seventeen minutes. Average flying speed was 206 mph. Wiley Post's old mark of seven days, nineteen hours had easily been surpassed.[10]

Howard Hughes was so tired he could barely speak above the cheers and only uttered a brief "thank you." Driven to Grover Whalen's home in Greenwich Village, he took his first bath in a week. After sneaking off to Katharine Hepburn's town house further uptown, he checked into a hotel and slept as if compensating for four sleepless days. On July 15th, in record heat, a crowd estimated at three quarters of a million people lined Broadway from the Battery to City Hall. The confetti shower was greater than it had been at Lindbergh's 1927 procession.

Hughes told the audience at a City Hall ceremony that the flight was not a stunt but the fulfillment of a careful plan. With apparent modesty, he was certain that other trained pilots could have completed it as well. He insisted that the speed record was secondary to the planning, which fulfilled the objective of no unscheduled stops. And best of all, he asserted, the achievement had reestablished the United States as the leading force in civil aviation. Indeed, Hughes's flight spurred sales of American-built planes, especially those built by Lockheed. Orders for the L-14 from airlines in Britain, France, and the Netherlands were particularly noteworthy. More ominous, Japan used models of the H-1 and H-2 for its Zeroes, and Germany adopted the Sperry gyroscope, which Hughes had used to maintain a level flight.[11]

Subsequent parades in Washington, Chicago, and Hughes's home town of Houston, along with massive press coverage, elevated him as a national hero similar to Lindbergh's elevation after his trans-Atlantic flight. Reporters described the young, tall, and handsome Texan as looking like Gary Cooper and flying like Lindbergh.[12]

Hughes was only thirty-two in 1938. Yet though his subsequent accomplishments as an airplane designer, defense contractor, real estate developer, and film producer were sometimes impressive, he never came close to duplicating his earlier feats. For example, the first movie he would produce (and direct) in eight years, 1940's *The Outlaw*, with Jane Russell, was essentially an early "soft porn" that was only released in 1945 after Hollywood censors eliminated a few salacious scenes. RKO, the company he bought in the late forties, produced mostly inferior, unprofitable films, because of his ill-advised intervention in the cinematic process. Hughes came close to being prosecuted for bribing influential politicians and high-ranking officers in order to promote the sale of warplanes manufactured at Hughes Aircraft. He never fully recovered from the crash of one of his planes in Beverly Hills in 1946, and by the time he was sixty he was suffering from obsessive-compulsive disorder and what appears to have been early-onset dementia. Before he died of kidney failure on April 5th, 1976, the tabloid press had devoted itself non-stop to coverage of his deterioration and his fortune.[13]

For the brief period from 1935 to 1938, however, Hughes could do no wrong; and during those years he may well have been the best flier in the world. Already worth millions, his primary aim was to publicize the reliability and safety of a twin-engine aircraft on long flights over both land and water. His was the most thoroughly planned private aviation endeavor of its time. In 1938 flying across the ocean was still a daring novelty. That it would eventually become commonplace was due, at least in part, to Howard Hughes.

The Reverend Dr. Ralph W. Sockman of New York's Christ Methodist Church placed Hughes's efforts in an interesting historical perspective:

> An achievement like that of Howard Hughes renders a human service far beyond scientific or commercial measurement. It lifts the emotional plane of a whole people. Such heroism delivers us from the drabness of the commonplace and the dull routine of money-grubbing. As Lindbergh gave a breath of spiritual exaltation to the booming prosperity of the 1920's, so Hughes helps to dispel the fog of the depressed 1930's ... The cult of the strong man is one of the besetting ailments of today. Hence in this day of dictators it is doubly heartening to have heroes of aviation and science. They reveal the greatness which can be won through this service of others rather than at the expense of others.[14]

Charles Lindbergh and Howard Hughes were linked, not only by their tall, lean physiques and retiring personalities but, above all, by their revolutionary flights. Lindbergh's was probably the more courageous of the two: a non-stop, solo jaunt across the Atlantic from New York to Paris in a small, frail single-engine plane – puny by comparison with Hughes's L-14.

Charles Augustus Lindbergh was born in Detroit, Michigan, his maternal grandparents' home town, on February 4th, 1902, the son of Charles August Lindbergh and Evangeline Land Lindbergh, his second wife. Lindbergh the elder, who had been a widower, was a lawyer who later represented a district in the vicinity of the family farm in Little Falls, Minnesota. He was a liberal Republican in the days when this was possible. Mrs.

Lindbergh, the daughter of an innovative dentist, was a high school chemistry teacher. Within a few years, little Charles's parents separated –unofficially—because an official separation or worse, a divorce, would not have been tolerated by the Representative's religiously conservative constituents.

Charles the younger was only an average student, but at his parents' insistence he enrolled at the University of Wisconsin. After a year and a half, however, he dropped out in order to learn the elements of aviation at a flight school in Nebraska. Despite the incompetence of the school's director, he quickly displayed a great aptitude for his chosen field. Leaving the school abruptly, he would spend the next year on his own barnstorming throughout the Midwest, which meant performing aerial acrobatics and giving rides to people drawn to the excitement of the early aviation era.

A desire for greater professional training led Lindbergh to enlist in the Army. The course, at an airfield in Texas, included experiences that rarely came a barnstormer's way, including formation flying, high altitude maneuvers, gunnery, bombing, and precision landing and taking off. After one year, in March 1925, he graduated and was commissioned a second lieutenant in the Army Reserve. Shortly thereafter, he signed a contract with a private company to pilot a plane that would carry U. S. air mail over a route between St. Louis and Chicago.

Lindbergh gained valuable experience flying in darkness and in all kinds of nasty weather, which implanted the notion that he might be capable of greater exploits. A number of prominent aviators were entering the contest for the Orteig Prize. Conceived by Raymond Orteig, the French owner of two New York hotels, it would award any flyer or group of flyers $25,000, then a handsome sum, if they could fly non-stop from New York to Paris or from Paris to New York. Financed by a group of St. Louis businessmen, Lindbergh supervised the construction by a San Diego aircraft company of a plane he called the "Spirit of St. Louis." Various problems delayed or eliminated his likely competitors, and on May 20th, 1927 the "Lone Eagle" took off from Roosevelt Field on Long Island heading for Le Bourget Field outside Paris. Overcoming serious navigational problems, he reached his destination on May 21st after a flight of thirty-three and a half hours.

Lindbergh's life changed forever even before his wheels touched down at Le Bourget. From utter obscurity he emerged as a figure of adulation and even adoration, not only in America and France but throughout much of the world. He was soon earning generous fees as a technical adviser to several airlines and from endorsement of a variety of commercial products. On May 27th, 1929 he married Anne Morrow, daughter of a wealthy family; and in thirteen months – on June 22nd, 1930 – they became the parents of Charles Augustus Lindbergh, III.

Lindbergh's marriage was evidently successful, as Anne became his partner in the air as well as on the ground. She learned how to read a chart, operate a radio, and use Morse code (which at the time was the means of communication between air and ground). At Charles's insistence and under his tutelage, she also became a competent pilot. They made many flights together, including one to China in 1931 which Anne, an aspiring author, wrote about in her first book, *North to the Orient*.[15]

Yet the early thirties were overwhelmingly tragic for the Lindberghs. Anne lost her father and older sister. But above all, there was the kidnapping and murder of the couple's first child, beginning with his abduction in 1932 and culminating in the trial and conviction of his killer in 1935. These events attracted constant, aggressive, and unprecedented press and radio coverage, as had Lindbergh since his historic flight. The earlier publicity had often annoyed the publicity-shy Lindbergh. But now, when his wife and he were in deep mourning, as well as apprehension about threats to themselves and their second son Jon (born August 16th, 1932), the press frenzy was becoming intolerable. They consequently decided to remove themselves from the situation and resettle in Britain, which they envisioned as more respectful of privacy than their homeland.

Arriving in December 1935, they settled in a rental property in a quiet corner of Kent, in southern England. Although disturbances of their privacy were indeed less common than before, the Lindberghs never felt completely comfortable in their host country. Charles, for one, deplored what he characterized as British apathy about many aspects of life. At the same time, he saw a tawdriness, as reflected especially on London's advertising billboards and in newspaper stories about murder, rape, and divorce.[16]

In 1938 the Lindberghs moved to a small home on the tiny island of Iliec a few miles off the coast of France. It had been bought for them by Alexis Carrel, a French biologist and physician who lived on the neighboring island of St. Gildas. Their friendship and collaboration dated back to 1932 when Charles had joined Carrel's research team at the Rockefeller Institute in New York. They worked together on a blood pump for an artificial heart (the Minnesota farm boy with little advanced education had evidently inherited the scientific inclinations of his mother and maternal grandfather).

Carrel was sixty-six years old in 1938. In 1912 he had won the Nobel Prize for pioneering a method of suturing blood vessels during surgery. Other surgical innovations followed; but what kept him in the public eye were his theories about genetics. He was a passionate believer in eugenics, views that included a white supremacist racial pecking order and the advocacy of euthanasia through the gassing of habitual criminals and the incurably insane. While Lindbergh did not share all of Carrel's extreme theories, he was apparently influenced by many of them. For instance, he accepted the Frenchman's conclusion that the western democracies were deteriorating due to loose living and lack of purpose.[17]

The Lindberghs continued their practice of flying off to foreign parts. Charles's racialism was sometimes evident during these trips, as in India whose inhabitants he compared to farm animals.[18] But Germany was the country he and Anne visited the most – six times during the period 1936-38. Major Truman Smith, the American military attaché in Berlin, requested invitations for them from the Hitler regime. An infantry officer with little knowledge of aviation, Smith wanted reports on Germany's air capability (notwithstanding the fact that he was not at all hostile to the Nazis).[19]

Whether attributable or not to Smith's influence, Lindbergh adopted a mostly positive attitude toward the Third Reich. These sentiments were reflected in his diary and later in his autobiography, which was written only a few years before his death. For example, he described Hermann Goring, head of the *Luftwaffe* (Air Force), with whom he socialized on numerous occasions and who was viewed as Hitler's principal subordinate, as a "dynamic political leader."[20] He considered Hitler himself a great man, though somewhat fanatical. Yet, given the post-World War I chaos in Germany, some fanaticism had been necessary – Hitler's moderation could emerge later. Lindbergh saw Germany (and Italy) as the most virile nations in Europe; and he favored the readjustment of European borders and the restoration of Germany's pre-war colonial empire.[21]

Years later, in his autobiography, Lindbergh tried to be more critical of Nazi Germany. But even here his allegedly *former* admiration managed to emerge:

> I shared the repulsion that democratic peoples felt in viewing the demagoguery of Hitler, the controlled elections, the secret police. Yet I felt that I was seeing in Germany, despite the crudeness of its form, the inevitable alternative

to decline ... It was a condition recorded in the past of every major nation ... Looking back through history, what nation does not find aggression in its origins? I was stirred by the spirit in Germany as I had been deadened by the lack of it in England and disturbed by its volatile individuality in France ....[22]

From the vantage point of his acquired expertise on the *Luftwaffe's* strength, Lindbergh played a role in great power European diplomacy and the war scare that culminated in the Munich Pact in September 1938. Above all, he wanted to prevent a conflict between Germany and the Anglo-French alliance. This was not because of any deep sympathy for Britain or France who would certainly be defeated by superior German air power. But then the civilized peoples of Western Europe would be weakened to the point where they would face an onslaught from the "Asiatic hordes" (by which he meant the Soviet Union). As for the present danger of Nazi aggression, he believed that it had been vastly exaggerated.

Lindbergh's outlook was shared by Britain's so-called Cliveden Set, a group of aristocrats meeting periodically at the country home of Lady Astor. Members of the Conservative government under Prime Minister Neville Chamberlain also leaned toward support of appeasing Hitler in the summer of 1938. Lindbergh spent much time telling influential people in Britain and France about what he deemed Germany's overwhelming air strength. He also sent a memo to American Ambassador to Britain Joseph Kennedy, whose views were similar to those of the British appeasers, requesting that it be shared with the prime minister, which it was. French premier Georges Bonnet was the recipient of a message too. Lindbergh warned him that in the event of a conflict over the Sudetenland, Czech and Soviet air assistance to the western allies would be totally inadequate. Lindbergh based his opinion on observations made during recent visits to Czechoslovakia and the U. S. S. R. All of these messages conceivably could have contributed to the Anglo-French decision to abandon the Czechs at Munich.[23]

Two weeks after Munich, the Lindberghs returned to Germany for their third visit of 1938. The Nazi greeting was warmer than ever, the greatest expression of which was the presentation of a medal to Charles on October 19th by Hermann Goring. The *Verdienstkreuz der Deutscher Adler* (Service Cross of the German Eagle) was a mark of gratitude to worthy foreigners. A few months earlier Henry Ford was a recipient, probably because of his earlier anti-Semitic writings in the *Dearborn Independent*. Ford later returned the medal. The award to Lindbergh was ostensibly for his 1927 transatlantic flight. Other governments had honored him for the same thing, but years earlier.

Lindbergh claimed not to have known beforehand about the German intention, which was probably true. But at a time when Nazi aggressiveness and racial intolerance were obvious, it was a public relations disaster in America and elsewhere. Anne recognized the probable long-term consequences for her husband – the medal, she feared, would become an "albatross" around his neck.

A few weeks after the medal ceremony, on the night of November 9th -10th, 1938, the Nazis released what can accurately be called a *pogrom* – an outbreak of violence against the Jews of Germany. *Kristallnacht,* or Night of the Broken Glass, allegedly was a spontaneous act of revenge for the murder of a German diplomat in Paris by a Jewish teenager. Stormtroopers in civilian clothes destroyed hundreds of Jewish shops, homes, and synagogues, attacked thousands of people (killing more than one hundred), and rounded up 30,000 Jewish men for transport to concentration camps. The "albatross" now seemed more offensive than ever, and denunciations of Lindbergh mounted. As one critic, Secretary of the Interior Harold Ickes, a fierce anti-Nazi, told a Zionist audience in Cleveland: anyone who accepts a medal from Germany "forfeits his right to be an American."[24]

After *Kristallnacht* Lindbergh wrote in his diary: "They (the Nazis) have undoubtedly had a difficult Jewish problem, but why is it necessary to handle it so unreasonably."[25] Still, his attitude toward the Jews of Germany, and later, toward those in the United States, was not compassionate but really more or less parallel to the Nazi line. German anti-Semitism, he believed, emanated from Jewish involvement in the country's collapse and revolutionary violence after the First World War. And, he added: "They (the Jews) had the best houses, drove the best automobiles, and mixed with the prettiest German girls."[26]

Lindbergh stubbornly refused to return the medal, which he described as a mark of friendship in a time of peace. Only later, when Germany and America were at war, did he make a halfway gesture by donating it to the Missouri Historical Society in St. Louis.[27]

A related issue arose shortly after *Kristallnacht*. The Lindberghs loved the wild beauty and privacy of their home on the island of Illiec but not the harsh winter weather. They decided that a stay in Berlin would be a pleasant alternative. Architect Albert Speer, chief Berlin city planner and later war industries czar, assured the couple that he would build a home for them anywhere they wanted it. But Anne's mother, who hated the Nazis, wrote to tell her daughter that emerging American public opinion would make it a terrible mistake for Charles and her to live in Berlin. An example of the growing coolness involved Trans-World Airlines, for whom Charles was a technical adviser. TWA dropped the promotional phrase, "the Lindbergh Line," from its marketing activity. Though the family soon left Berlin for an apartment in Paris, Charles continued to believe that living in the Nazi capital would have benefitted German-American relations.[28]

Lindbergh was no longer a totally beloved national hero. His status became even clearer in 1940-41 after he became the most prominent figure in the America First movement, which advocated absolute U. S. neutrality in the European war. After the fall of France in June 1940, he spoke to large audiences at Madison Square Garden in New York, Soldiers' Field in Chicago, and other locales, as well as making frequent radio addresses. Strong support was forthcoming from isolationists in general, FDR haters, Socialists, Communists (until the German invasion of Russia), and home-grown fascists such as Father Coughlin and the German-American Bund. Media supporters included many newspapers, the *Reader's Digest*, and the *Saturday Evening Post*, and well-known individuals such as Henry Ford, World War I ace Eddie Rickenbacker, actress Lillian Gish, among many others.

After Pearl Harbor, however, the opposition to President Roosevelt's policies virtually disappeared, including Lindbergh's. He applied for the return of his Army Air Corps commission that he had resigned in 1940 when the president compared him to a Civil War Copperhead (basically a traitor). Following the orders of the commander-in-chief, the War Department rejected his application. Still, Lindbergh managed to contribute to the war effort by working on the development of the B-24 bomber at the Ford plant in Willow Run, Michigan. In 1944 he went to the Pacific Theater as a technical adviser of United Aircraft but was unofficially allowed to fly combat missions – fifty of them – by commanding officers in the field. He shot down Japanese aircraft on two occasions.

Lindbergh lived in Darien, Connecticut after the war and served as a consultant to the U. S. Air Force Chief of Staff and to Pan American World Airways. In 1954, on the recommendation of President Eisenhower, he received a commission as a brigadier general in the Air Force Reserve. Also in that year, he served on a panel that chose the future site of the U. S. Air

Force Academy (Colorado became the site). His deep interest in the Apollo program of the 1960s, which had its greatest success with the moon journey of Apollo 11, earned him a place as commentator on Walter Cronkite's TV news program.

Lindbergh's last years were much concerned with the environment, particularly with saving the humpback whale and other endangered species. Together with Laurence Rockefeller, he helped establish the Haleakala National Park in Hawaii. He died in 1974 and is buried in Hawaii. Anne Morrow Lindbergh died in 2001.[29]

Douglas Corrigan bore a few surface resemblances to the two aviators previously discussed. Like Howard Hughes, he was born in Texas, spent much of the rest of his life in California, and lost his parents at a relatively early age. And, like his hero Lindbergh, he had been a barnstormer and a total unknown before making his unique flight across the Atlantic in a small, single engine plane.

Douglas Corrigan was born Clyde Corrigan, Jr. in Galveston, Texas on January 22nd, 1907, the eldest of three children born to Clyde Corrigan, Sr., a civil engineer, and Evelyn Nelson Corrigan, a former elementary school teacher. The elder Clyde Corrigan failed in business and deserted the family when his sons were nine and eight and his daughter four. At his mother's request, Clyde, Jr. became Douglas.

Mrs. Corrigan made a meager living running a series of rooming houses, while her young sons supplemented her earnings through various odd jobs. After his mother's early death, Douglas quit school so he could work full-time. In his late teens, he took a few flying lessons while also learning much about aeronautical mechanics. Much of the latter resulted from his job at the Ryan Airplane Factory in San Diego.

In early 1927 Corrigan had one of the most formative

experiences of his life. Charles Lindbergh had hired the Ryan company to build a plane that would take him from New York to Paris. The future "Lone Eagle" was present for much of the two months it took to complete the construction project. Corrigan worked on the wings, the cabin, and then on installing the gasoline tanks. A bit later, when news of the fateful flight reached San Diego, Corrigan and the entire Ryan workforce celebrated what for them was a triumph too. The twenty-year-old Corrigan, who did not yet have a pilot's license, began to dream of the day when he would be able to duplicate Lindbergh's achievement.[30]

Between 1927 and 1938 Corrigan made his living as a barnstormer, aeronautical mechanic, flying instructor, and commercial pilot. His resume included several cross-country flights. In 1935, while in New York City, his dream took a long step toward reality when he purchased a much-used OX-5 Curtiss Robin for the bargain price of $325. With his brother Harry on board, he flew the plane to Los Angeles, a trip that took them eighteen days. They were slowed by numerous landings for refueling, emergency repairs, and giving people rides to earn desperately needed cash. Once in Los Angeles Corrigan replaced the aircraft's ninety horsepower engine with a 165 h-p model cobbled together from two old engines. Another key improvement was the addition of five extra fuel tanks.[31]

Corrigan openly speculated with friends about a flight either to Dublin or London (even with its enhanced fuel capacity, he knew that the Robin could not make it all the way to Paris). But his plans seemed to collapse altogether when federal regulators declined permission for a trans-Atlantic flight. Their chief rationale was the plane's generally flimsy condition (reporters later nicknamed it an "airborne crate" or a "flying jalopy."[32]).

Corrigan arrived in the New York area from California in time to take his place among the huge crowd assembled at Floyd Bennett Field to witness Howard Hughes and his crew depart for their world-circling adventure. A week later, at a quarter past five in the morning on July 17th, 1938, a few people watched the little Robin take off for what was supposedly a non-stop return trip to California. Inexplicably, when the plane emerged from the clouds over Floyd Bennett, it headed east rather than west, as the flight plan indicated it should have done.

Twenty-eight hours, thirteen minutes, and 3,150 miles later, the young man landed at Baldonnel Airport in Dublin, Ireland. "I'm Douglas Corrigan," he told a group of startled airport workers. "Just got in from New York. Where am I? I intended to fly to California." From that momentous landing, he earned the nickname "Wrong Way Corrigan," claiming that heavy fog and a misreading of his plane's compass were responsible for the gigantic miscalculation.[33]

Although Corrigan was obviously fibbing (which he never admitted), the Irish people, their political leaders, and the U. S. Ambassador to Ireland all laughed a lot and appeared to enjoy themselves immensely. The Irish government assured him that his lack of a passport was no problem. Irish Airlines granted him a free flight to London where he saw the sights and had an audience with Ambassador Kennedy.

After returning to Ireland, he received free passage to New York on the U.S. liner *Manhattan* (passage included his crated-up plane). A cablegram from the Assistant Secretary of Commerce informed him that his pilot's license was suspended for a total of four days, until August 4, for violation of numerous laws. But the suspension happened to expire on the same day the *Manhattan* docked in New York.[34]

The day after his arrival the city gave Corrigan a ticker-tape parade rivaling those for Lindbergh and Hughes. He visited many towns of various sizes throughout the country where he received a hero's welcome. They presented him with numerous gifts, some of which were comical "wrong-way" items; one was a watch that ran backwards. A Native American leader in Tulsa,

Oklahoma initiated him into his tribe as Chief Wrong-Way. Also forthcoming were lucrative contracts for an autobiography, entitled *That's My Story* (1938), and a movie, *The Flying Irishman* (1939), in which he played himself.[35]

Except for his work as a test pilot during World War II, the rest of Corrigan's long life was relatively uneventful. But his one bizarre flight struck a chord with the American people. In the words of Robert Thomas, his *New York Times* obituary writer:

This was because he (Corrigan) was seen as an engaging and impish young pilot who had boldly thumbed his nose at authority, then baldly denied it, and partly because he had made the flight not in a state-of-the-art aircraft with cutting edge instruments, but in a rickety plane ... precariously patched together ....[36]

Corrigan's flight, in the middle of 1938, was also comic relief that momentarily pushed aside depressing newspaper and radio coverage of an economic downturn at home, brutal wars in Spain and China, and an impending one in Europe. Our last aviator was certainly unique too. Unlike the others, he could not pass as an all-American boy, despite many visits to the country – mainly for fund-raising and a teaching assignment at a seminary in Illinois. The seminary was Catholic, and Father Paul Schulte (1896-1975) eschewed the aviator's snappy leather jacket in favor of traditional clerical garb.

Born in Germany, induction into the army in World War I interrupted Schulte's education for the priesthood. After suffering a wound during his service in an infantry unit, he transferred to the air force. He trained as a pilot and served in Palestine with German forces who were assisting their Turkish allies against the British. When the war ended, he resumed his priestly studies and was ordained in 1922. His first assignment was as a missionary in South Africa.

In 1925 a fellow priest and good friend of Schulte's died in Africa of pneumonia complicated by malaria. He died at a

Protestant mission hospital that it had taken his bearers five days to reach. Schulte estimated that the trip would have taken two and a half hours by air! This thought inspired him to found the Missionary Vehicular Association (MIVA), the purpose of which was to provide modern vehicles – its motto was "Toward Christ by land and sea and in the air." By 1936 MIVA had bought twelve aircraft and more than 150 autos and motorboats that were used by Catholic missions across the world.

The Church later transferred Schulte to a parish in Churchill, a town situated on Hudson's Bay in the northern part of Canada's Manitoba province. From there, in August 1938, he undertook a series of rescue efforts, flying more than several thousand miles over land and water and parts of which were north of the Arctic Circle. During the few respites he had, Schulte described salient aspects of his flights for the *New York Times*. He flew mostly over desolate and sparsely populated territory in northern Canada, now known by the Inuit name Nunavut.

Learning of the critical illness of fellow priest, Father Julien Cochard, Schulte flew twelve hundred miles from Churchill to a remote hospital in the Arctic, at Chesterfield Inlet, to pick up a physician, Dr. Thomas Melling. In spite of Melling's own serious illness, the two of them flew eight hundred miles to Baffin Island to retrieve Father Cochard. It was "summer" in the Arctic, but fog obscured visibility and ice covered much of the ground. Schulte still managed to fly a total of 2,200 miles to reach the sick priest and bring him and the doctor to the hospital at Chesterfield.[37]

Another rescue effort took Schulte and Dr. Melling back to the same hospital, after 1,200 miles of an Arctic flight during which an impenetrable fog forced them down and later made them turn back temporarily. The patient this time was an Inuit named Okumaaluk who had been accidentally shot by Nupuyark, one of his five children.

A different type of mission took Schulte and Henri Haffmans, a radio engineer, to the Arctic Ocean. Their objective was to chart a course for the *Therese*, a ship laden with a year's supply of food and fuel destined for one of the Church's northernmost missions. The *Therese's* captain was satisfied with the scouting report and proceeded on his way. Still, the ship briefly became ice-bound until a powerful northeast gale blew it free.[38]

Difficult experiences were not confined to the year 1938 for the man known as "the flying missionary" and also as "the blond giant" because of his physique and striking hair color. On August 1, 1937, for instance, while flying west from Detroit, he had to make a forced landing on the Hudson River to escape a severe electrical storm. Both before and after his Arctic experiences, Father Schulte flew over many isolated regions of Africa as part of his MIVA endeavors. He died in Namibia in 1975.

Notes: Chapter 5

1   Donald L. Bartlett and James B. Steele, *Empire. The Life, Legend, and Madness of Howard Hughes.* New York: W. W. Norton Co., 1979, 67-68.

2   *Ibid.*, 75.

3   *Ibid.*

4   *Ibid.*, 82, 86-87; Charles Higham, *Howard Hughes. The Secret Life.* New York: G. P. Putnam's Sons, 1993, 75-76.

5   George J. Marrett, *Howard Hughes. Aviator.* Annapolis, MD: Naval Institute Press, 2004, 34; Bartlett and Steele, *op. cit.*, 88, 94.

6   *NYT,* July 4, 1938, 15.

7   Bartlett and Steele, *op. cit.*, 94; Higham, *op. cit.*, 83; Marriett, *op. cit.*, 36.

8   Higham, *op. cit.*, 84.

9   Bartlett and Steele, *op. cit.*, 96; Higham, *op. cit.*, 85; Chelsea Fraser, *Famous American Flyers.* New York: Thomas Y. Crowell Co., 1941, 305-306.

10 Bartlett and Steele, *op. cit.*, 96-97; Higham, *op. cit.*, 85; Marrett, *op. cit.*, 36.

11 Bartlett and Steele, *op. cit.*, 99; Higham, *op. cit.*, 91.

12 Marrett, *op. cit.*, 38.

13 Higham, *op. cit.*, *passim.*

14 *NYT,* July 14, 1938, 3.

15 Leonard Mosley, *Lindbergh. A Biography.* Garden City, NY: Doubleday and Co., Inc., 1976, 145, 156.

16 Wayne S. Cole, *Charles A. Lindbergh and the Battle Against American Intervention in World War II.* New York and London: Harcourt Brace Jovanovich, 1974, 38.

17 Mosely, *op. cit.*, 219-220. Carrel was a quasi-fascist, but his French nationalism prompted a deep hatred of Germany. Nor was he anti-Semitic. Some of his best friends, for example, Albert Einstein, were indeed Jewish.

18 Charles A. Lindbergh, Autobiography *of Values.* Ed., William Jovanovich. Co-ed., Judith A. Schiff. New York and London: Harcourt Brace Jovanovich, 1977, 149.

19 Cole, *op. cit.*, 31-32.

20 Lindbergh, *op. cit.*, 146.

21 Cole, *op. cit.*, 34, 38.

22 Lindbergh, *op. cit.*, 156.

23 Mosely, *op. cit.*, 227-228; Kenneth S. Davis, *The Hero. Charles A. Lindbergh and the American Dream.* Garden City, NY: Doubleday and Co., Inc., 1959, 377-379. Lindbergh in 1938 had an exaggerated idea of *Luftwaffe* strength, partly because Goring packed factories, air fields, and flying squadrons to impress him. Lindbergh and Major Truman Smith sent a report to General H. H. (Hap) Arnold, Chief of Staff of the U. S. Army Air Corps, that the *Luftwaffe* possessed 10,000 planes and was building 500-800 a month. Two years later, in 1940, real German air strength was actually 4,665 planes.

24 Quoted in A. Scott Berg, *Lindbergh.* New York: G. P. Putnam's Sons, 1998, 376.

25 Quoted in Mosely, *op. cit.*, 235.

26 Quoted in *ibid.*, 238.

27 Cole, *op. cit.*, 44.

28 Mosely, *op. cit.*, *237-238;* Davis, *op. cit.*, 381-382; Cole, *op. cit.*, 45.

29 Lindbergh also led a secret life. As a young barnstormer, cadet, and air mail pilot, he had been critical of associates who spent much of their time pursuing women. His marriage to Anne seemingly was characterized by mutual respect and faithfulness. Yet in the latter years of the 20th century the Lindberghs' younger daughter Reeve discovered shocking evidence about her late father. Apparently, he had sired seven children by three German women between the years 1958 and 1967. This confirmed earlier evidence provided by one of her half-sisters. DNA tests in 2003 verified these strong suspicions. *Wikepedia, The Free Encyclopedia:* "Double Life and Secret German Children"

30 Fraser, *op. cit.*, 322.

31 *Ibid.*, 328. See also Robert M. Thomas, Jr., "Douglas Corrigan Obituary," *NYT,* Dec. 14, 1995, B. 18.

32 Thomas, *op. cit.*, B. 18.

33 *Ibid.*

34 Douglas Corrigan, *That's My Story.* New York: E. P. Dutton & Co., Inc., 1938, 206.

35 Fraser, *Op. cit.*, 341-342.

36 Thomas, *op. cit.*

37 *NYT,* Aug. 10, 1938, 21; Aug. 12, 1938, 34.

38 *NYT,* Aug. 22, 1938, 15; Aug. 29, 1938, 15.

CHAPTER 6

Advent of the Superhero

Heroes of the air won the plaudits of millions. But the era also gave rise to the first and most renowned superhero whose feats no ordinary mortal could hope to match. Superman, in comic book form, first entered America's consciousness in the spring of 1938.

The "man of steel" actually had many mythological and literary forbears. For example, the biblical figure of Sampson slew numerous enemies of the Israelites, and the ancient Greek demigod Herakles (the Roman Hercules) defended society against evil, tamed wild beasts, and rescued women in distress. In more recent times the pulp fiction magazines (a name derived from the coarse paper on which they were printed) sometimes centered around heroes with supernatural powers. These pulps were popular from the 1890s to the 1930s. More skillful writers, such as Edgar Rice Burroughs and Philip Wylie, also devised heroes with superhuman powers. Played in the movies by the former Olympics swimming champion Johnny Weissmuller, Tarzan cavorted through "jungles" created by Hollywood set designers. Additional superhero types included the cartoon character Popeye, made invincible by spinach, and radio's "The Shadow," who fought bad guys by becoming invisible.

Superman, as the world came to know him, emerged from the collaboration of two young men from the lower middle class

Cleveland neighborhood of Glenville. Writer Jerome (Jerry) Siegel and artist Joseph (Joe) Shuster were the offspring of Jewish immigrants from the *shtetls* (small towns) of Eastern Europe. They met through their involvement in *Torch*, Glenville High School's student magazine. Both of them were short, somewhat homely, myopic, and less than ideal in weight – Jerry was chubby, while Joe was very thin. These disadvantages, plus an inherent shyness, limited their appeal to girls. Students of psychology, professional or otherwise, might speculate that their physical imperfections impelled them, subconsciously at least, to create a superman.

Jerry and Joe collaborated for the first time in 1931 on a story in *Torch* entitled *Goober the Mighty*, which was about a heroic, semi-human son of a lioness. Daydreaming in class made Jerry a poor student. But he read voraciously, especially the ten cents pulp magazines available at the neighborhood pharmacy and the relatively new genre of science fiction. Both Joe and he also loved the comics page in the *Cleveland Plain Dealer*. The business-oriented *Fortune* magazine also encouraged them through an article on how to launch a comic series which, the author declared, could earn them at least $1,000 a week. Not a pittance even today, that sum was fantastic, in every sense of the word, during the on-going Great Depression.[1]

In 1932, while still in high school, Jerry wrote and Joe illustrated a story that appeared in their self-published magazine called *Science Fiction*. "The Reign of the Super-man" contained many elements of the later Superman, especially the central character's enormous strength, telescopic vision, and mind-reading ability, as well as an ambition to rule the universe. In subsequent months the character would drop "the" and the hyphen, along with his evil intentions. He became simply Superman – a bulletproof fighter of bullies who won the hearts of girls and used his super powers to help those most in need.[2]

Many years later, in the first decades of the twenty-first

century, a scholarly debate arose over Superman's possible Jewish identity. To be sure, he didn't "look" Jewish, with his up-turned nose and bright blue eyes. The name of his alter ego, Clark Kent, could only be WASP. Nor had anyone ever heard of a Jewish strongman. (Actually, there were Jewish strongmen besides Sampson. One, the Golem, was a mythic giant of a man, shaped from clay, who supposedly appeared from time to time in medieval Central Europe to save Jews from persecution. More believable, in modern America, there was Siegmund Breitbart, a Polish-born circus performer sometimes referred to as the strongest man in the world. His talents included pounding nails into wood with his fists and pulling a wagon full of people with his teeth).

In spite of Superman's apparent identity, there were hints to the contrary. One was his Kryptonian name: *Kal-El. El* is a much used Hebrew suffix, one of several (substitute) words for God, as in Isra-el, Samu-el, and Dani-el. *Kal* is similar to the Hebrew words for voice and vessel. Taken together, these two words suggest that *Kal-El* was not just a Jew but a unique one at that, a voice or vessel of God. So just as the baby Moses was floated in a reed basket by a mother desperate to spare him from a pharaoh's death warrant, *Kal-El's* doomed parents, before the planet Krypton blew up, placed him in a spaceship that carried him to the safety of Earth. Both babies were raised in foreign cultures – Moses by Pharaoh's daughter and *Kal-El* by Kansas farmers named Kent. The destruction of Krypton and its inhabitants also may call to mind the Nazi Holocaust that was gathering momentum when Jerry and Joe were publishing their first comics, as well as the *Kindertransports*, the exodus by rail of Jewish children from the rising terror in Germany and in German-occupied Austria and Czechoslovakia.[3]

As with many American Jews, Superman was evidently left-of-center politically, championing causes from disarmament to the welfare state. He was the ultimate foreigner, escaping from an "intergalactic *shtetl*" and shedding his "Jewish" name for Clark Kent, as obviously WASPish as the pen names that Jerry had periodically chosen for himself.

Much of the above, of course, is speculation, and neither Jerry nor Joe was an observant Jew. But in his memoir Jerry acknowledged that his writing was strongly influenced by the anti-Semitism that he saw and felt in his younger years, and that Sampson was a role model for Superman. He was also proud that his anti-Nazi superhero provoked a hostile reaction in Germany. Moreover, as Jerry asserted repeatedly, he wrote about his world, a strongly immigrant neighborhood that was seventy percent Jewish and consequently saturated with Jewish culture and tradition.[4]

Jerry and Joe graduated from Glenville High School in 1934. Family poverty necessitated paying jobs, so Joe delivered groceries for five dollars a week and also sold ice cream, while Jerry earned five dollars weekly for moving paper at a printing plant. But they still worked on their dream of comic book success. They created a variety of characters, while continuing to develop aspects of the Superman story, such as the hero's childhood and adolescence as Clark Kent. Beginning in 1934 they contributed stories to a comic book called *New Fun*, which was published by Malcolm Wheeler-Nicholson, a retired army officer. Pay for this work was minimal, and worse, not very timely.

During these years Joe was putting the finishing touches on Superman's attire. First, he essentially adopted the space suits of Flash Gordon and Buck Rogers with emblems on their chests. Below the waist the tights were a mixture of a weight lifter's outfit and those of wrestlers and boxers, who sometimes wore tights under their shorts. Superman's belt-buckled shorts looked like those in the Jantzen swimsuit advertisement, not surprising since Joe had used this particular model. The lace-up leather boots were similar to those worn by circus strong man Breitbart.

Superman's overall physical appearance reflected images of Tarzan-actor Johnny Weissmuller as he appeared in movie magazines. But his smile was basically that of comic page detective Dick Tracy. The name Clark came either from Clark Gable, an Ohio boy who often played macho film roles, or possibly from a comic book character named Clark, a convict who had a secret heroic identity.[5]

While still working for Major Wheeler-Nicholson, Jerry and Joe tried to sell the idea of Superman to newspaper syndicates but without success. Then, on March 1st, 1938, the proprietors of *Action Comics* – who had forced out the bankrupt major – purchased the rights to Superman. The prior publishing ventures of Harry Donnenfeld and Jack Liebowitz were mainly works of pulp fiction. The payment to Jerry and Joe took the form of a check for $412: $282 of this was for money owed to them for work done for the major, and $130 for Superman. In practice, it turned out to be a huge underpayment for the right to control the character, whose astounding success launched a multibillion-dollar superheroes' industry.

Action Comics #1, dated June 1938, actually went on sale in April. The Superman story's length was only thirteen of the sixty-four pages in the whole comic book, but the longer segment was far less memorable. Donnenfeld and Liebowitz had printed 202,000 copies of *Action* #1. They were taking a chance but had guessed right. Vendors sold 130,000 comic books, or sixty-four percent of the print run, at a time when anything over fifty percent was considered a success.

When a survey asked readers which of the eight features they thought had driven sales, 404 of 542 respondents named Superman. Sales continued to rise. A year later *Action* 13 printed 725,000 copies and sold 625,000. Most of the buyers were children and adolescents. Superman became their hero because his causes were just, he always won, and the price at ten cents a comic book was right too.[6]

The cover of the first issue of Superman showed him lifting an auto off the ground, which no real-life muscle man could do. Joe copied the vehicle, a 1938 Hudson, from an advertisement and the superhero's lifting position from a fitness manual. Many of Superman's adventures reflected real events. For example, the story entitled "San Monte" resembled the seemingly endless Chaco War (1932-38) between Paraguay and Bolivia over a piece of oil-rich territory. Other realities were reflected in Superman's leveling of slums and confrontation of wife-beaters, corrupt politicians, and manufacturers of accident-prone autos, and his freeing of inmates wrongfully convicted of murder.

In the opinion of Ian Gordon, a recent author, the Superman of the first two years of *Action Comics* was basically a reformist liberal, though one inclined toward direct action in support of his causes. The spirit of the New Deal and the reality of life in 1930s Cleveland were the inspiration for many of Jerry's Superman stories.[7]

Within two years of his appearance, Superman had surpassed Little Orphan Annie, Dick Tracy, and Popeye in the world of comics. Through the efforts of Donnenfeld and Liebowitz, the superhero's exploits secured coverage in media other than comic books. In a contract dated September 22nd, 1938, the McClure Syndicate purchased the right to market a Superman comic strip to newspapers (one newspaper carrying it was the *Cleveland Plain Dealer*, which Jerry had read and written to as a kid). This was the first time a hero had jumped from a comic book to a comic strip – until then it was the other way around. Syndication lasted until May 1966. At its peak, the strip appeared in more than three hundred dailies and ninety Sunday papers. Soon after its inauguration, Jerry and Joe had to hire additional artists to assist with the work load.[8]

Superman's popularity eventually led to a radio show, a cartoon movie short, a weekly movie serial, a television program (1950s), and four full-length feature films of the late 1970s and early 1980s. "Superman, Inc." also spread into merchandising, as numerous companies manufactured Superman toys, games, dolls, jigsaw puzzles, and clothing. Cereal boxes, milk containers, and even high-octane gasoline took on the Superman label. This commercialism added considerably to the income of Donnenfeld and Liebowitz.[9]

Meanwhile the influence of Jerry and Joe over Superman faded continuously during the five years after the publication of *Action* #1. In a letter of September 28th, 1938, Liebowitz reminded Jerry, who had complained against low pay rates, that *Detective Comics* (the new name of *Action Comics*) could replace Joe and him at any time. In conjunction with the McClure Syndicate, the publishers increasingly forced changes on the creators. So, for instance, new guidelines in 1940 prohibited the destruction of private property and required more concern for the views of parents. Artistic criticism dictated that Joe reduce the size of Superman's backside and trim down the bust and hips of Lois Lane, the apple of Clark Kent's eye, so that she appeared less sexy. More significantly, perhaps, they dictated that Superman cut down on social crusading.[19]

By late 1942 *DC* was exercising almost complete control over the production of all Superman ventures. True, Jerry and Joe were making good money by 1940s' standards: Jerry earned $28,000 a year, about $475,000 in 2016 dollars, and Joe got $15,000, or about $250,000 by the same measure. Yet aside from their comic book and newspaper strip work, they got nothing from the handsome proceeds of "Superman, Inc." activities.

On June 28th, 1943 Jerry entered the Army and was stationed in Hawaii. His military duties (on the staff of the Army newspaper *Stars and Stripes*) and the long-distance communication between Hawaii and corporate headquarters in New York City soon ended his connection with Superman. Joe's art work suffered the same fate, in his case largely because of his fading eyesight. Superman, however, not only survived the withdrawal of his creators but thrived during and after the war. Comic books outsold all other reading material at U. S. military bases, and Superman was the most popular of all comics figures.[11]

Jerry and Joe struggled to survive. Jerry worked sporadically writing for a number of comics productions before moving from New York to California, where he took employment at dead-end jobs, such as mail-sorting. Joe was so desperate at one point that he sold all of his furniture. And, though hardly able to see, he drew illustrations for under-the-counter soft porn publications. One of them eerily resembled a scantily-clad Lois Lane wielding a whip over Superman.

After a number of lawsuits initiated by Jerry and his wife, he and Joe ended up with enough money to live in modest comfort. The also got the credit they deserved as Superman's creators, including during the enormously popular Superman movie of 1978. Joe died in 1992 and Jerry in 1996. The latter never fully forgave his former employers for, in his opinion, cheating him out of millions.

The first appearance of Superman in 1938 essentially marked the beginning of a golden age of comic books that lasted into the 1950s. A key part of this age were other superheroes, such as Batman, Captain Marvel, Spider Man, and Wonder Woman, whose creation was undoubtedly inspired by the success of Superman. Superman himself has endured into the twenty-first century, buoyed up by four full-length movies and three successful TV shows. Comics writer Edward Nelson Birdwell summarized a number of cogent reasons for this success:

> Superman's exploits held something for everyone. There was his science-fiction background and his ancestry on the planet Krypton. There was high adventure in his incredible feats of strength and daring, each one topping the last. There was a maddening romantic triangle, wherein Clark

Kent, reporter for the *Daily Planet,* fell in love with co-worker Lois Lane, who, it seemed, had eyes only for Clark's secret identity as Superman! How perplexing! Clark was his own competition for Lois's affections, his own rival ....[12]

Notes: Chapter 6

1   Brad Ricca, *Super Boys. The Amazing Adventures of Jerry Siegel and Joe Shuster, The Creators of Superman.* New York: St. Martin's Press, 2013, 46-47.
2   Larry Tye, *Superman. The High-Flying History of America's Most Enduring Hero.* New York: Random House, 2012, 6.
3   *Ibid.*, 65-66. In 2000 Pulitzer Prize-winning author Michael Chabon published a novel, *The Amazing Adventures of Kavalier and Clay,* in which two young Jewish men create a comic book superhero who combats the Nazis.
4   *Ibid.*, 66-67.
5   Ricca, *op. cit.*, 114-115, 128, 130.
6   Tye, *op. cit.*, 23, 31, 35-37.
7   Ian Gordon, *Superman. The Persistence of an American Icon.* New Brunswick, NJ and London: Rutgers University Press, 2017, 18.
8   *Ibid.*, 99; Tye, *op. cit.*, 38, 47; Ricca, *op. cit.*, 162.
9   Tye, *op. cit.*, 124.
10 Gordon, *op. cit.*, 99; Tye, *op.cit.*, 49. In addition to lack of control over Superman, Jerry and Joe (who was mostly affected) gave up their art work, which was destroyed soon after it was used. There would be no chance to sell it or to preserve it for posterity.
11 Gordon, *op. cit.*, 105-106; Tye, *op. cit.*, 66.
12 Quoted in Boardman, *op. cit.*, 215. Edward Nelson Birdwell (1931-87) was a writer for *Mad* magazine and various comic books published by *DC Comics* and for the *Batman* comic strip.

CHAPTER 7

Political Extremism, American Style

C omic book heroes would eventually spend some of their time fighting fictitious fascists and communists. But the real-life counterparts of these extremists were not absent from these shores; and, in fact, 1938 may have been the year in which they experienced some of their greatest successes.

The Communist Party of the United States (CPUSA) was born in 1919, in the aftermath of the Bolshevik Revolution in Russia. Many of its adherents had seceded from the American Socialist Party, which was non-violent and whose pacifism during the war years (1917-18) had provoked government prosecution of its leader.

Postwar strikes and terroristic attacks, the latter mostly by anarchists, gave rise to a national mood of anti-radicalism, which included CPUSA as a target. Deportation of foreign-born Communists to Soviet Russia and other countries of origin was one consequence. Still, the foreign-born element constituted the majority of a party that during the 1920s never had more than a few thousand members and who were enlisted in organizational units based on ethnic identity. Nor were many Communists union members, African Americans, or women. Bitter leadership quarrels were common, along with complete subservience to the Comintern (Communist International). This organ of the Soviet state exerted overwhelming influence over the American and other non-Russian Communist parties.[1]

The CPUSA underwent modest change during the period 1930-34. Spurred by the onset of the Great Depression, membership rose from 7,000 to 26,000. Many newcomers came from the ranks of the unemployed; and the Unemployed Council movement of this period, which agitated for greater relief efforts, was dominated by the party. As employment increased, Communists became more active in unions.

Although American-born membership grew, a majority of the party remained foreign-born. Geographically CPUSA was concentrated in New York, Chicago, San Francisco, Seattle, and other big cities. The following statistics illustrate these realities: one-third of party members lived in New York City; no party Central Committee was less than one-third Jewish; and few Communists lived between the Mississippi River and the West Coast.[2]

Until 1935-36 CPUSA leaders regarded left wing competitors as "social fascists" and democratically-elected leaders, including President Roosevelt, as "stalking horses for fascism." But with the absolute victory of Nazism in Germany and the rise of fascism elsewhere Communist views, from the Comintern down, began to change. The leftist regime in France, an alliance between Socialists, Communists, and "Radical" bourgeois democrats that came to power in 1934, gave a great boost to the "Popular Front" idea.

The view that competitive left wingers had to be absorbed remained part of Communist ideology, but with the rise of fascism this goal had to be postponed indefinitely. The 1936 presidential election campaign introduced a new, somewhat subtle but still significant attitude toward President Roosevelt. As articulated by leader Earl Browder, the party would oppose Republican candidate Alf Landon and all other FDR foes without openly supporting the president.

This approach broadened considerably in 1937 as the Popular Front (or People's Front) morphed into the Democratic Front. According to Browder, the new American political reality consisted of liberals and laborites versus reactionaries, not simply Democrats vs. Republicans. The CPUSA would support progressive elements within the Democratic or Republican Parties or in other parties too. Only when suitable candidates from these groups were not available would Communists run on their own ticket.[3]

The year 1938 was a remarkable one for the CPUSA, especially by contrast with its extremism and numerical weakness only a few years earlier. Membership had increased to 75,000, from 26,000 in 1934. Attachment to the New Deal and to the union movement became open and even enthusiastic. Underlying this in large measure was Comintern approval, prompted by fear of potential Nazi aggression against the Soviet Union (these antagonists already were fighting a proxy conflict in the Spanish Civil War).

Although CPUSA criticized the president for his unwillingness to ship arms to the Spanish Republicans, they placed most of the blame on his subordinates, notably Secretary of State Cordell Hull and Undersecretary of State Sumner Welles. By contrast Communists praised FDR for his occasional anti-fascist remarks and avoided blaming him for the outbreak of a strong recession in 1937-38 (overlooking the Administration's cutback of funds for relief projects). Meanwhile the *Daily Worker*, the major CPUSA organ, printed the president's speeches in their entirety, and scarcely a week passed without him being praised in its pages.

The growing collaboration between the party and the CIO (Congress of Industrial Organizations) was another manifestation of the Democratic Front. By 1938 industrial workers had largely seceded from the craft-oriented American Federation of Labor. John L. Lewis, president of the United Mine Workers, had become leader of the CIO.

Lewis and the CPUSA leadership previously had despised each other. He accused the party of being dominated by Moscow, and they denounced him for being an autocrat. Both allegations were basically true. What changed the situation was Lewis's commitment to organizing the unorganized into industrial unions and CPUSA's quest for legitimacy through association with the CIO. The need for organizing was particularly great in the steel industry, and Communists had already demonstrated their aptitude for it by their leadership with transport workers and with state, county, and municipal employees. By 1938 forty percent of the industrial unions were led by Communists or "fellow travelers." No CIO-affiliated unions had a majority or even a substantial minority of Communists within their ranks, but there was much appreciation for those party members who were there and contributing much to the general welfare.[4]

Perhaps even more astounding was CPUSA's Americanization makeover. Its 1938 national convention featured numerous U. S. flags, maps of the states, the singing of the "Star Spangled Banner," a catchy slogan ("Jobs, Security, Democracy, and Peace," and deletion of the word *Soviet* from the traditional Communist anthem *Internationale*. Testifying before the New York State Legislature, Browder declared: "Communism is the Americanism of the twentieth century." He also upheld the party's defense of democracy and opposition to the use of violence. The message seemed to be clear: CPUSA was firmly rooted in American traditions.[5]

The apparent transformation was sometimes startling. Familiar old catchwords, such as "proletarian" and "dictatorship of the proletariat," gave way to new ones – "progressive," "anti-fascist," and "democracy." The notoriously anti-religious party reached out to mollify religious groups, including Catholics (many CIO union members were Catholic). Non-political subject matter now appeared in the *Daily Worker*, for example, movie reviews and sports, while the Young Communist League held women's fashion shows and danced to the latest Swing rythms.[6]

In state-level politics, no state was as congenial to the Democratic Front concept as Washington. Its CPUSA succeeded in electing more members to the legislature than in any other state; and Communists and fellow travelers were active in the Democratic Party and in the strongest CIO-affiliated unions. But New York still had the largest concentration of Communists in America (30,000 by 1938). Together with the American Labor Party, which had been founded by several labor unions to support FDR but to vote for him on a separate ticket, CPUSA constituted a formidable political force. In 1937 these allies had helped elect (Republican) reformer Thomas Dewey as Manhattan district attorney and re-elect long-term New York City Mayor Fiorello LaGuardia.[7]

On the other hand, CPUSA was weakest in the South, which was solidly Democratic by affiliation but strongly conservative politically and socially. In 1938 there were only three thousand party members in the southern states, a figure that actually represented a gain and included a modest number of union activists. Communists were one of the few groups in the United States to object publicly to anti-black racism. Among their protests was the case of the nine "Scottsboro boys," wrongfully arrested for raping two white women, as well as the horrendous lynching that continued throughout the South. Anti-lynching bills periodically failed in Congress because of southern filibusters and half-hearted leadership by the Roosevelt Administration. Racial segregation and discrimination, whether official or not, were very much part of the fabric of American life. [8]

By 1939 the American Communist Party had a registered membership estimated at 100,000. Few liberal and left-wing organizations and labor unions were without a Communist presence. Even a number of mainstream politicians (albeit quietly) vied for CPUSA support. Moreover, hundreds of intellectuals, performers, and artists applauded the Soviet Union, despite Stalin's purge trials that ended with the execution or imprisonment of several million party members. The trials fell far short of judicial standards in democratic nations.[9]

Everything changed abruptly and dramatically after August 23rd, 1939, the day Nazi Germany and the U. S. S. R. signed a Non-aggression Pact. Publicly the two states agreed not to attack each other, but events soon demonstrated the pact's true intentions. Hitler could proceed with the planned invasion of Poland without concerning himself with Soviet opposition (no two front war would hamper Germany as it had in the First World War). Consequently, within days – on September 1st, 1939 – German forces struck the Poles, and since Britain and France had allied themselves to Poland the Second World War began. Stalin's real reward was German acquiescence in the Soviet occupation of eastern Poland and the Baltic republics of Lithuania, Latvia, and Estonia – these territories had been part of Tsarist Russia before 1914. A few months later Stalin was also free to invade part of Finland, which the Finns defended vigorously before being overwhelmed.

President Roosevelt became the target of a strong CPUSA attack after he expressed shock at the Soviet invasion of Finland. For weeks American Communist Party leaders had been confused over what policy to follow with respect to the transformation of European great power politics. But this changed after a Comintern message provided guidance: the U. S. should adhere strictly to its Neutrality Acts *since there was no real difference between Nazi Germany and the British and French governments!* Therefore, Roosevelt's push to revise this legislation in order to aid Britain and France effectively ended the notion of a "Democratic Front."

CPUSA's *volte face* cost them many members and especially previously sympathetic liberal and leftist fellow travelers. Yet most party leaders did not resign, in spite of their initial dismay.

Perhaps more surprising, thousands of ordinary members remained loyal. The Nazi-Soviet Pact ended the most successful period in American Communist history, clearly revealing that loyalty to Moscow took precedence over everything. This became evident again when the Germans invaded Russia in June 1941, and more so after Pearl Harbor in December of that year when the U. S. and the U. S.S. R. became allies. According to the CPUSA, America's involvement in the war was now not only necessary but noble.[10]

◆

Extremism of the Right was also part of American political life in the 1930s. There were probably several hundred hard right organizations (though many of them were tiny). They were separated from conservative groups by their focus on white supremacy, conspiratorial anti-Semitism, and open praise for Hitler and Mussolini. Like their conservative cousins, they hated Marxism, organized labor, and the New Deal; but their racism was crucial. They perceived blacks as a sexual threat to white women; and behind the scenes rich, clever, or radical Jews were even more dangerous. Rich Jews, they believed, were manipulating the economy for their own benefit, while radical Jews were encouraging mayhem among blacks and guiding FDR's "Jew Deal."[11]

Most of these ideas had antecedents in American history, from the Anti-Mason Party of the 1820s and 1830s, the Know-Nothing Party of the 1850s (anti-immigrant and anti-Catholic), the anti-Chinese hysteria of the late 19th century, the Populist Party of the 1890s (agrarians with anti-immigrant, anti-Semitic tendencies), and perhaps most of all, the Ku Klux Klan. The Klan reached its first peak in the late 1860s as a reaction against black emancipation in the South, and again, in the 1920s as a mass organization that was anti-black, anti-Semitic, anti-Catholic, and anti-immigrant.

Though much diminished, the KKK was still active in the thirties, once again mainly in the South where African Americans were the principal, though not the only focus of its venomous speech and behavior. For example, in Florida's Bradford County, two hundred Klan members held a parade and burned two crosses in an effort to warn blacks against voting in municipal elections (this was only partly successful). And two months later, in the congressional elections of 1938, Klan leaders from Maryland's predominantly Protestant Eastern Shore criticized Catholic Democratic candidates from the western part of the state.[12]

Gerald B. Winrod, a Protestant fundamentalist preacher, was one of the more active right-wing extremists of the thirties. He had founded Defenders of the Christian Faith in 1925 and later became a pro-Nazi. Indicative of Winrod's success were the 52,000 votes he received in the 1938 Kansas Republican primary, which was third in a four-way race, and a circulation of 100,000 for his *Defender Magazine*. Most of Defenders' supporters were denizens of small towns or rural areas.[13]

William D. Pelley, also a fundamentalist turned fascist, was the son of a Methodist minister. He started out as a writer of newspaper and magazine articles and a few movie scripts. A fellow writer, Donald S. Strong, deemed him a frustrated literary hack.[14]

Until 1933 Pelley was not openly anti-Semitic. But that year, influenced by the Hitler revolution in Germany, he came to see FDR as a communist backed by Jews. He consequently founded the Silver Shirts, a name derived from the Brown Shirts, a mass organization of Nazi street thugs. At their peak in 1934, the Silver Shirts numbered fifteen thousand, but by 1938 they had declined to only five thousand, with most of their strength in parts of California and Oklahoma. Their signature racist scheme called for blacks, Native Americans, and immigrants to be formed into separate castes and deprived of the vote and other citizenship rights. Jews would be disenfranchised and ghettoized in one city in each state.[15]

Originally founded in 1932 as the Friends of the New Germany, the German-American Bund adopted its new name in 1936. It was ethnically, ideologically, and sartorially more akin to Nazi Germany than any other proto-fascist group in the U. S. Most of its members were German-born aliens who wore swastika armbands and military-style gray shirts similar to those of the Brown Shirts. After 1936 they were led by a *Fuhrer* (Leader), Fritz Kuhn.

Born in Munich in 1895, Kuhn served in the German army during World War I. He emigrated to Mexico in 1923, supposedly for economic reasons but probably because of his record as a petty thief. Relocating to the U. S. in 1927, he got a job with the Ford Motor Company as a chemist (he had a chemistry background) and became an American citizen.[16]

Bund strength was greatest in cities with substantial numbers of recent German immigrants. The organization was especially visible in the New York City Boroughs of Brooklyn, Queens, and Manhattan. One of its biggest rallies was in Madison Square Garden, where hundreds of police had to be summoned to prevent a hostile street mob of Jewish war veterans and others from breaking into the premises. Also in 1938, a group of teenage boys hurled "stink bombs" to disrupt a smaller Bund meeting in White Plains, New York.[17]

The Bund tried to maintain close ties to the Nazi leadership in Germany, which furnished it with modest cash support and propaganda materials, such as Hitler's memoir and political manual *Mein Kampf* (My Struggle). German consuls in the U. S. were another source of guidance, and the Bund also patterned its summer youth camps on those of the Hitler Youth. But documents reveal that officials of the German Foreign Office were somewhat embarrassed by the imitative behavior and occasional violence associated with the Bund (maintaining satisfactory relations with Washington was a Foreign Office objective until the late thirties).[18]

By far the most popular and effective of right-wing extremist organizations was that connected with a Canadian-born radio personality. Charles Edward Coughlin was born to Irish Catholic parents in Hamilton, Ontario on October 25th, 1891. He was a graduate of St. Michael's College in Toronto and studied theology at St. Basil's College in Waco, Texas. His first parish priest's position was at a church in the Detroit suburb of Royal Oak, Michigan. Sensing the potential of the new medium of radio, Father Coughlin delivered his first on-air sermon on Station WJR on October 17th, 1926. It did attract attention and marked the start of a long radio career.

Within a few years Coughlin was no longer confining his talks to religious themes. On January 12th, 1930, for example, he preached against communism and socialism – without distinguishing between them. Yet for the next six years, as he became a national radio figure, he could probably be defined as more left than right in his political perspective. As the Great Depression worsened, he became more critical of capitalism, especially of the banking system, and of President Herbert Hoover's reluctance to embrace whole-hearted federal relief activities. He advocated an expanded currency, including remonetizing silver (as backing for the dollar). He endorsed presidential candidate Roosevelt and accepted his invitation to attend the 1932 Democratic National Convention.[19]

This warm relationship did not last through Roosevelt's first term. Coughlin broke with him when the president rejected "free silver" and declined to accept him as one of his advisers. Instead, on December 11th, 1934, the priest organized his own National Union for Social Justice (NUSJ). Its principles included a living wage, abolition of the privately-owned Federal Reserve Banking System and its replacement by a government-owned Central Bank, the right to organize unions, profit-sharing between labor and management, and a federal role in mediating labor-management disputes.[20]

In 1936 the NUSJ began publication of *Social Justice*, a weekly that was intended to promote Coughlin's choice for president in 1936 – North Dakota Congressman William Lemke. A new Union Party would encompass NUSJ, the followers of old age pension advocate Dr. Francis Townsend, and those of the assassinated Louisiana politician Huey P. Long (now led by the anti-Semitic Gerald L. K. Smith). Coughlin predicted nine million votes for the Union Party, but it was buried in the Roosevelt landslide.

The electoral defeat failed to diminish Coughlin's popularity as a radio figure. By early 1938 his broadcasts were carried by over sixty-three stations; and some programs may have attracted as many as forty million listeners. What did change, however, was Coughlin's message, as he became a scarcely concealed anti-Semite with strong fascistic tendencies. In becoming more open, he may have been influenced by German and Italian propaganda and, perhaps more so, by what he sensed were half-formed but widely held views among a substantial portion of the American population.

The year 1938 bore witness to Coughlin's emerging extremism. In March, for example, borrowing a concept from Fascist Italy, he proposed the U. S. government be reorganized into a corporate state, in which occupational groups would elect members of Congress, while political parties would disappear. Coughlin's newspaper, *Social Justice*, in July 1938 began publishing excerpts from the notorious anti-Semitic forgery, *Protocols of the Elders of Zion*. When confronted about the writing's veracity, he declared that although the details might be false, the analysis of nefarious Jewish behavior was not. Later that year Coughlin used his radio pulpit to defend Germany's vicious persecution of its Jewish population, during and after *Kristallnacht*, as a necessary defense mechanism against communism.[21]

By late 1938 the amount of explicit anti-Semitic, pro-Nazi material during Coughlin's radio programs and in the pages of *Social Justice* was unrelenting. Among other things, he praised Hitler's annexation of Austria and, after Munich, his partial annexation of Czechoslovakia, Mussolini's negation of the citizenship rights of Italian Jews (which Coughlin defended on grounds that most Jews were anti-fascist), the Rome-Berlin Axis as a rampart against communism, and support of intervention against the Spanish Republic. The priest's adherence to the Nazi line was so faithful that the *New York Post*, on December 30th, 1938, was able to show that an article of his in *Social Justice* had been lifted, almost word for word, from a speech delivered by Propaganda Minister Josef Goebbels. The context pertained to alleged Jewish involvement in the leadership and financing of the Russian Revolution of 1917 and in fomenting postwar unsuccessful revolutions in Germany and Hungary.[22]

Also in 1938, Coughlin established the Christian Front, which was much closer to a disciplined fascist organization than the NUSJ. Its purpose, he declared, was to save America from communism, FDR, and the Jews. Concentrated in New York and other northeastern cities, the Front's membership was largely lower middle class and Catholic. Although Coughlin maintained that violence should only be a last resort, members of this new body advocated it without reservation and attacked Jews on the streets. Much of this violence took place in Brooklyn where the first chapter of the Front had been organized. The Brooklyn Archdiocese claimed the group was beyond its control, but the editor of the *Brooklyn Tablet*, the official Archdiocesan newspaper, consistently lauded Coughlin and the Front. Nor did New York's Cardinal Spellman do anything to counter Coughlin's influence on Catholics. A minority of Catholic clergy in the country denounced the radio priest's canards. But, at best, others either remained silent or said that he did not speak for the Church. However, Coughlin's extremism did make powerful enemies in the media, and by early 1939 radio stations that broadcast his programs had dropped to forty-six from sixty-three a year earlier.[23]

Coughlin continued his political career over the next few years, principally by consistently spouting his anti-Semitic, pro-fascist line and making common cause with the isolationists associated with the "America First Committee." He retained much of his influence, though never matching the popularity he had gained during his pro-New Deal period.

Social Justice's criticism of the U. S. government and the Jews persisted even after Pearl Harbor. For instance, on February 2nd, 1942 an editorial blamed the latter for playing a major role in fomenting the war. Since Coughlin had already been deprived of his access to the air waves (by government and station owners), *Social Justice* was now his only outlet. His political career therefore ended abruptly in May 1942 when his superior, Archbishop Mooney of Detroit, ordered him to cease his writing and all non-religious activities. Simultaneously the U. S. Post Office revoked *Social Justice's* mailing privileges on grounds that it was guilty of sedition.

Coughlin lived the rest of his life in obscurity before dying in 1979 at age eighty-eight. But he had been a major figure in American history, a trailblazer in radio communication who used the medium skillfully to attract millions of supporters. In this respect he was unique among right wing extremists of the pre-World War II period. The Catholic Church, including the Vatican, tolerated him because of their shared fervent anti-communism. In the opinion of historian Sheldon Marcus, Coughlin caused much harm. As a propagandist for fascism, Marcus asserts, "he weakened the will and numbed the understanding of millions of Americans. Especially dangerous, his diatribes were delivered under the guise of religion and piety …."[24]

Extremists of the left and right provoked an official response. Specifically, the German-American Bund and the Communist Party were targets of congressional investigations by the House Un-American Activities Committee (HUAC). The U. S. House of Representatives created HUAC in May 1938 during a surge of panic over Nazi style summer camps in New York and New Jersey. The Committee's chairman was Representative Martin Dies, Jr., a conservative Democrat from west Texas who was a leader of the anti-New Deal bloc in the House. Two other Democrats and two Republicans – all conservatives – were Dies' committee colleagues. Dies offset HUAC's small budget of $25,000 by hiring volunteers to collect information; all of them were vehemently anti-New Deal too.[25]

The Bund was a subject of concern to HUAC because of its obvious connection to a foreign power. But most of its attention was devoted to revealing the particulars of what was deemed the dire threat to America posed by Communists, fellow travelers, and other CPUSA sympathizers. There were occasional gaffes, such as the name of ten-year-old Shirley Temple appearing on a list of Hollywood figures who had sent a message of support to *Ce Soir*, a French Communist newspaper. Secretary of the Interior Harold Ickes, a bugaboo of HUAC members, could not contain a sarcastic commentary: "They (HUAC) even went to Hollywood and made the amazing discovery that little Shirley Temple is a dangerous Red. Imagine the great committee raiding her nursery and seizing her dolls as evidence …."[26]

James B. Matthews, a former Socialist, was a favorite HUAC informant who ultimately became its director of research. His investigations presented a picture of an America overrun by Reds, fellow travelers, and dupes. One target of Matthews' "research" was the prominent newspaper columnist Heywood Broun, whom he accused of being a secret Communist. At a committee hearing, Dies and other HUAC members would not allow Broun to utter more than a few words, which he used to deny the principal allegation. He admitted his support for the C. I. O. and for the Spanish Loyalists fighting fascism but denied any CPUSA affiliation, secret or otherwise.[27]

HUAC continued its work despite criticism from many quarters. On November 14th, 1938, for example, Chairman Dies published a list of what he termed "purveyors of hate." Joseph Stalin headed the purveyors of class hatred, while Hitler and Mussolini were the top proponents of racial and religious hatred. Although the American list included Fritz Kuhn and William Pelley, New Deal figures Ickes, Works Progress Administrator Harry Hopkins, Paul Sifton of the Federal Wages and Hours Administration, National Labor Relations economist David Saposs, and CIO head John L. Lewis were on the list as well.[28]

Whatever its blunders, inconsistencies, and prejudices, HUAC enjoyed support in conservative-leaning newspapers and in Congress, particularly after the defeat of many New Dealers in the congressional elections of 1938. The Federal Theatre Project, a subsidiary of WPA, soon became the subject of intense Committee scrutiny. As already discussed, (in Chapter 4), the Project provided employment for actors, directors, and writers whose careers had been devastated by the depression. It was a vehicle to keep the arts alive, not only in New York and other major cities but in rural areas and small towns whose residents had seldom, if ever, experienced live theater.

Appointed by Harry Hopkins in 1935, Hallie Flanagan was the only director of the Federal Theatre Project. During a full-day hearing on December 6, 1938, she skillfully refuted the charges of HUAC members and a few witnesses that nearly every play performed since 1935 was an example of Communist propaganda. Nevertheless, in the spring of 1939, a majority of the House Appropriations Committee voted to kill the Project by totally eliminating its budget.[29]

HUAC was a major player in Washington through the 1950s,

not expiring till 1969. Its inquisitorial methods encouraged the practice of blacklisting and ultimately led to the McCarthy Era, both of which probably harmed America far more than any real or alleged Communist conspiracy.

Notes: Chapter 7

1   The Comintern was often short-sighted. For example, it directed the Communist Party of Germany to focus its wrath on the SPD (Socialist Party), a rival for working class support. At a time when there should have been an emphasis on creating as broad an anti-Nazi coalition as possible, this was suicidal.

2   Harvey Klehr, *The Heyday of American Communism. The Depression Decade.* New York: Basic Books, Inc., Publisher, 1989, 102, 161, 163.

3   *Ibid.,*191, 196; Fraser M. Ottanelli, *The Communist Party of the United States From the Depression to World War II.* New Brunswick, NJ and London: Rutgers University Press, 1991, 111-113.

4   Klehr, *op. cit.,* 218, 220, 222, 234-235, 238, 240.

5   Ottanelli, *op. cit.,* 115, 117, 123, 125.

6   *Ibid.,* 126-127.

7   Klehr, *op. cit.,* 253-254, 265-269.

8   *Ibid.,* 273, 275, 327.

9   *Ibid.,* 386.

10   *Ibid.,*387, 400, 404, 409; Ottanelli, *op. cit.,* 300. The Anglo-American-Soviet alliance did not extend to the Pacific war, which the U. S. S. R. did not join until the eve of Japan's defeat in August 1945.

11   Chip Berlet and Matthew Lyons, *Right Wing Populism in America. Too Close for Comfort.* New York and London: The Guilford Press, 2000, 131.

12   *NYT,* Sept. 1, 1938, 46; Sept. 15, 1938, 20; Nov. 2, 1938, 7.

13   Berlet and Lyons, *op. cit.,* 132.

14   David S. Strong, *Organized Anti-Semitism in America. The Rise of Group Prejudice During the Decade 1930-40.* Westport, CT: Greenwood Press, 1979, 44.

15   Strong, *ibid.,* 40, 47, 51; Berlet and Lyons, *op. cit.,* 133.

16   Strong, op. cit., 23-24.

17   *NYT,* op. Cit., Apr. 26, 1938, 3.

18   Strong, *op. cit.,* 26, 36, 38-39; Berlet and Lyons, *op. cit.,* 136-137.

19   Sheldon Marcus, *Father Coughlin. The Tumultuous Life of the Little Flower.* Boston, Toronto: Little Brown and Co., 1973, 14-15, 26, 28, 31, 36, 44, 46.

20   *Ibid.,* 71-72, 78. Despite his apparent pro-union stance, Coughlin used non-union labor to rebuild his parish church, denounced the United

Auto Workers' efforts to unionize General Motors, and opposed his own employees' inclusion in Social Security.

21 Berlet and Lyons, *op. cit.*, 141; Marcus, *op. cit.*, 160.

22 Marcus, *op. cit.*, 169, 189, 191-192; Charles J. Tull, *Father Coughlin and the New Deal*. Syracuse: Syracuse University Press, 1963, 197, 206. Coughlin also supported Japan against China (the latter supposedly backed by "international" bankers), and his Irish background manifested itself in his hatred of Britain.

23 Marcus, *op. cit.*, 154, 160, 162, 173; Strong, *op. cit.*, 66-68; Berlet and Lyons, *op. cit.*, 141. An astonishing forty percent of New York City policemen joined the violence-prone Christian Front.

24 Marcus, *op. cit.*, 230. See also Berlet and Lyons, *op. cit.*, 143; and Strong, *op. cit.*, 64.

25 Michael Hiltzik, *The New Deal. A Modern History*. New York, London, Sydney, and New Delhi: Free Press, 2011, 396.

26 *NYT*, Aug. 28, 6. Dies' political sentiments were made clear by his closeness to a number of KKK figures, notably Imperial Wizard James Colescott, whom he urged to lead the Klan "back to its original objectives." See also Berlet and Lyons, *op. cit.*, 152.

27 Hiltzik, *op. cit.*, 398-399. See also *NYT. op. cit.*, Aug. 23, 1938, 2.

28 *NYT, op. cit.*, Nov. 14, 1938, 12.

29 Eric Bentley, ed., *Thirty Years of Treason. Excerpts from Hearings before the House Committee on Un-American Activities, 1938-1968*. New York: The Viking Press, 1971, 3, 6, and *passim*; Hiltzik, *op. cit.*, 398-399; John Gladchuk, *HUAC and the Evolution of the Red Menace, 1935-1950*. New York and London: Rutledge, 2007, 68, 87, 112.

CHAPTER 8

Dealing with Nazi Anti-Semitism

T he Dies Committee made a half-hearted effort to highlight the character of the German-American Bund. But the Roosevelt Administration faced a perplexing problem in dealing with the intermittent, yet increasingly painful Nazi persecution of the Jews in Germany. It had to reconcile protection of America's economic interests, isolationist stance toward European affairs, and discouragement of immigration with the moral challenge represented by Nazi policy.

Various actions, or inactions, illustrate the Administration's stand-offish behavior. For example, the refusal to endorse anti-Nazi resolutions of censure in Congress ensured that these would fail. Nor did the State Department officially protest anti-Semitic actions that it conceded were regrettable but had to be considered part of Germany's internal affairs. Secretary of State Hull went further by apologizing to German Ambassador Dieckhoff who had complained about New York City Mayor LaGuardia's characterization of Hitler (on March 4th, 1937) as a "brown-shirted fanatic who is threatening the peace of the world."[1] To be fair, Hull was not as apologetic to Dieckhoff as he may have appeared, telling him that many Americans viewed the racial situation in Germany as a "temporary abnormality," and that he hoped that the "old German type," presumably the civilized variety, would reassert itself.[2] Other Administration spokesmen went far beyond the point that Hull was inclined to go, leaving no doubt about the target of their attacks. President Roosevelt himself, in a San Diego address of October 2nd, 1935, declared that the American people could not be indifferent to acts suppressing freedom of conscience and equality before the law. This statement came on the heels of the Nuremberg Laws, which had relegated Jews in Germany to the legal status of a despised caste. Secretary of the Interior Ickes later disclosed in his *Secret Diary* that the White House had overruled the State Department in granting him permission to deliver an anti-Nazi speech to a Jewish audience at the University of Chicago on March 30th, 1938.[3]

U. S. Ambassador William E. Dodd, a former professor of history at the University of Chicago, a southerner, an admirer of Jefferson, and a personal friend of the late President Wilson, was openly sickened by the persecution in Germany. Because he was an embarrassment to the State Department, it forced his retirement in January 1938 and replaced him with career diplomat Hugh R. Wilson. The German Foreign Office termed Wilson a "moderate" in his attitude toward the Nazi regime. Nevertheless German-American relations actually deteriorated in 1938, largely due to the exploding crisis over would-be Jewish emigrants.

In 1930 520,000 Jews lived in Germany, out of a general population of approximately seventy-two million. Jewish emigration began shortly after Hitler assumed power, tapered off markedly in the spring of 1933 after the initial panic, and rose again sharply after enactment of the Nuremberg Laws in September 1935. By then 80,000 Jews had left their homeland.

The Nuremberg legislation was an ugly landmark in Germany's persecution of its Jewish population. But even worse was the hatred and violence that occurred during 1938, behavior associated with the Nazi annexation of Austria and the event known in German as *Kristallnacht,* in rough English translation, Night of the Broken Glass (see also Chapters 5 and 7). On March 12th Hitler's troops marched unopposed into neighboring German-speaking Austria and incorporated its territory into the *Reich*. The undisguised brutality of what the Nazis called the *Anschluss* (union) shocked American public opinion. Undersecretary of State Welles warned Ambassador Dieckhoff on March 15th that it would grow even more hostile unless the violence against Austrian Jews and political foes of the Nazis subsided. Nevertheless, as already noted (in Chapter 2), the U. S. and other nations recognized the *Anschluss* as a *fait accompli*.

The chain of events leading to *Kristallnacht* began in Paris on November 7th. Herschel Grynszpan, a seventeen-year-old Jewish refugee, went to the German embassy intending to kill the ambassador. Gryszpan's parents had been among 10,000 Polish-born Jews long resident in Germany recently stripped of their assets and deported to Poland in boxcars. The young man was seeking revenge. But instead of the ambassador, it was Ernst vom Rath, the third secretary of the embassy (and a secret anti-Nazi) who appeared in the doorway and was gunned down. His death spelled disaster for the Jews of Germany. On the night of November 9th - 10th, "spontaneous demonstrations" well-organized by Propaganda Minister Goebbels and utilizing paramilitary S. A. police in civilian garb brought terror and destruction to homes, shops, and synagogues. Scores of men, women, and children were shot to death while attempting to flee the flames and clubs. The next day the hundreds of survivors who lined up for visas at U. S. and British consulates continued to be harassed by storm troopers.

The November pogroms finally caused Washington to reconsider its policy of official silence with respect to Nazi anti-Semitism. Assistant Secretary of State George S. Messersmith, a former consul-general in Berlin, recommended the immediate recall of Ambassador Wilson "for consultations," and President

Roosevelt took that step on November 14th. He coupled his action with a statement expressing "disbelief that such things could happen in a twentieth century civilization."[4] The Germans responded to Wilson's recall by recalling Ambassador Dieckhoff. Although the president told British Ambassador to the U. S Sir Ronald Lindsay that he did not intend to detain Wilson indefinitely, neither of the affected diplomats ever returned to their respective posts and were replaced by *charges d'affaires*. The U. S. response to this major episode of Nazi violence was a singular development because the nations of western Europe could not afford the breach in relations with Germany likely to follow any strong protest.[5]

The pressure on Jews to emigrate became irresistible after the events of 1938. Yet the German government's refusal to allow them to leave with more than a tiny fraction of their resources and the determination of potential countries of refuge to reject people who might become "public charges" was a cruel dilemma.

The restrictive quota legislation of the early 1920s governed immigration to the U. S. Under the 1924 law, the German annual quota stood at 25,957; and during the early Hitler years Washington did nothing to ease the entry of German refugees. Consequently, from July 1st, 1932 to June 30th, 1938 only 45,953 quota emigrants from Germany entered the country, of whom approximately two-thirds were Jewish. President Hoover's Executive Order of September 8th, 1930 was a large part of the reason why the quotas were not filled. Designed to curtail immigration at a time of acute economic crisis, it had instructed consular officials responsible for issuing visas to interpret, *in the strictest possible sense*, the provision prohibiting admission of persons likely to apply for relief. The significance (or insignificance) of German immigration to the U. S. during this period is perhaps best illustrated by comparison with the situation in tiny Palestine, at the time a British mandate under the League of Nations. Beset by Arab-Jewish conflict Palestine, with British acquiescence, absorbed about 200,000 Jews, 63,000 of them from Germany.[6]

The restrictive policy of the U. S. government was an accurate reflection of a large segment of public opinion. Opposition to liberalization of the immigration laws was particularly intense in the south and west, which were strongholds of isolationism. Here, as elsewhere in the country, it was fear of aggravating the unemployment problem that was crucial. American Federation of Labor President William Green supported the boycott of German goods organized by Jewish groups to protest Hitler's anti-labor and anti-Jewish policies (and also because it might help create more jobs for American workers). When it came to admitting the victims of Nazi persecution, however, he found himself on the other side of the debate. After all, he argued, immigrants were foreigners who might take jobs away from citizens.

An attitude of caution characterized even those most anxious over the plight of the German Jews.. Samuel Rosenman was a case in point. This presidential adviser and speech writer was afraid that introduction of bills in Congress designed to facilitate immigration might result instead in further restrictive legislation. And Emmanuel Celler, who represented a heavily Jewish congressional district in Brooklyn, expressed the same sentiment that he had heard voiced directly by southern and western colleagues.[7]

Though reluctant to lift its own immigration barriers, America nonetheless played a major role in the last effort before the Second World War to solve the refugee problem. The State Department announced, on March 24th, 1938, that it had asked thirty-three governments to join in establishing an international committee to deal with the question – primarily by seeking ways to increase resettlement opportunities in non-European countries. But the proposal was not a radical departure from the earlier initiative of the League of Nations. Two mandates were decisive: (1) That the search for places of settlement had to fall within the bounds of prevailing immigration laws; and (2) That private sources should provide the necessary funding. The U. S. initiative occurred against the backdrop of the recent German occupation of Austria and the obvious danger now facing its Jewish population. Something had to be done, or at least an attempt had to be made, and President Roosevelt knew that leadership could not be left to the moribund League of Nations.

The Intergovernmental Committee on Refugees (ICR) was the outgrowth of the American proposal of March 24th, with personnel from the State Department assigned to do most of the leg work. The widely-publicized conference held in Evian, France, from July 6th - 15th, 1938, marked the inauspicious beginning of the Committee's labors. Against the scenic beauty of the French Alps, the delegates expressed profound sympathy for the victims of terror. Informal discussion of settlement prospects, however, revealed a harsher reality. The correspondent of the *New York Times* likened the gathering to a poker game. Most of the participating governments, he suggested, seemed to agree in regarding it as a burden to receive these refugees; and the bargaining among them is mainly on how to share the burden and, more bluntly, how to limit or reduce the total supply...."[8]

The delegates were nearly unanimous in stressing the generosity of their countries in having accepted small numbers of refugees, few of whom, they implied, were contributing anything of value to their new homelands. Nor were more malign motives lacking, such as the one reflected in a statement by Australia's representative who pointed out that his nation had no racial problem and no wish to import one. At the same time France, Belgium, and the Netherlands announced that they had reached the end of their capacity to admit refugees and implored New World nations to reopen their doors. Meanwhile, from Germany, Nazi propagandist Alfred Rosenberg admonished the delegates to find a home for *future* as well as present Jewish emigrants.[9]

At a London meeting of August 3rd, the ICR's Executive Committee named George Rublee, a Washington attorney and personal friend of President Roosevelt, as the organization's director. Since capital transfer was a key issue, the U. S. used its diplomatic facilities to initiate negotiations between Rublee and German officials. Berlin's response seemed at least somewhat promising, as Minister of Economics Walther Funk conceded that the Jewish question was stirring up animosity against Germany. Even during the height of the Czech crisis, there were possible signs of optimism. For instance, Hitler's chief crony Mussolini informed British Foreign Secretary Lord Halifax that the *Fuhrer* was so eager to get rid of the Jews that he would do anything to expedite their departure.[10]

More encouraging still was a report by U. S. *charge d'affaires* Prentiss Gilbert on the apparent views of Hermann Goring, head of the *Luftwaffe* and the Four Year (industrial) Plan, an obvious power in the Nazi hierarchy. Goring had confided to his intimates that he no longer viewed the Jewish question as simply a German internal matter but rather as a technical and economic situation with international ramifications. In this light it was absurd to expect emigrants to leave Germany completely destitute; and therefore, a Rublee visit and an exchange of information on the entire subject of Jewish emigration might prove useful. Goring assured his listeners that he had not become a sentimentalist, yet undeniably certain German exports were decreasing at an alarming rate as a result of boycotts. Could this trend be reversed, he wondered, if the refugee issue were divested of its emotional overtones.[11]

However, other documentary evidence reveals that the desire to mitigate the effects of boycotting was not the sole, much less the chief cause of this ostensible change of heart. A bizarre gathering of cabinet ministers and ranking officials on November 12th, 1938, presided over by Goring, levied a fine of one billion marks against the Jews for complicity in Rath's murder and decided to "kick the Jew out of Germany" and to promote emigration "by all possible means." Goring did not exclude collaboration with "trusteeships organized abroad" if it would hasten the attainment of this goal; and in spite of opposition from the Foreign Office he was able to obtain Hitler's approval for talks with the ICR.[12]

Negotiations between Rublee and various Foreign Ministry spokesmen occurred in November and December of 1938 and early 1939. There was a complex, tentative deal that called for an international loan to support the sale of German exports and an increase in the amount of funds available for emigrating Jews. Still, nothing moved forward. The ICR met frustration in its attempts to broaden resettlement prospects; and the German government, though professing eagerness to have the emigrants accepted abroad, did nothing to facilitate the release of a reasonable portion of their property,

As with the quest for negotiations, the U. S. aided the ICR in its endeavors to resettle the refugees. A decision to allow the German immigration quotas to be filled was a move that theoretically would enable approximately 100,000 of them to enter the country over a five-year period. Although President Roosevelt, at a press conference of November 15th, 1938, excluded any enlargement of the quotas, the State Department believed America had set an example of generosity.

Whatever the merit of this assertion, it failed utterly to induce other governments to lower their bars. The attitudes of Latin American republics were especially disappointing. Between 1933 and 1938, for example, Argentina had absorbed 18,000 German Jews, which was more than any other country in Latin America. But after Evian the Argentine government made immigration more difficult by ordering its consuls in Germany to refer all visa applicants to a special board in Buenos Aires for approval. When the U. S. ambassador protested this regulation, which threatened to leave six hundred persons with newly invalidated visas stranded, the Argentine foreign minister grew vexed. Why, he asked, had the U. S. not doubled its German quota. The implication was clear enough: his country too would be guided by its own interests in devising immigration policies; and Argentina needed farmers, not "artists and musicians." However, an exception was made for the six hundred.[13]

On November 22nd, 1938 Secretary Hull addressed a circular to all Latin American nations expressing the wish that they would find it possible to make "specific and generous" statements regarding the number of refugees they would admit. Fidelity to the principles upon which they were founded, he said, dictated acceptance of people fleeing oppression. Yet as the secretary understood quite well, governments were (and are) rarely motivated by moral considerations, and the appeal went unheeded.[14]

The huge British Empire also remained closed to large-scale Jewish immigration. Partial to British immigrants and beset by economic troubles, the dominions admitted only 12,000 German refugees from 1938 to 1940. Of the many paper schemes to organize refugee resettlement in remote and sparsely inhabited regions of the world, the British Guiana project probably received the most fanfare. The British Colonial Office was optimistic, and a report by an Anglo-American commission was favorable, but there were no tangible results. "Expert" opinion aside, it was obvious that the hot, humid savannahs were not likely to draw people acclimated to urban life in a temperate climate. Another proposal – by Americans Bernard Baruch and Herbert Hoover – to create a refugee haven to be formed from parts of the British colonies of Kenya, Tanganyika, and Northern

Rhodesia foundered largely on the resident white population's "dim view of civilization crowding in upon them."[15]

◆

By the outbreak of World War II in September 1939, the ICR had become a paper organization only. To be sure, the vague promise of Nazi cooperation on the question of refugee assets never materialized. Lacking that, no half-hearted prodding could persuade potential countries of resettlement to act against what they conceived to be their own best economic interests. Also involved was an element of latent and not-so-latent anti-Semitism, including in the U. S., as reflected by unfavorable attitudes toward Jews in public opinion polls and by the popularity of professional anti-Semites such as Father Coughlin (see Chapter 7).

The power of the Great Depression over the minds of people was enormous, but it was not wholly responsible for the world's failure to act more decisively. Historical perspective reveals that there was little sense of immediacy with regard to the situation of the Jews in Europe during the pre-war years. Initially the Nazis favored their dispersion all over the world which, they believed, would provoke anti-Semitic reactions and win adherents to their propaganda line. "The more pauperized and the more burdensome the emigrant appears in the land of his destination," Foreign Minister Ribbentrop reasoned, "the stronger the new land will react and the better it will serve the propaganda interests of Germany ...."[16]

Only as World War II progressed did the policy of forced emigration give way to one of physical extermination. Hitler prophesied in a speech to the *Reichstag* on January 30th, 1939 that a new world war would mean "the annihilation of the Jewish race in Europe."[17] But few took him at his word. When the immensity of the deed still confounds human comprehension, it is somewhat unfair to attribute lack of foresight to the generation of the thirties.

As early as 1938, several perspicacious individuals did indeed anticipate the worst. The American boycott leader Joseph Tenenbaum in April of that year worried about "a campaign of extermination of the six million Jews living under the shadow of Hitler ...."[18] And Swedish Diplomat Olof Lamm advised the U. S. to drop the quota system temporarily and admit 100,000 refugees at once, warning that something must be done quickly "so that we may catch the refugees alive."[19] If these forebodings had been more widely shared, funds might have flowed more readily, immigration barriers might have crumbled, and thousands more might have survived the Holocaust.

Notes: Chapter 8

1   *NYT*, Mar. 5, 15, 1937.

2   *Foreign Relations (FR) 1937* (5 vols., Washington, 1954. Memorandum by the Secretary of State, II, Aug. 5, 1937, 376.

3   Harold L. Ickes, *The Secret Diary of Harold L. Ickes.* 3 vols. New York: 1953-54, II, 347-348.

4   *FR 1938*, II, Assistant Secretary of State George S. Messersmith to the Secretary of State, Nov. 14, 1938, 396-398; *NYT*, Nov. 16, 1938, 1.

5   *FR 1938*, II, Memorandum by the Undersecretary of State (Welles) of a Conversation with the British Ambassador (Sir Ronald Lindsay), Nov. 18, 1938, 402. On Britain's attitude toward a protest of *Kristallnacht* see, for example, Great Britain. Foreign Office, *Documents on British Foreign Policy (DBFP)*, Third Series (10 vols.), London: 1949-61, III, 264, Nov. 9, 1938.

6   U. S. Dept. of Labor, *Annual Reports of the Secretary of Labor*, Washington, D. C.: 1933-38, *passim;* and *American Jewish Year Book XLI*, 1939, 385-386. American consular officials were also influenced by traditional anti-Semitism. See, e. g., Arthur D. Morse, *While Six Million Died.* New York: 1968, *passim.*

7   Franklin D. Roosevelt Library (FDRL), O. F. 133-A Miscellaneous (Immigration) 1933-45. William Green to the President, Sept. 22, 1933; P. P. F. 64, Samuel Rosenman 1933-45, Samuel Rosenman to the President, Dec. 5, 1938.

8   *NYT*, July 6, 1938, 1.

9   *Actes du Comite Intergouvernmental, Evian, du 6 au 15 Juillet 1938.* Evian 1938; *NYT*, July 8, 1938, 1.

10 *DBFP*, Third Series, III, p. 519, No. 500, Conversations between British and Italian Ministers, Rome, Jan. 11-14, 1939.

11 *FR 1938*, I, The *charge d'affaires* in Germany to the Secretary of State, Dec. 9, 1938, 864-865.

12 *Documents on German Foreign Policy (DGFP)*, Series D, V, Memo by the Director of the Political Department, Nov. 12, 1938, 904-905, No. 649s.

13 *FR 1938*. The Ambassador in Argentina to the Secretary of State, Sept. 5, 1938, I, 786; The Secretary of State to the Ambassador in Argentina, Sept. 24, 1938, 790.

14 Kurt Grossman and Arieh Tartakower, *The Jewish Refugee.* New York: Institute of Jewish Affairs, 1944, 316-318.

15 *Contemporary Jewish Record*, March-April 1939, 82, 120.
16 *DGFP, op. cit.*, Circular of the Foreign Ministry, Jan. 25, 1939, 926-933, No. 664.
17 Norman H. Baines, ed., *The Speeches of Adolf Hitler, April 1922-August 1939.* 2 vols. London, New York, Toronto: 1949, 741.
18 *Boycott. Nazi Goods and Services*, Mar.-April 1938, 3.
19 FDRL, P. P. F., Hendrik Willem Van Loon. Olof Lamm to H. W. Van Loon, Nov. 1, 1938.

CHAPTER 9

Our Own Racism: Black Life in America

The Nazi rejoinder to American criticism of anti-Semitism in Germany frequently was a reminder of lynching and other injustices inflicted on African Americans. All too often, these barbs had the ring of truth.

By the 1930s, more than seventy years had passed since the emancipation of the slaves and the enactment of what should have been the empowering Fourteenth and Fifteenth Amendments to the Constitution. Reconstruction Era federal actions against the Ku Klux Klan and similar hate groups and the Civil Rights Act of 1875, which had prohibited racial discrimination by private citizens, were not even distant memories. Congressional inaction, Supreme Court decisions, most notably Plessy v. Ferguson (1896) proclaiming the "separate but equal" doctrine, and state laws enacting "grandfather clauses," poll taxes, and "lily white" primaries, ushered in an age of segregation, discrimination, and disenfranchisement. The doctrine of states' rights offered legal support, augmented unofficially by the horrors of lynching and "chain gang" incarceration. The inequities of sharecropping tenancy and other forms of economic discrimination ensured widespread black poverty.

During the first three decades of the twentieth century, the situation of African Americans in their own country failed to improve. The "Southern Way," somewhat less formalized, became the "American Way," even among northern liberals. For example, progressive journalist Ray Stannard Baker asserted that the place of Negroes had been defined and settled and that the less said about it the better. The pseudo-scientific racialism of the period, which gave rise to the popular movement of eugenics, placed people of African descent (together with Asians and southern and eastern Europeans) in an inferior category. A few members of the tiny northern black elite continued the civil rights movement they had inherited from the nineteenth century abolitionists and Radical Republicans. But they lacked adequate funding, public support, and access to centers of political and media power; and without these they could not hope to succeed.[1]

The country's political system completely failed African Americans. Southern Democrats were the embodiment of the "Solid South," while their northern Democratic partners either remained silent on civil rights issues or openly supported the southern racial regime. Virginia-born Woodrow Wilson, president from 1913 to 1921, segregated white and black federal office workers in Washington, D. C. and hosted a White House showing of the landmark (and highly racist) film *Birth of a Nation.*

Though still supported by a large majority of those blacks who could vote, the Republican Party had completely abandoned its Reconstruction Era image. The party simply did not need black votes to elect presidents or control Congress. Presidential behavior reflected this reality during the terms of Warren G. Harding (1921-23), Calvin Coolidge (1923-29), and Herbert Hoover (1929-33). Harding, for instance, denounced what he viewed as the bugaboo of social equality and racial amalgamation and declined to take a stand on an anti-lynching bill introduced into Congress. "Silent Cal" remained silent on the issues of lynching, disenfranchisement, and discrimination in federal employment. Yet he still won the black vote in 1924 because the Democrats and the Progressive Party were regarded as even worse. The former's convention defeated an anti-KKK plank and permitted no black delegates to participate in the proceedings, while the latter's "most liberal party platform to that date" said nothing about racial injustices. For his part, Herbert Hoover appointed almost no blacks to federal office and excluded them from jobs on the massive Boulder Dam construction project.[2]

Hoover's presidency coincided with the onset and intensification of the Great Depression. Although suffering was widespread, blacks were affected earlier and, statistically speaking, they endured more than their fellow citizens. For example, the fall in agricultural prices included cotton, the cultivation of which had provided a meagre living for black tenant farmers and laborers. As the job market shriveled, moreover, white males increasingly took positions previously defined as "black." One southern town posted this sign: "No nigger work until all white men have jobs." Many white women entered the job market for the first time and competed with African American women, notably in the textiles and garment industries. These developments help to explain why, by 1932, the general unemployment rate stood at twenty-five percent while the black figure was approximately fifty percent.[3]

The "Great Migration" -- the movement of African Americans from the rural South to northern cities that had begun at the turn of the twentieth century – continued into the 1930s when about 400,000 people became part of this exodus. This was only half the number that came in the twenties but big enough to increase the black population of the North by about twenty-five percent.

Many of these migrants survived in part on relief payments, which paid little. Harlem, in New York City's Borough of Manhattan, was one of the largest of the northern ghettos. As late as 1941, a study found that 10,000 residents lived in cellars and basements with no toilets or running water. Not surprisingly, Harlem had the highest mortality rate in the city. Rents were high because the amount of housing available to African Americans was limited by discriminatory rental policies.

People in Harlem and other ghettos supplemented relief payments in various ways, legal or otherwise. These included growing vegetable gardens, throwing rent parties (which often featured gambling), running the "policy" or numbers racket, taking in boarders, and receiving food and other forms of assistance from relatives, neighbors, or local churches.

The presidential election of 1932 took place in the darkest period of the Depression, but President Hoover still managed to win sixty-six percent of the black vote. Only in New York City and Kansas City, Missouri did that vote go to the Democrats. This was in spite of the economic crisis and Hoover's lackluster performance in dealing with it, his refusal to be photographed with black leaders, his disbandment of the U. S. Army's (black) Tenth Cavalry unit, and the small number of blacks attending the Republican convention.

Pro-Hoover articles in African American journals apparently had an impact on the electoral count. So did Democratic candidate Franklin Roosevelt's prior record as Assistant Secretary of the Navy and Governor of New York. In the latter capacity, for instance, he had largely ignored blacks in making appointments to state jobs. The early years of his presidency (1933-35) were not much better, as he opposed anti-lynching and civil rights bills and declined to receive black delegations at the White House.[5]

Equally aloof were federal agencies, such as the National Recovery Administration (NRA), which exempted domestic service workers and unskilled laborers from its support of a minimum wage. Also, under NRA codes, wages paid by private companies were lower for blacks simply because this was traditional. The Department of Agriculture, another agency deeply involved in economic recovery issues, did nothing to prevent landowners from cheating sharecroppers and tenants out of their fair share of payment benefits. Of all cabinet departments, Agriculture had the smallest percentage of black employees and was the last to hire a black adviser. The fact that patronage appointments to federal relief projects were under the control of local officials also translated itself into much discrimination. At the same time, because of the seniority system southern Democrats were a powerful force in Congress. FDR needed them to ensure passage of New Deal legislation. As he explained to Walter White, executive secretary of the National Association for the Advancement of Colored People (NAACP), he did not choose the "tools" with whom he had to work.[6]

However, the period of the "Second New Deal" (1935-38) brought measurable if modest Improvements. Many of them emerged from the efforts of the Works Progress Administration (WPA) and its subsidiary, the National Youth Administration (NYA), and from the passage of the Social Security Act and the National Labor Relations Act. Older agencies such as the Public Works Administration (PWA) and the Civilian Conservation Corps (CCC) were also instrumental in extending benefits to blacks, whose income from New Deal programs by the late thirties equaled that from the occupations of agriculture and domestic service. There were also new racial attitudes among educated whites (inspired in part by the scientific work of Franz Boas and his graduate students on race at Columbia University). These advances led to a dramatic change in electoral politics: seventy-six percent of the black vote in the 1936 presidential election went to FDR and the Democrats. More receptive attitudes toward blacks on the part of urban Democratic political machines were also evident.[7]

No individual did more than First Lady Eleanor Roosevelt to change the relationship between the New Deal and the cause of civil rights. Although her understanding of racial problems was limited when she came to Washington in 1933, her concern for underdogs drew her in. She soon developed friendships with prominent African Americans, especially with NAACP leader Walter White and black college president Mary McLeod Bethune, both of whom visited her often at the White House and at the Roosevelt homestead in Hyde Park, New York. Mrs. Roosevelt endorsed abolition of the poll tax, anti-lynching legislation, increased aid to black schools, the minimum wage, and a decent quota for African Americans in government employment and in access to public housing. She spoke frequently at "Negro" colleges and often made the point about the inequities associated with education in the South.[8]

With the exception of Mrs. Roosevelt, Secretary of the Interior Ickes was the New Dealer with the strongest ties to African Americans. It was to Ickes, for example, that the NAACP and the National Urban League took their problems. He often addressed their conventions, gave commencement talks, and campaigned in their neighborhoods. He stressed relief (and delivered it through the PWA, a subsidiary of the Interior Department). An advocate of federal farm aid, low-income housing, and employment for blue- and white-collar workers, Ickes tied New Deal ideas to the theme of social justice. The New Deal was a blessing, he believed, because it would bring social and economic reform to all ethnic groups.[9]

Harry Hopkins, the head of WPA and a close adviser of the president, was another Administration activist on racial issues. Hopkins' achievements included the adoption of WPA policies making it illegal for relief officials to discriminate on the basis of race, creed, or skin color. Another was the WPA Education program that employed five thousand blacks, who taught another 250,000 of them to read and write.[10]

By 1938 nearly one hundred African Americans had served the New Deal in a (non-clerical) white collar capacity. Most of them were middle class college graduates and/or highly trained professionals who were chosen because they had the background to deal with issues important to their people. Collectively they were nicknamed the "Black Brain Trust." The primary function of these "race advisers" (another nickname") was to provide information concerning the black community to federal agencies and also to act as spokespersons for New Deal programs. Few of them were actually directly responsible for implementing government policy.

Mary McLeod Bethune and Robert Weaver were the two most influential of these appointees. From 1935 to 1943 Bethune was in the NYA, which helped find employment for high school students – she was head of its "Negro Affairs" section. Her support of New Deal reforms was fervent. As she asserted in 1938, even if they were not specifically aimed at uplifting blacks, they warranted support because "the Negro was the real sick man of America and therefore in need of every liberal program designed to benefit the masses."[11]

Harvard Ph.D. graduate Robert Weaver, whose tenure lasted from 1935 to 1944, was probably the most powerful black adviser. He was Ickes' chief racial adviser at Interior and PWA before joining the newly created U. S. Housing Authority in 1938. There he concentrated on inadequacies in housing and employment, which he viewed as the greatest obstacles to African American progress.[12]

The year 1938 was an important one in the struggle to expand civil rights, and one issue – lynching – continued to draw national attention. This flagrant violation of the law, which was really murder under a different name, dated back to the nineteenth century. Though there were instances of it in a few northern states, such as Illinois, lynching was overwhelmingly a southern phenomenon. And, as the severity of the Depression worsened, the number of them rose (seven in 1929, twenty-one in 1930, and a decade-high of twenty-eight in 1933). Several southern-based organizations, such as the Southern Commission on the Study of Lynching, particularly debunked the defenders' argument that it was a deterrent against potential black rapists of white women. But since the southern political establishment would not undertake corrective action, the only hope seemed to be congressional legislation.[13]

The NAACP had made anti-lynching its most urgent legislative objective since 1933. In fact, a bill sponsored by Senator Robert Wagner (D-NY) and Representative Edward Costigan (D-CO) was largely drafted by the NAACP's Walter White. The greatest obstacle to passage was the Senate rule requiring a two-thirds majority to cut off debate and allow a floor vote. Because of this weapon, southern Democrats and their emerging Republican allies were able to filibuster the bill to death in 1934 and 1935. The House of Representatives, which lacked a filibuster rule, easily passed the bill in 1937 by a margin of 277-120. Public opinion polling indicated that seventy-two percent of Americans nationally and *fifty-seven percent of them in the South* actually supported the legislation. But on January 6th, 1938 southern senators launched another filibuster.

There was a big difference between the1935 filibuster and that of 1938. During the earlier one, neither northern nor southern Democrats considered civil rights important enough to risk splitting the party and thereby jeopardizing the New Deal. This filibuster ended calmly after six days. But the 1938 filibuster lasted nearly seven weeks, with northern Democrats insisting on night sessions and twice seeking to invoke cloture. None of these moves succeeded. Almost every southern senator blamed President Roosevelt for alienating the South, and they linked demands for civil rights to pro-leftist (read *Communist*), pro-union, and pro-black forces. Southerners turned the debate into a paean to their women folk and an attack on the New Deal programs benefiting blacks. It was in this context that Senator Theodore Bilbo (D-MS) introduced his scheme for colonizing

African Americans in their ancestral continent. Sensing success, Senator Allen Ellender (D-LA) talked for six days, then exulted: "It was costly, it was bitter, but oh, how sweet the victory ...."[14]

Finally, on February 16th, 1938, the Senate finally took a cloture vote, which was far short of the needed two-thirds majority. Conceding defeat on February 21st, FDR and most Democrats turned their attention instead to an emergency appropriation to combat a resurgent Depression. The defeat was not total, however. Lynchings actually declined to six in 1938 and two in 1939. Roosevelt also ordered the Justice Department to investigate all cases of mob violence that possibly involved a denial of federal rights. The campaign against lynching taught activists much about public relations, fund raising, and legislative lobbying. Many of them joined the NAACP or other organizations to fight against the poll tax, discrimination in defense jobs, and segregation in education and housing. Their struggle became more professionalized.[15]

Reports in the *New York Times* during 1938 reveal a mixed record with respect to racially-connected issues. For example, John D. Byrd, mayor of the small town of Snow Hill, Maryland, warned unemployed blacks to leave the community in the aftermath of a race riot in which one of them was killed and twenty-one arrested. The town's police chief claimed that he was forced to fire on the nineteen-year-old victim who was one in a group that had insulted a police officer (a coroner's jury exonerated the chief). Mayor Byrd announced that he would take a census of all African Americans in Snow Hill. Those not employed would be given the choice of leaving immediately or of being detained in the House of Correction on vagrancy charges.[16]

North of the Mason-Dixon Line, in Elizabeth, New Jersey, the mood was only somewhat better. The Board of City Recreation Commissioners closed the public pool indefinitely following disputes between white and black youths. A delegation of community leaders protested that the black boys had been "ducked" and that water had been poured into the locker room where they had left their clothes. A supporting letter from the Communist Party of Elizabeth charged that the recent drowning of a boy in Staten Island Sound had been the direct result of his fear of entering the city pool.[17]

Another article, datelined East Orange, New Jersey, reported that the manager of a local movie theater had been arrested for violating a 1935 ordinance that prohibited the showing of films that promoted hostility against persons based on race, color, or religion. The film in question was the previously cited *Birth of a Nation*. A petition bearing 609 signatures had brought the complaint.[18]

On the national level by 1938, the judges of the federal judiciary had come to reflect the political supremacy of the New Deal; and this resulted in a number of pro-civil rights decisions. A number of suits in Federal District Courts in Maryland and Virginia, for instance, resulted in decisions ruling that the rights of African American teachers had been violated due to large salary differentials favoring whites. In another case, the U. S. Supreme Court, in Hale v. Kentucky, restated the constitutional guarantee of a jury of one's peers and overturned the murder conviction of a defendant because no blacks had sat either on the grand or trial juries.

Later that year, in the legalese-inflected case known as Missouri ex rel Gaines v. Canada, the Supreme Court struck what might be characterized as a preliminary blow against the doctrine of "separate but equal." Reversing the Missouri Supreme Court, a six to two majority ruled that Lloyd Gaines, a St. Louis black man, must either be admitted to the Law School of the University of Missouri, or a law school must be established at the state-run black Lincoln University. The decision held that under the Fourteenth Amendment Gaines was entitled to an education in the law equivalent to that provided for white students. Nor had he received equal protection under the law by Missouri's offer to pay his tuition at a law school in another state where racial segregation was not the rule.[19]

In another 1938 case, New Negro Alliance v. Sanitary Grocery Company, the Supreme Court overruled the Washington, D. C. Court of Appeals, declaring that use of injunctions to stop picketing against businesses with racial hiring practices was *not* permissible.[20] This decision was useful to a movement in Harlem and other centers of African American population originally known by the admonition: "Don't buy where you can't work." By 1938 a Harlem group named the Greater New York Coordinating Committee for Employment had taken up the battle. It claimed the backing of 206 organizations representing 170,000 members. Also involved were the NAACP, the Urban League, and the local Communist Party branch. Two young clergymen – Adam Clayton Powell, Jr. of the Abyssinian Baptist Church and William James of the St. James Presbyterian Church – led the Committee's efforts to secure white collar jobs for Harlem residents. Their campaign gained momentum from the Supreme Court's picketing decision.

The facts seemed to demand corrective action. On the main commercial thoroughfare of 125th Street, for example, there were approximately 250 businesses refusing to employ blacks. In the neighborhood generally, only five percent of the stores hired blacks, though residents provided ninety percent of business revenue.[21]

Backed by the threat of picketing, the Coordinating Committee 's first success came against the Consolidated Edison Company, the giant New York-based utility. Pressure against the New York Telephone Company produced similar results. At the end of April 1938 firms not yet hiring blacks received a letter from the Reverend Powell holding out the prospect of picketing. The big breakthrough occurred after four months of negotiations with the Uptown (Harlem) Chamber of Commerce.

The deal stipulated that stores not yet employing thirty-three to forty percent of blacks would work toward that goal through the resignation or discharge of white personnel (however, no whites would be dismissed simply to make room for blacks). In stores with closed shop agreements, employers agreed to prevail upon unions to admit prospective black employees. Stores would experience no picketing unless they violated the pact. Within two months of the Memorandum of Agreement, three hundred African Americans had found white collar jobs in Harlem.[22]

The "Don't buy ..." campaign was an empowering experience, one that revealed the *potential* of mass action. Yet it certainly did not persuade the vast majority of white citizens to support black equality. Despite the decisions of the Supreme Court and a somewhat sympathetic New Deal, the *patterns* of race relations in the thirties did not change. In the words of historian Harvard Sitkoff, "the depression decade proved to be a time of planting, not harvesting."[23] The caste system still stood, as did the accompanying oppression and humiliations. Gains in the administration of justice, education, housing, public acomodations, and the right to vote were minor by later standards.

A number of additional points stand out. In the nation's capital, for instance, African Americans could not attend a movie theater, stay at a hotel, or buy a cup of coffee at most eateries. Proposed changes in race relations encountered a political system better constructed to *impede* change, characterized by the poll tax, the "lily white" primary, states' rights and, in Congress, the seniority system and the filibuster. The fact that less than fifteen percent of Americans went beyond high school slowed the dissemination of new ideas. Again, citing Sitkoff: "It would take twenty-five years of prosperity, a world war, a protracted Cold War, the end of colonialism in Africa, and a mass exodus of blacks from the South before the basic conditions of life for blacks would change significantly. These would make it possible to alter racial relations to an extent not conceivable in the 1930s ...."[24] Even so, from the perspective of 2020. The road to racial equality remains uncompleted.

Notes: Chapter 9

1   Harvard Sitkoff, *A New Deal for Blacks. The Emergence of Civil Rights as a National Issue.* Vol. I. The Depression Decade. New York: Oxford University Press, 1978, 6-7, 10-11.
2   *Ibid.*, 27-28.
3   Joe William Trotter, Jr., *"From a Raw Deal to a New Deal? 1929-1945,"* in Robin D. G. Kelley and Earl Lewis, eds., *To Make Our World Anew. A History of African Americans.* Oxford, New York City: Oxford University Press, 2000, 410-411.
4   Trotter, *op. cit.*, 426-427; Cheryl Lynn Greenberg, *"Or Does It Explode?" Black Harlem in the Great Depression.* N. Y., Oxford: Oxford University Press, 1991, 176, 179, 181, 186.
5   Sitkoff, *op. cit.*, 40-41.
6   *Ibid.*, 44, 47-51, 54; Trotter, *op. cit.*, 413-415.
7   Trotter, *op. cit.*, 416-417; Sitkoff, *op. cit.*, 68, 75.
8   John B. Kirby, *Black Americans in the Roosevelt Era. Liberalism and Race.* Knoxville: The University of Tennessee Press, 1980, 75, 77.
9   Kirby, *op. cit.*, 25-27.
10 Trotter, *op. cit.*, 419.
11 Quoted in Kirby, *op. cit.*, 113. Though Bethune served in government a relatively long time, her patience was not unlimited. Later in 1938, she openly despaired over the status of her people who, she declared, were losing their jobs, farms, and homes and were sunk in peonage, virtual slavery, ill health, and exclusion from unions.
12 Kirby, *ibid.*, 121-123. Later in life – 1966-68 – Weaver served as the first black cabinet appointment, as Secretary of Housing and Urban Development (HUD) under President Lyndon Johnson.
13 Sitkoff, *op. cit.*, 269, 271-272.
14 *Ibid.*, 118, 269-271, 278, 288, 290-292.
15 *Ibid.*, 295.
16 *NYT,* Spt. 20, 1938, 24.
17 *Ibid.*, July 20, 10.
18 *Ibid.*, May 19, 1938, 23.
19 *Ibid.*, Dec. 13, 1938, 1; Sitkoff, *op. cit.*, 238-239; Trotter, *op. cit.*, 424. Gaines never attended the University Law School. In fact, he would never be heard from again. According to some rumors, he had been murdered. Others claimed that he had accepted a payoff and fled to New York City or Mexico City. Neither local authorities nor the FBI

looked into his disappearance. Fifty-five years later the University of Missouri Law School would grant Gaines an honorary law degree as a symbolic apology for the past injustices. See Patricia Ball-Scott, *The Firebrand and the First Lady. Portrait of a Friendship. Pauli Murray, Eleanor Roosevelt and the Struggle for Social Justice.* New York: Alfred A. Knopf, 2016, 40.

20 Greenberg, *op. cit.*, 132.

21 *Ibid.*, 133-134; *NYT, op. cit.*, Apr. 29, 1938, 8.

22 *NYT, op. cit.*, Apr. 29, 1938, 8; Greenberg, *op.cit.*, 134-137. The CPUSA strengthened its base in Harlem through its backing of black economic opportunity but then lost much of it because of its support of the Nazi-Soviet Pact and for leaving the Democratic Front.

23 Sitkoff, *op. cit.*, IX.

24 *Ibid.*, 329. The limits of 1930s liberalism were discernible in a letter from a Brooklyn resident to the *New York Times* (Aug. 9, 1938) on desegregating major league baseball: "So many ballplayers come from below the Mason-Dixon line and would object to have a colored player on the same team. Why couldn't the major leagues have one all-colored club? …This suggestion at least does not run against the grain of prejudice … Not only from the standpoint of justice but also from the viewpoint of sporting curiosity, I am eager to see the colored Hubbells and Medwicks given the chance to compete on an even basis against the nation's best talent."

CHAPTER 10

The Kings of Swing

R ace relations influenced many aspects of life in American society during the Depression years, and Swing, an immensely popular form of jazz, was one of them. For a long time, there was no agreed-upon definition of Swing. Benny Goodman, crowned by admirers as the "King of Swing," said that it cannot be defined, only recognized. Years later a somewhat scholarly definition emerged. Swing was "a stage in the development of jazz characterized by written arrangements and performed by big bands and small ensembles culled from these bands during the 1930s and 1940s."[1]

Early twentieth century Blues, Ragtime, Dixieland, and especially the "Hot Jazz" of 1920s dance bands were all part of Swing's ancestry. The last category included contributions from the black musicians Joe "King" Oliver, Fletcher Henderson, Louis Armstrong, and "Duke" Ellington. Oliver had one of the "hottest" bands, which for several years employed the improvisational genius Armstrong. Henderson's group was a model for the later bands of Benny Goodman and others. And as early as 1932, Ellington recognized the sound with the opening lyrics to one of his hits: "It don't mean a thing if it ain't got that swing." Another influence was the (white) Casa Loma Orchestra, founded in 1929, which reigned as the country's leading dance band until the mid-thirties.[2]

Then Benny Goodman came along. Born in Chicago of impoverished Russian Jewish immigrants, he was already playing clarinet professionally as a teenager and, in 1934 at the age of twenty-five, he founded his own band. Although he did not create the demand for Swing, his version of it suited the youthful taste more exactly than those of his older contemporaries. In fact, he was only a few years older than the college students who were attracted to the music, which was heard on the radio show "Let's Dance" and other venues. A cross-country tour in 1935, which at first seemed a miserable failure, exploded into meteoric success in California, first in Oakland and particularly at the Palomar Ballroom in Los Angeles. The musically creative Fletcher Henderson, now a former band leader, wrote the arrangements that set Goodman's style.

A *gig* a few months later in 1935 and 1936 at Chicago's Congress Hotel also boosted the band's popularity. It was accompanied by heavy press coverage, excellent new records, and live radio broadcasts from the Congress. The Hotel soon extended the band's booking from one month to six months. This significant musical event also became a landmark in racial history.

Goodman was not the only white bandleader to feature black musicians before a paying audience – Charlie Barnet had done so earlier in 1935. But it had also happened occasionally in the twenties and even as far back as the 1890s on Hudson River cruise lines. The non-prejudicial attitude of German-born clarinet teacher Franz Schoepp influenced the young Benny, whose jam sessions with black musicians taught him many useful techniques. Still, on the eve of the Congress appearance, fearing a public uproar, he hesitated to hire splendid black pianist Teddy Wilson. Benny's friend and promoter John Hammond, a Vanderbilt descendant, socialist, and jazz lover, had recommended Wilson. He finally agreed to do it, and Wilson, drummer Gene Krupa, and BG himself formed the

Benny Goodman Trio. Success at the Congress followed, and nobody seemed to care about Wilson's skin color.[3]

Wilson became a permanent member of a previously all-white orchestra, a relationship that should be judged against the day's racial realities. One of these was the separation of the Chicago Musicians' Union into white and black locals. Another was in New York where blacks played in the jazz clubs on 52nd Street, but black patrons were unwelcome.[4]

The Benny Goodman band won first place in the jazz magazine *Down Beat's* 1936 readers' poll. However, other bands were beginning to provide competition, including those led by Artie Shaw, Woody Herman, Tommy Dorsey, Charlie Barnet and, a bit later, Glen Miller. In 1937 the Goodman group had another engagement at the Palomar Ballroom, site of the 1935 breakthrough performance. While having dinner at a nearby restaurant, they enjoyed the distinctive sound of Lionel Hampton. His instrument was the vibraphone, or vibes, not to be confused with the xylophone, which was unamplified and had wooden rather than metal keys. Signed up immediately, Hampton became part of the Goodman Quartet, along with Wilson, Krupa, and BG.

The inclusion of another black musician caused very few negative audience reactions, not even in the southern city of Dallas, Texas. Goodman was also quick to reject attempts by several of his employers to drop or segregate his black band members. For instance, he ignored the request by the manager of the New Yorker Hotel to force Wilson and Hampton to enter the building through the kitchen rather than the lobby (he said he would quit first, and the request was withdrawn). There were occasional incidents (involving other bands), and segregation did not vanish. But integration in Swing music generally proceeded more smoothly than would the later Jackie Robinson experience in baseball. The success of the Trio and Quartet brought fame to Wilson and Hampton as great jazz musicians.[5]

The advent of a style of dancing that matched the exuberance of the music gave an even greater popularity to the Swing bands. There were eventually a number of distinct dances – the Shag, the Big Apple, the Suzie-Q, and others – but they all resembled the Lindy-hop. That name dated back to Harlem in the late twenties and was derived from Charles Lindbergh's (nickname Lindy) hop across the Atlantic. By the mid-thirties black teenagers were jitterbugging (a later term) at the Savoy Ballroom to the music of the Chick Webb band. Joined by their right hands, the boy and girl danced separately but came together periodically to twirl or effect maneuvers in which the girl would be thrown in the air or slid between the boy's legs.

White kids were soon imitating the new style, most notably on March 3rd, 1937 during the first day of a two-week BG engagement at New York's Paramount Theater. This was not the first appearance of a big band at a movie house, but it was certainly the most memorable. The audience, many of whom danced in the aisles, consisted mainly of truant high school students who had arrived at the theater at seven in the morning. to line up for twenty-five cent tickets. The price was within their reach, whereas slightly more affluent college students had the option of attending big band performances at hotels and jazz clubs.

The Swing phenomenon really took off after Goodman's show at the Paramount. For example, the winter of 1937-38 in New York City had the Dorsey brothers, Chick Webb, Cab Calloway, Louis Prima, and Art Tatum all appearing somewhere. Swing's popularity lasted through World War II, but 1938 was probably its heyday. Fans of the music, nicknamed hepcats, were similar to followers of sports. They had their favorite "teams," whose activities they followed avidly; and they knew, sometimes in minute detail, about the lives of principal band members. Their fan clubs were unique in that most of them had young women as presidents (the old "Hot Jazz" of the twenties had been a male-dominated activity). Jitterbugging "uniforms" for boys consisted of jackets and ties, in imitation of band members' outfits. Girls were more inventive, sporting white buck shoes, short white "bobby sox," and short dresses or skirts that rose when the wearers twirled on the dance floor.[6]

January 16th, 1938 was one of the greatest days in the history of jazz and one of several in the historical record of popular music. The idea of a Benny Goodman concert at New York's Carnegie Hall was originally conceived by publicist Wynn Nathanson but was also a way to give American popular music parity with the classics. Nathanson persuaded impresario Sol Hurok to present the event. Ticket prices ranged from eighty-five cents to $2.75. All 2,760 seats were sold out, as well as one hundred extra seats.

Goodman himself was nervous about the forthcoming event. "What the hell would *we* do there," he exclaimed. Carnegie Hall, after all, was for the likes of Toscanini, Stokowski, and others whom Benny actually idolized. Fearful that nobody would show up, he decided to ask well-known British comedienne Bea Lillie to act as mistress of ceremonies to add an element of humor (she declined). Just before the curtain went up, trumpeter Harry James commented: "I feel like a whore in church."[7]

The trepidation turned out to be totally unwarranted. While a small group of pro-Franco demonstrators picketed outside (Goodman had played a few benefits for the Loyalist cause), the paying crowd filed in. It consisted of a few classical musicians but mostly of college and high school kids. The show opened with a piece originally written for the Chick Webb orchestra, "Don't be That Way," which subsequently became a Goodman staple. Other staples followed, including "Sing, Sing, Sing" and "One O'clock Jump," a "history of jazz" medley, a jam session on "Honeysuckle Rose," performances by the Goodman Trio and Quartet, and guest appearances by musicians from the Count Basie and Duke Ellington bands.[8]

Reviews of the concert were mostly favorable, with a major exception being newspaper classical music critics whose sense of decorum seems to have been challenged. But the generally positive impact led to the opening of Carnegie Hall to jazz entertainers throughout 1938, among them Ethel Waters, Louis Armstrong, Artie Shaw, and Count Basie. Twelve years later, in 1950, a recording of the most famous Carnegie Hall Jazz Concert, not made public till then, became one of the best-selling jazz albums, selling one million copies in the U. S. as well as large numbers abroad.[9]

In spite of a few predictions of its pending demise, the Swing era not only continued but thrived. A "Carnival of Swing" at Randall's Island in New York City in May 1938 drew 24,000; and a few months later a crowd roughly estimated at between 100-200,000 jammed Soldier Field in Chicago for a "Swing Jamboree." Nor did the ongoing Depression prevent approximately 700,000 Swing records from being sold every month. A huge recording event took place on July 24th, 1938: Artie Shaw's band recorded "Begin the Beguine," and almost overnight it became a sensation.[10]

The poorly controlled crowd at Soldier Field caused the "Jamboree" to be ended early. This was symptomatic of the fact that Swing, and particularly jitterbugging, were becoming the subject of an emotional controversy. Critics viewed some of the lyrics as suggestive in an era when premarital sex was unacceptable, for example, lyrics from "All or Nothing at All" and "That Old Black Magic." Jitterbugging inescapably offered glimpses of thighs and panties. Blue Barron, a bandleader of calmer dance music, declared: "Swing is nothing but orchestrated sex ... a phallic symbol set to sound ... music that cannot shake off its origins in the lower sporting spots of the deep South." The *Chicago Tribune* asserted: "Swing deals largely with eroticism." Other commentators, such as the notoriously anti-Semitic Henry Ford, also decried Jewish and black influences (in fact, black influence *was* overwhelming, Eastern European Jewish *Klezmer* folk music much less so).[11]

Another negative interpretation of Swing compared its "mass hysteria" to the behavior of youthful fascists in Germany and Italy. But there were positive interpretations as well, according to which Swing was one or more of the following: the voice of youth striving to be heard; a youth rebellion similar to that of the 1920s Jazz Age; a protest against mechanization; or a joyful way of transcending the misery of the Depression.

For their part, the naysayers not only spoke out but took, or tried to take, stronger action. For instance, in October 1938 the Bach Society of New Jersey launched a campaign to halt radio broadcasts of jazzed-up versions of European concert music. The organization's president suggested suspending the offending station's license for a first offense, while a second offense would bring revocation of the station's license. Radio stations in Detroit, Cleveland, and Los Angeles, in fact, did ban jazzed-up traditional favorites. Organizers of the 1938 St. Patrick's Day festivities in New York City also banned Swing along the parade route. And members of the New York State Legislature proposed a general ban on Swing, which failed to pass.

The practice of "swinging the classics" was a distinctive part of the pop musical scene, such as Tommy Dorsey's rendition of Rimsky-Korsakoff's "Song of India" and Strauss's "Blue Danube." Defenders of the practice rested their case on the basis of freedom of expression, and they won out. Two prominent bandleaders disagreed on this issue. Benny Goodman argued that popular treatment of the classics actually increased public interest in the originals. But Count Basie was critical, describing the practice as a desecration of beautiful old melodies.[13]

The age of Swing continued through the war years, but by 1945 it was clearly faltering. Aside from the fact that many musicians had enlisted or were drafted into the armed forces, gasoline rationing had rendered going on the road difficult if not impossible. The Musician Union's strike of 1942-44 against the record companies was a huge blow because it kept Swing from fans who largely depended on recordings. Meanwhile, singers such as Frank Sinatra, were not part of the union, and they recorded new songs while the Swing bands stagnated. At the same time new (and older) styles of music were siphoning off jazz audiences from the big band sound. In particular, younger audiences were attracted to the new Bebop.[14]

Benny Goodman biographer James Lincoln Collier believes that Swing was the finest kind of popular music, rivaled only by the waltzes of the late nineteenth century. He described it as carefully rehearsed, with close attention to detail and often brilliantly played by thoroughly trained musicians.[15]

The remarkable Gunther Schuller, a composer, conductor, teacher, and classical and jazz musician (on French horn and flute) cogently summed up the Swing era:

> That remarkable period in American musical history when jazz was synonymous with America's popular music, its social dances and its musical entertainment ... Jazz in the thirties spread through expansion of the recording industry and of network radio and its nightly broadcasts of jazz groups from hotel and ballrooms. A vast array of musical talent was directed at satisfying the American consumer (black and white) ... It was the only time in American history when jazz was completely in phase with the social environment and when it both captured and reflected the broadest musical common-denominator of popular taste in the nation. This music provided an alluring escape from the often-depressing real world ....[16]

Notes: Chapter 10

1   Cited in David W. Stowe, *Swing Changes. Big Band Jazz in New Deal America*. Cambridge, MA. And London: Harvard University Press, 1994, 5.
2   Ross Firestone, *Swing, Swing, Swing. The Life and Times of Benny Goodman*. New York, London: W. W. Norton and Co., 1993, 150.
3   James Lincoln Collier, *Benny Goodman and the Swing Era*. New York: Oxford University Press, 1989, 172.
4   *Ibid.*
5   *Ibid.*, 174, 176.
6   *Ibid.*, 190-193.
7   *Ibid.*, 215; Firestone, *op. cit.*, 209.
8   Scott Yanow, *Swing*. San Francisco: Miller Freeman Books, 2000, 60.
9   Collier, *op. cit.*, 217-218; Firestone, *op. cit.*, 217.
10 Firestone, *op. cit.*, 238-239.
11 The citations are in Firestone, *op. cit.*, 242. Benny Goodman, Artie Shaw, and many lesser-known Swing musicians were Jewish.
12 Stowe, *op. cit.*, 94-97.
13 Firestone, *op. cit.*, 242-244.
14 Yanow, *op. cit.*, 305.
15 Collier, *op. cit.*, 361.
16 Gunther Schuller, *The Swing Era. The Development of Jazz 1930-1945*. New York, Oxford: Oxford University Press, 1989, 4-6.

CHAPTER 11

LIFE (September 19, 1938)

J ust as Swing enlivened the popular musical scene in the
1930s, so did LIFE magazine give popular journalism a
significant boost. During its heyday from 1936 to 1972, LIFE
was a lively general interest weekly known especially for its
photographic excellence. The name itself dates back to 1883,
when it was founded as a humor magazine based largely on
the British publication *Punch*. That all changed in 1936 when
Henry Luce, the owner of TIME, acquired the rights to its name
and transformed it thoroughly and successfully. At one point
its circulation reached 13.5 million copies a week. The best
known of its illustrations was probably Alfred Eisenstaedt's
photograph of a nurse and sailor kissing enthusiastically on a
New York City Street as they celebrated Victory over Japan Day
on August 14th, 1945.

The magazine's Contents in the September 19th, 1938 issue
divided subject matter into the following sections: The Week's
Events; Close Up; The Photographic Essay; Movies; Other
Departments; and Letters to the Editor. The Week's Events
naturally were varied in character. Two stories dealt with the
so-called Czech Crisis, when Germany was demanding cession
of the little republic's Sudetenland region and threatened a
war that could have involved much of Europe (see Chapter 2).
One ominous photograph shows a previously secret German

artillery piece with a forty-foot barrel that was probably the longest in the world. Since foreigners were not allowed to take pictures of the gun, LIFE reproduced a photo lifted from the *Berliner Zeitung.*

A more extensive photographic essay on the same crisis discussed the views of British Prime Minister Neville Chamberlain, Foreign Secretary Lord Halifax, and Ambassador to Germany Sir Nevile Henderson. This was accompanied by a photo that LIFE labeled "a rather glum shooting party," a typically English aristocratic scene featuring *London Times* editor Geoffrey Dawson with family members, guests, and hunting dogs. The *Times* had close ties to the Conservative government, and Dawson had already suggested that the Czechs surrender the entire Sudeten territory outright to Hitler (a policy that Chamberlain ultimately adopted).[1]

LIFE featured a more personal tragic scene shot at the Lido Beach in Venice, but one that seems just the opposite. The attractive American young woman, *nee* Barbara Hutton, cavorts happily with a group of friends while she awaits the arrival of a decree finalizing her divorce from the Danish Count Georg von Haugwitz-Hardenberg-Reventlow. Hutton's difficult early years had earned her the nickname "poor little rich girl." She was the only child of Edna Woolworth, who was the daughter of chain store founder Frank W. Woolworth.

A bad marriage to Franklyn Laws Hutton contributed to Edna's decision to commit suicide, as a result of which young Barbara was passed from one set of indifferent relatives to another. She herself would go on to have seven unsuccessful marriages. The press dubbed her and third husband, actor Cary Grant, "Cash and Cary," a play on the description of a revised U. S. arms embargo act of 1939. In 1972 her only child, Lance Reventlow, was killed in a plane crash. An impoverished Hutton died of a heart attack in 1979 at the age of sixty-six.[2]

Another brief photographic essay reminded readers that

men, such as Howard Hughes (see Chapter 5), were not the only competitive fliers in 1938. Jacqueline Cochran flew from Burbank, California to Cleveland, Ohio in eight hours and ten minutes to win the Bendix Trophy and $12,500. Not that Cochran needed the money, inasmuch as she was the wife of a multi-millionaire investment banker.

Football undeniably was a thoroughly male sport, with the college version far surpassing the professional one in popularity. The College All-Stars – National Football League game was a major annual event; and in 1938 the All-Stars beat the Washington Redskins by a score of twenty-eight to sixteen. A LIFE photo shows University of Colorado All-American Byron "Whizzer" White as he broke away for an eleven-yard gain. A runner-up for the Heisman Trophy in 1937, White was a first-round pick in the 1938 National Football League draft. In his rookie season with the Pittsburgh Pirates, he would lead the NFL in rushing yards.

White played two more seasons (for the Detroit Lions) before serving as a U. S. Navy intelligence officer in World War II. After the war he attended Yale University Law School, had a successful legal career, and in 1962 he was nominated by President John F. Kennedy for a seat on the Supreme Court. He retired from the Bench in 1993.[3]

A final photographic essay on the opening of the 1938-39 academic year bore the following title: "California Opens Fall Semester with Pageantry and Fun." The action took place at the University of California's Berkeley campus which, decades later, became notorious for youthful radicalism. But in 1938 freshmen apparently had more pressing concerns, which was whether they could secure admission to prestigious fraternities or sororities. LIFE focused on coeds "rushing" the latter. Most of them were fashionably outfitted in below-the-knee dresses or skirts, bobby sox, and saddle shoes. In the first major event, incumbent sorority sisters selected pledgee Jane Jackson as the "Sweetheart of Sigma Chi."[4]

The highlight of the Close-ups Section was an article about the key New Deal figure James A. Farley, a piece written by the *New York Herald Tribune's* political columnists Joseph W. Alsop and Robert E. Kintner. From 1938 to 1941 they collaborated in writing a nationally syndicated column called "Capital Parade." Both of them enjoyed later success – Alsop as a journalist (sometimes in conjunction with his brother Stewart), an intelligence agent, and an art collector; Kintner as president of the American Broadcasting Company (1949-56) and the National Broadcasting Company (1958-65).

The Alsop-Kintner heavily illustrated article was entitled "Farley and the Future," as it looked ahead to the presidential election of 1940 and particularly to the question of who would be the Democratic candidate. The authors concentrated on detailing Farley's important political role.

Born in upstate New York in 1888, the grandson of Irish immigrants, James Aloysius Farley ascended through the ranks to become a leading behind-the-scenes activist before the age of forty. He worked on Franklin Roosevelt's 1928 gubernatorial campaign and was among those engineering his victory in the 1932 presidential election. Roosevelt rewarded him with an appointment to the cabinet as Postmaster General. At the same time, Farley became Chairman of the Democratic National Committee and also retained his position as chair of the New York State Democratic Committee.

In those days of machine politics, Farley's skills helped maintain the loyalty of party bosses to the New Deal. In the words of Alsop and Kintner:

> Jim Farley had done more favors and made more friends than any politician in American history, and his power is proportionately vast ... Is there a thorny problem involving a federal project? The local Democratic leaders notify Jim, and he straightens it out. Is there a detail of legislation

troubling a particular community? The bosses telephone Jim, and he puts in a good word on Capitol Hill. Is there a difficult patronage matter? Jim makes sure the man who gets the job has organization clearance... Twelve hours a day, weekdays, Sundays, and holidays, Jim has labored as the Washington agent of the Party organizations ... And with the health of a horse, he can do three times the work of an ordinary man ....[5]

By 1938, however, differences within the Democratic Party were widening, as Farley's friends in the urban machines and southern conservatives were increasingly being challenged by left-leaning intellectuals on the White House staff and in the cabinet. And more and more, FDR was leaning in their direction.

Alsop and Kintner emphasized the affection between Farley and the president, noting the former's oft-repeated statement: "Roosevelt made me, and I'm never forgetting that." They also asserted that if FDR chose to run for an unprecedented third term, Farley would support him (he had said as much a number of times). They concluded: "It would take a strange set of circumstances to make Farley change his mind. He would have to disavow the big loyalty of a lifetime of extremely, rather touching loyalties."[6]

As excellent as their article was, Alsop and Kintner fell far short of accurately predicting the future Farley-Roosevelt relationship. Farley's successes evidently convinced him that he could be a plausible successor to his boss, whose 1940 endorsement he anticipated. It never came because FDR, while disavowing a plan to run again, declared that he would accept a "draft" at the convention. Given his continued popularity, and backstage maneuvering, that "draft" did materialize. The embittered Farley resigned his positions as Postmaster General and Democratic National Chairman and denounced the president for breaking the two-term tradition. In his 1948 memoir, *Jim Farley's Story: The Roosevelt Years*, he extolled his own legacy while criticizing FDR's. He spent most of his later years as chairman of the Coca Cola Export Corporation, a sinecure created for him by big business allies.[7]

In 1938 and other Depression years, Americans temporarily escaped their dire economic circumstances by going to the movies. This medium was therefore a natural one for LIFE to cover, and it did so regularly. Featured in this issue was *You Can't Take it With You*, a comedy directed by Frank Capra, the son of Italian immigrants, whose cinematic success dated back to the silent film era. The cast was a distinguished one. It included Lionel Barrymore, Edward Arnold, Jean Arthur, Mischa Auer, Spring Byington, an incredibly youthful-looking James Stewart, Eddie "Rochester" Anderson (Jack Benny's "butler"), and many others. Originally a Broadway play by George S. Kaufman and Moss Hart, the plot centers around a love affair between a young man (Stewart) and young woman (Arthur) who come from extremely different family backgrounds. He is the son of an avaricious businessman (Arnold), and she is a member of an impoverished, bizarre, but joyful extended family. Through a series of comic yet also serious contacts between the families, Arnold's character eventually reaches the conclusion that "you can't take it with you."

This LIFE essay focuses heavily, and very positively, on the directorial skills and character of Capra. For example, he always stayed within the budget, never lapsed into displays of temperament, remained loyal to members of the technical crew, precisely remembered every scene, and frequently displayed a good sense of humor. As actor Gary Cooper once remarked: "On a Capra set, you'd never pick Frank as the director."[8]

Finally, LIFE's advertisements revealed much about everyday life in 1938. Women's fashions, for instance, were far more formal than those of today. Dress gloves and assorted hats were in vogue, as were dresses and skirts with hemlines modestly falling several inches below the knee. Outfits of Carolyn's Fashions, which were available at numerous stores across America, sold for an average price of $19.95. This might remind us that in 1938 an annual salary of $4-5000 was far above average. So should the following sample of prices: a Serta Sleeper ($39.50); a "giant size" of Colgate Dental Cream (35 cents); men's Arrow shirts ($2.25—5.00); and Bostonian men's shoes ($7.50—11.00). With regard to male fashions, the well-dressed man wore a suit (single or double-breasted), a tie, and a fedora hat (even at baseball games). LIFE itself sold for ten cents an issue. With a product not yet revealed as a public health danger, cigarette manufacturers advertised wherever and whenever they could. In retrospect, of course, their claims about the health benefits of smoking were totally absurd.[9]

Notes: Chapter 11

1   LIFE, Sept. 19, 1938, 12-13, 16.
2   *Ibid.*, 17.
3   *Ibid.*, 21.
4   *Ibid.*, 22-23.
5   *Ibid.*, 24-25.
6   *Ibid.*, 24.
7   *Ibid.*, 56-57.
8   *Ibid.*, 42-47.
9   *Ibid.*, 2-5, 8, 41, 56-57, back page.

CHAPTER 12

Major League Baseball Highlights

A s is the case today, sports in 1938 were an important part of life in America. Professionally, baseball was "the national pastime," with prize fighting (boxing) and horse racing probably tied for second place. By contrast, the National Football League was in its infancy, hockey was mainly a Canadian sport, and there was no National Basketball Association. The 1938 Major League season was a lively one, with a very competitive National League pennant race and a number of outstanding individual achievements.

Two consecutive no-hitters thrown by Cincinnati Reds' lefthander Johnny Vander Meer was certainly one of the latter. He threw his first one on June 11th against the Boston Bees (Braves) and his second four days later, on June 15th, against the Brooklyn Dodgers. The Dodger game suddenly became suspenseful in the bottom of the ninth inning. With one out Vander Meer suddenly lost his control and walked the bases loaded. A force-out at home plate on an infield grounder became the second out. Now only Dodger shortstop Leo Durocher stood between Vander Meer and a second consecutive no-hit game. A good-fielding, light-hitting player, Durocher hit an easy fly ball to center field, and Vander Meer's accomplishment became a record that stands to this day.[1]

Vander Meer's second no-hitter at Brooklyn's Ebbets Field

was also the first night game there and only the second one ever played in the major leagues – the first was at Cincinnati's Crosley Field on May 24th, 1935, with the Reds beating the Phillies, two to one. Vander Meer's catcher for both of his no-hitters was Ernie Lombardi, another outstanding performer in 1938. He had a league-leading .342 batting average, nineteen homers, and ninety-five runs-batted-in, achievements that earned him the National League's Most Valuable Player award. At six feet, three inches tall and (at least) two hundred and thirty pounds, he was handicapped as a base runner. But defensively he had a strong and accurate arm and the ability to "call a game" (select the pitches thrown).[2]

Lombardi was not the most celebrated Italian-American ballplayer of his day. That description belonged to the New York Yankees' center fielder Joe DiMaggio who, after only two seasons in the majors, had already earned the nicknames "Jolting Joe" and "the Yankee Clipper." In 1941 he would establish a record that probably will never be broken by hitting safely in fifty-six consecutive games.

In the early spring of 1938, DiMaggio decided to "hold out" for more money in light of his excellent 1937 numbers. He asked for $40,000, nearly triple his previous salary, while the Yankees' ownership offered only $25,000. Holding out was the only leverage a player had in those days of the "reserve clause," under which management could hold on to players indefinitely or trade or release them at any time. Signing with a rival team was not an option. After more than a month, DiMaggio agreed to sign for $25,000 and even professed sincere (or perhaps insincere) joy to be back with such a wonderful club. The Yankees got their money's worth: Joe batted .324 with thirty-two homeruns and one hundred and forty RBIs. But in those Depression days, his teammates resented him, and Yankee fans booed him through much of that season.[3]

The 1938 Yankees were indeed an excellent team. They won

their third straight American League pennant by nine and a half games over second place Boston – the clinching date was a relatively early one, on September 18th. There was a much closer race in the National League where the Chicago Cubs climbed from seven games behind league-leading Pittsburgh at the beginning of September to only one and a half games behind on September 27th. The Pirates proceeded to lose three straight games at Wrigley Field, the first two of which were memorable.

The Cubs' starting pitcher in the first game was Dizzy Dean, who had been acquired in a pre-season trade with the St. Louis Cardinals for what was then the incredible sum of $200,000 -- $185,000 in cash and three players. This was especially noteworthy because Dean's live fast ball had vanished. Returning too soon from a toe injury, he had hurt his arm by adopting a new and completely unnatural pitching motion. Consequently, in 1938, he was able to start only ten games and appear in relief three times. Yet through determination and guile, he won seven of eight decisions and had a very low earned run average of 1.81. In that key game against the Pirates, Dean managed to pitch eight and two-thirds innings and win, two to one.

The second game of the series was tied five to five after eight innings and, with dusk descending, Pittsburgh failed to score in the top of the ninth. The home plate umpire would have called an ordinary game on account of darkness, but he allowed this crucial one to continue into the bottom of the ninth. The Pirate pitcher got the first two outs and had two strikes on the Cubs' third batter – catcher and player-manager Gabby Hartnett. Somehow, in almost total darkness, Hartnett lined a pitch into the left field stands to win the game. Chicago took first place and perhaps more important, the Pirates' morale collapsed and they were crushed in the next game by a score of ten to one. The Cubs easily clinched the National League pennant on October 1st. In the World Series, however, the Yankees outclassed them completely, four games to none. This was the third straight

Series win for the Yankees, a record that would increase to four straight Series with a win over Cincinnati in 1939. A later version of the club would surpass this achievement with five straight Series wins (1949-53).[4]

    While the Cubs and Pirates were competing for the National League pennant, another drama was taking place in American League ballparks. The Detroit Tigers' Hank Greenberg was striving to overturn Babe Ruth's 1927 Major League record of sixty homeruns. Born Hyman Greenberg in 1911 in New York City, the son of Romanian Jewish immigrants, he became Hank early in his athletic career. He kept his last name, though, unlike most of the twenty-two previous Jewish big-league players who changed theirs in response to the anti-Semitism common among fellow ballplayers, owners, and fans. Undoubtedly, he was the first *important* Jewish player and one of only two elected to the Baseball Hall of Fame (the other was Los Angeles Dodger pitcher Sandy Koufax).[5]

    A muscular six feet four, Greenberg starred in baseball and basketball at his Bronx high school. Not a natural athlete, he had to work hard to hone his skills. He began attending New York University after graduating from high school and also spent much of his time playing in a semi-pro baseball league. The Yankees tried to sign him, but he ultimately turned them down to sign with the Tigers. Lou Gehrig's overwhelming presence at first base was behind this decision. A first baseman himself, Greenberg easily recognized as false a Yankee scout's reassurance that Gehrig's tenure at first would soon end (in fact, he would excel for another ten years until crippled by amyotrophic lateral sclerosis, better known as Lou Gehrig's disease).

    Greenberg advanced from the minor leagues to the Tigers in 1933. During his first eight years – until 1941 when he entered the army – his numbers were outstanding. He hit over .300 every season and had excellent homerun and RBI totals. He always believed that 1937 was his best year, and statistics seem to confirm this. Besides a colossal 184 RBIs, only one below Gehrig's American League record, he batted .337, scored 137 runs, and hit forty homers (second that year only to Joe DiMaggio's forty-six). Still, he started the 1938 season slowly. For example, by May 3rd his batting average had dropped to a mediocre .234. However, by the end of June there had been noticeable improvement, including a handsome total of twenty-two homers.[6]

Though selected for the 1938 American League All-star team, Greenberg declined to play or even show up. This was in part because of Yankee manager Joe McCarthy's failure to insert him in the 1937 game, notwithstanding his superb numbers, and due to medical appointments to have his eyes and wrist examined (they were fine). But he also used the break to take special batting practice, which may have helped boost his subsequent performance. He proceeded to bat .382 for the month of July. Fifteen of his twenty-nine hits were homeruns, and from July 23rd, 1938 he hit nine homers in seven days. The last streak included homers in four consecutive at-bats, equaling the mark set by Jimmy Foxx in 1934. Also in July, he hit two homers in a game four times. This caused a few observers – journalists and others – to start mentioning Greenberg in connection with the Babe's record year.[7]

By the end of July, Greenberg already had thirty-seven homeruns for the season, which put him seventeen days ahead of Ruth's pace. Then, from August 9th - 18th, he had a homer "drought;" but on the 19th, in a double header against the St. Louis Browns he hit three of them. This brought his total to forty-one, and Ruth did not hit that many until August 27th.[8]

Greenberg ended August with forty-six homers. As would be the case with Roger Maris and Henry Aaron decades later, Hank would become tied to Babe at the hip, particularly after the Yankees clinched the 1938 pennant and the "chase" could now dominate sports journalism. Incidentally, Babe himself was paying a lot of attention. Now forty-three years old and a coach with the Dodgers, he asked his team to activate him, probably because of all the attention that his record and Greenberg's quest were drawing. The Dodgers left the decision to manager Burleigh Grimes, who rejected the proposal, insisting that this would be best for Ruth's and the team's welfare.[9]

Greenberg's efforts drew a lot of attention from his co-religionists, even from the immigrant generation that had shown little interest in the sport till then. There was major coverage in the Jewish press. The following commentary, for instance, appeared on the op-ed page of the *Boston Jewish Advocate*:

> For the next few weeks, the incidents in Palestine (Arab attacks), in Germany (intensified anti-Semitism), in Czechoslovakia (a possible European war) take a back seat .... We have had *pogroms* before; we have had wars before; we have had trouble with the Arabs before. *But never before have we had a Jewish home-run king...* (italics mine). At a time of rising anti-Semitism, Hank Greenberg is a goodwill emissary for the Jewish people in America. He doesn't make speeches, doesn't give money to non-Jewish causes, doesn't sponsor brotherhood meetings. He simply hits homeruns and the crowd goes wild.[10]

Feelings of non-Jews towards Greenberg breaking Ruth's record were mixed. A number of opposing players, such as the Yankees' Gehrig and catcher Bill Dickey and manager Joe McCarthy were rooting for him (Dickey even tipped him off on pitches). The Browns' first baseman George McQuinn deliberately dropped a Greenberg pop fly to give him another chance to hit it out (he made out anyway during that at-bat). But just as the African American Hank Aaron received hate mail and death threats while chasing Ruth's career mark of 714 homeruns, so did the Jew Greenberg for a similar challenge.[11]

Controversial in a less noxious sense was the fact that Hank walked more times in 1938 (119 times) than during any other years. The closer he came to the record, the more he walked: 20.4 percent of his at-bats in September compared to 15.9 percent in previous months. He had three games with three walks in September 1938, as opposed to 1937 when he had no three walk games. He did have one in 1935, the year he won his first Most Valuable Player Award, and three also in 1940, a second MVP season.

Greenberg always denied that the walks were due to anti-Semitism. Yet in 1932 pitchers walked Jimmy Foxx less when he hit fifty-eight homers; nor did Foxx's walk rate increase much in September of that year. On the other hand, pitchers in 1938 walked Foxx the same number of times as Greenberg, a season in which the Red Sox star would lead the league in batting average (.349), RBIs (175), hit fifty homeruns, and be chosen as MVP. Pitching sensation Bob Feller of the Cleveland Indians later commented on the allegation that pitchers would not throw strikes to Greenberg because they opposed the possibility of a Jewish player overtaking Babe's mark: "With a very successful hitter, the pitchers were anti-Semitic? That's a joke … We played the Tigers about a week before and Hank got a homer or two in that series."[12]

In offering their opinions on Greenberg's prospects, a number of baseball writers mentioned the difficulties facing hitters in the month of September. It was tough, they said, because of the fatigue of a long season, more shadows on the field, colder temperatures, windier conditions, the earlier onset of dusk, and more frequent rainouts. They also noted that the Babe had seventeen homers in September 1927, a record until it was broken by Detroit's Rudy York in 1937. Greenberg's lack of homer production from September 1st – 8th seemed to corroborate the general tenor of these views.

The Detroit first baseman himself believed that the odds against him were about ten to one. But then, on September 9 in Cleveland, he challenged these odds a little with his forty-seventh homer of the year. Then came a hot streak that would continue during the next two-and-a-half weeks. Some of its highlights were as follows: Number fifty on September 12th against the Chicago White Sox (at that time, only the third player who had reached fifty); numbers fifty-two and fifty-three on September 17th against the Yankees; on September 23rd numbers fifty-five and fifty-six against the Indians (the second game was called after the seventh inning because of darkness). Greenberg now had fifty-six homers in 145 games compared to Ruth's fifty-six in 148 games. This put him three games ahead of Ruth's pace, and this remained the same after Hank hit numbers fifty-seven and fifty-eight in a double header against the Browns on September 26th.[13]

Another double header, at Cleveland's cavernous Municipal Stadium, would be the last opportunity for Greenberg to tie or break Ruth's record – two to tie it and three to overturn it. In game one he faced Bob Feller, striking out three times and hitting a long fly ball to center field (where the fence was 467 feet from home plate) and a double estimated at 450 feet on the fly. In game two, he had three singles, including one that traveled 420 feet on the fly. All three of the long drives might have been homers elsewhere. By the seventh inning, it was obviously getting dark as Greenberg came to bat. Home plate umpire Cal Hubbard made a decision: "I'm sorry, Hank," he said, "but this is as far as I can go." To which the reply was: "That's all right. This is as far as I can go too." It was all over! [14]

Before this finale a number of baseball writers and fans

were saying that if Greenberg tied or beat Ruth's mark in 154 games, while the latter had played in only 151 games in 1927, it would be unfair. It turned out that Greenberg would actually have *fewer* trips to the plate (681) than the *Bambino* had had in 1927 (691). The former also lost twenty at-bats to rain or darkness in 1938. Statistically these lost at-bats could have cost Greenberg at least two homers, given his season average of one every 9.6 times at the plate.[15]

In spite of his excellent season, Greenberg finished third behind Jimmy Foxx and Bill Dickey in the American League voting for MVP. It was a plausible decision. Foxx had fifty homers (second to Greenberg), led the majors in total bases (398), on-base and slugging percentages (.462 and .704), and won the batting title (.349). Dickey did not win in any category, but he was the heart of the pennant-winning Yankees.

After the 1938 season, Tigers' owner Walter Briggs offered Greenberg $35,000, which was the same salary he had received *before* hitting fifty-eight homeruns. Years later Hank told the *Los Angeles Times*: "I squeezed an extra $5,000 out of them, but it wasn't easy."[16]

Greenberg had a decent season in 1939; but 1940 was one of his best years. He helped the Tigers win another pennant by batting .340, hitting forty-one homers, and driving in 150 runs. He also won his second MVP and had an outstanding World Series, although Detroit lost to Cincinnati in seven games.[17]

Greenberg missed most of 1941 because of his military service, from which he did not return until mid-1945. He did not look like his old self, but before the season was over, he had contributed to Tiger victories in the pennant race and over the Cubs in the World Series. Returning to form in 1946, he would lead the American League with forty-four homers and 127 RBIs. Much to his chagrin, the Tigers sold his contract to the Pittsburgh Pirates for the minimum price of $10,000. Perhaps the most notable aspects of his 1947 season were his tutelage of the youthful Ralph Kiner, who would proceed to lead the National League in homers for seven straight years, and his support for Jackie Robinson of the Dodgers during his difficult year of breaking the color bar. Greenberg's experience with anti-Semitism in his days with the Tigers, though not as extreme as the prejudice Robinson encountered, gave these two superb ballplayers a lot in common.

Notes: Chapter 12

1   Boardman, *op. cit.*, 217. Vander Meer's 1938 won-lost record was 15-10, with a 3.12 earned run average. His next best year was 1941, with a 16-12 record, six shutouts, and a league-leading 202 strikeouts. However, his overall career mark of 119 wins, 121 losses was mixed at best. For his part, Leo Durocher went on to become a combative and moderately successful manager, mostly with the Dodgers and New York Giants.

2   *NYT, op. cit.*, Nov. 1, 1938, 31.

3   *Ibid.*, Apr. 1, 18; Apr. 21, 23; May 21, 1938, 11. Twenty-five thousand dollars, about $402,000 in today's purchasing power, is less than the current major league minimum salary. Ted Williams, another great ballplayer four years younger than DiMaggio, was demoted to the minors by the Boston Red Sox during 1938 spring training. He would have huge numbers with the Minneapolis Millers and go on to become one of the best major league hitters of all time. He remains the last player to hit over .400, with a .406 average in 1941.

4   *Ibid.*, Oct. 2, 1938, V, 1; David S. Neft and Richard M. Cohen, *The Sports Encyclopedia: Baseball. 1992 Edition.* New York: St. Martin's Press, 196. Until a generation ago, player-managers, such as Hartnett, were not unusual because club owners could pay one salary instead of two.

5   Mark Kurlansky, *Hank Greenberg. The Hero who Didn't Want to Be One.* New Haven and London: Yale University Press, 1990, 14.

6   John Rosengren, *Hank Greenberg. The Hero of Heroes.* New York: New American Library, 2014, 150-151, 154. Greenberg's 1937 numbers may have been augmented by third base coach Del Baker tipping him off on pitches. Baker's *modus operandi* was primitive and quite open compared to more recent sign stealing. "All right, Hank, you can do it" meant a fastball. "Come on, Hank" meant a curve. Baker took credit for Hank's hits, which annoyed him. He later wrote: "There's a big difference between knowing what's coming and hitting it." Before the 1938 season, Greenberg had sworn off Baker's signs. As *Detroit News* sports writer Harry Salsinger put it: "Hank Greenberg announces that he will no longer play Charlie McCarthy to Del Baker's Edgar Bergen."

7   *Ibid.*, 156-157; Ron Kaplan, *Hank Greenberg in 1938. Hatred and Home Runs in the Shadow of War.* New York: Sports Publishing, 2017, 97-98; Rosengren, *op. cit.*, 160.

8   Kaplan, *op. cit.*, 115.

9   *Ibid.*, 105; Hank Greenberg, *The Story of My Life.* Edited and with an Introduction by ira Berkow. New York and Toronto: Times Books, a Division of Random House, 1989, 109. Disappointed with not being able to secure a manager's position and bored with an inferior team, Ruth retired from baseball again after the 1938 season.

10   Quoted in Kaplan, *op. cit.*, 127-128. The *Advocate* editorial writer was unaware of Lipman Pike, the New York-born son of Dutch Jews who played in the nineteenth century and led the "majors" of that day in homeruns four times. But in those days of the "dead ball," he never hit more than seven in any season.

11   Rosengren, *op.cit.*, 168-169, 173.

12   Greenberg, *op. cit.*, 112-114. The fifty-seventh homer was an inside-the-park variety. In those days before instant replay, the umpire's "safe" call stood despite a vigorous protest by the Browns. Forty years later, Greenberg received a letter from former Browns' catcher Sam Harshaney, who wanted his college-age sons to know that their father had tagged out Hank in time for the out. The latter replied: "I was out by a mile and had no business being called safe."

13   Rosengren, *op. cit.*, 176. With eighteen strikeouts, Feller broke the strikeout record, though losing 4-1 to Detroit's young (and Jewish) Harry Eisenstat who pitched a four-hitter.

14   Kaplan, *op. cit.*, 137-138, 152.

15   Quoted in Greenberg, *op. cit.*, 126. This made Greenberg the highest paid player in major league baseball.

16   Kaplan, *op. cit.*, 163; Kurlansky, *op. cit.*, 46.

CHAPTER 13

The Written Word: Books, Plays, Newspapers, and Magazines

While Americans in 1938 were spending much of their time on sports-related activities, they were also reading a lot. And, to be sure, there were many books – of all categories – readily available.

Carl Van Doren (1885-1950), a historian, biographer, literary critic, and university professor, won the 1939 Pulitzer Prize for Biography for his *Benjamin Franklin*. Published in 1938, it is still regarded as one of the finest biographies of Franklin. Another 1938 publication was *My America*, by Louis Adamic (1898-1950), who immigrated from Slovenia in 1913. Then part of the Austro-Hungarian Empire, Slovenia became a constituent part of Yugoslavia and still later an independent republic. Essentially a left-leaning journalist, Adamic focused on his labor experiences in the United States and on developments in his former home. He kept up with conditions throughout the Balkans, giving many Americans their first real knowledge of the region.

The fictional works of Pearl S. Buck (1892-1973) also dealt with foreign parts. She spent most of her life before 1934 in China as the daughter of missionaries. Her novel, *The Good Earth*, was the best-selling work of fiction in the U. S. in 1931-32, winning the Pulitzer in the latter year. In 1938 she became the first American woman to be awarded a Nobel Prize for her general contributions to literature.

Women were not unique among 1938's successful authors. Daphne du Maurier (1907-69) spent the greater part of her life in the western English county of Cornwall, where most of her stories were set. Its rugged landscapes and turbulent seascapes formed a suitable backdrop for her dark romantic novels, which were also characterized by hints of the supernatural. Published in 1938, *Rebecca* was her most popular work, a status reflected by the sale of nearly three million copies between publication date and the year 1965. The American Booksellers Association chose it for the 1938 National Book Award. *Rebecca* and several of du Maurier's other writings eventually made it to the movies and to high quality television shows. The Alfred Hitchcock film *The Birds* (1963), for example, was based on one of her short stories.

Also adapted for the screen was *All This and Heaven Too*, a 1938 novel of passion and murder by American author Rachel Field (1894-1942) – the 1940 film starred Bette Davis and Charles Boyer. Field based her novel on the true story of her French great-aunt's experiences as a governess in mid-nineteenth century Paris.

One of the world's greatest writers of mysteries was English and female. Agatha Christie (1890-1976) was incredibly prolific, authoring sixty-six detective novels and fourteen short story collections. Her best-known works involved the unique detectives, Hercule Poirot, a dapper Belgian refugee during the First World War who remained in England, and Miss Marple, an elderly resident of the small (fictional) town of St. Mary Mead. Both provided invaluable assistance to the police. Their dramatic incarnations appeared in numerous movies and TV programs. Christie also wrote the world's longest-running play, *The Mousetrap*, which was performed in London's West End from

1952 to early 2020. Her 1938 publications were *Appointment with Death* and *Hercule Poirot's Christmas* (the U. S. title for the latter was *Murder for Christmas*).

American writers of detective fiction were also excellent. Despite not publishing anything of note in 1938, perhaps three of them deserve special mention: Dashiell Hammett (1894-1961), Raymond Chandler (1888-1959), and James M. Cain (1892-1977). Their private detective heroes, particularly Hammett's Sam Spade and Chandler's Philip Marlowe, would contribute much to the Film Noir genre of the 1940s. Humphrey Bogart played both Sam Spade in *The Maltese Falcon* and Philip Marlowe in *The Big Sleep*.

Two talented young writers did publish in 1938: James T. Farrell (1904-79) and Richard Wright (1908-60). Both of their works had strong ethnic overtones. Farrell's *Studs Lonigan Trilogy*, set in the Irish working-class section of Chicago's South Side, was largely based on the author's own experiences (his father was a teamster, his mother a domestic servant). The African American Wright's first publication, *Uncle Tom's Children*, was a collection of short stories that all took place in the deep South. Written in the southern black dialect prevalent in the thirties, Wright's vivid presentation of his people's cruel oppression and their terrible poverty bring the writing to life.[1]

Thomas Wolfe (1900-38), who would later be recognized as a major American literary figure, died an early death. His novels appeared at a time when the hard-boiled, naturalistic school of writing exemplified by Hemingway, John O'Hara, and others mentioned above was dominant. Critics described Wolfe either as poetic and descriptive, or overly wordy and overly dramatic, or both.

A native of Asheville, North Carolina, Wolfe was a graduate of the University of North Carolina and of the Harvard Graduate School. He taught English for a few years at New York University before becoming a full-time writer. His best-known novel was

Look Homeward Angel (1929) followed by *Of Time and the River (*1935), and two posthumous works thanks to the efforts of Harper and Brothers editor Edward Aswell – *The Web and the Rock* (1939) and *You Can't Go Home Again* (1940). Wolfe owed a lot to Aswell and perhaps even more to Charles Scribner's Sons editor Maxwell Perkins. With great difficulty, Perkins persuaded the author to make massive cuts to the manuscripts of his first two novels, which made them far more readable.[2]

The greatest American novel in terms of readership in the 1930s, and for decades thereafter, was Margaret Mitchell's *Gone With the Wind*. This tale of the old South and of the adventures of a manipulative "southern belle," Scarlett O'Hara, during and after the Civil War, came out in June 1936. It became the fiction bestseller of 1936-37; and many years later, in 2014, a poll identified it as the second all-time favorite book of American readers (behind the Bible). Mitchell's writing experience before beginning work on the novel in 1926, while recuperating from a serious auto accident, had been limited to feature articles for the *Atlanta Journal*. By December 1936 the book had sold one million copies, and in 1937 Mitchell won both the Pulitzer Prize and the National Book Award. The Hollywood film of the same name, which was released in December 1939, won ten Academy Awards out of thirteen nominations and was re-released periodically at home and abroad as a perennial box-office favorite.

In 1938, despite the impact of a major recession, live theater productions enjoyed success on Broadway and in other venues too. A number of them were of excellent quality, such as *Of Mice and Men,* by John Steinbeck (1902-68). He was better known as a novelist, in particular for *The Grapes of Wrath* (1939). The play opened in late 1937 and ran to the spring of 1938; after a break, it resumed in the fall.

Of Mice and Men is the story of two wandering, unemployed farm workers in California, Steinbeck's birthplace. The clever one, George, frequently complains about having to look after Lennie, who today would be described as mentally challenged. When Lennie inadvertently commits what the authorities will probably see as a horrible crime, George must choose an equally horrible way to look after Lennie. The New York Drama Critics Circle gave *Of Mice and Men* its annual award for Best Play of American Authorship.

Our Town, by Thornton Wilder (1897-1975), opened early in 1938 and won the Pulitzer as the Best American Play of the Year. Its theme is life in the small (imaginary) town of Grover's Corners, New Hampshire during the early years of the twentieth century. The settings were unique, with a bare stage and the stage manager also playing the role of narrator. Performers placed in the audience question cast members about happenings in their town, such as religious life, drinking habits, weather patterns, voting, and more. A cemetery scene features banter among the town's ghosts about the satisfactions and frustrations of their mortal years.[3]

Abe Lincoln in Illinois, by Robert E. Sherwood (1896-1955) was a third outstanding play. It opened on October 15th, 1938. The initial objections to a foreigner playing the American presidential icon vanished, as it became obvious that Canadian actor Raymond Massey was a huge asset. Burns Mantle, among other drama critics, praised this Lincoln play as the best one to date; and consistently enthusiastic audiences seemed to confirm this opinion.

The Little Foxes, by Lillian Hellmann (1905-84), was yet another high-quality production of the 1938-39 season. Southern-born actress Tallulah Bankhead led the cast. This was appropriate because the play could be termed a psychological horror story about a hateful Southern family around 1900 and the rise of a more industrialized South that scorned antebellum romanticism.[4]

Of course, lighter fare – comedies, musicals, or both – were available too. *The Boys from Syracuse*, a musical that opened on November 23rd, 1938, owed its success to composer Richard Rodgers, lyricist Lorenz Hart, and librettist George Abbott (besides being based on Shakespeare's *The Comedy of Errors*). "Falling in Love with Love" and "This Can't Be Love" were two of the show's best-known songs.

Another hit was *The Merchant of Yonkers*, which opened on December 28th, 1938. Written by Thornton Wilder, this comedy about a matchmaker and her wife-seeking client served as the inspiration for *The Matchmaker*, a hit play of 1955, and for an even bigger hit, the 1964 musical *Hello, Dolly*, which ran on Broadway for 2,844 performances.[5]

As in the realm of novels, social consciousness played a part in theater productions (though much eclipsed by the escapism that was the driving force behind most 1930s novels, plays, films, and radio programs).

Two Broadway plays emphasizing social issues were surprisingly successful. *Tobacco Road*, written by Jack Kirkland (1902-69) and adapted from the 1932 novel by Erskine Caldwell (1903-87), opened on December 4th, 1935. This story of a poverty-stricken and degenerate southern tenant farmer family seemed about to fail but gradually found its public. To the amazement of theater aficionados, by the autumn of 1939 it had broken the record for successive New York performances set by *Abie's Irish Rose* in the 1920s. Certainly, the openly sexual dialogue helped attract audiences, but so did the play's emphasis on the relationship between poverty and moral failure.[6]

Pins and Needles, an initially obscure musical revue, also revealed the attraction of audiences to the social consciousness theme. It opened on November 27th, 1937 and was produced by Labor-Stage, Incorporated, a company consisting of garment workers, none of whom received a theater salary of more than fifty-five dollars weekly. Yet, as with *Tobacco Road*, it was still running at the end of 1939. Its catchiest song was entitled "Sing Me a Song of Social Significance."[7]

◆

Despite the fanfare surrounding novels and plays, newspaper readers vastly outnumbered book worms and playgoers. As historian Frederick Lewis Allen points out, newspapers had a bit of a split personality. Their owners tended to be conservative because publishing had become a branch of big business. This included a tendency toward monopoly, so that in all but the largest cities -- New York City led these exceptions – there were only three dailies at most.[8]

Although publishers were overwhelmingly conservative, editors and especially reporters were mostly supporters of the New Deal or even more left-leaning. But they had to control themselves at a time when job opportunities were scarce. Editorial pages, therefore, warred against FDR, as did most political columnists, while "factual" reports of events were often slanted against labor. The smaller contingent of liberal columnists included Drew Pearson, Dorothy Thompson, and Mrs. Roosevelt in her "My Day" column. At least as popular as political columnists were those who gossiped about show business personalities and gave advice to readers with personal problems.

The majority of magazines, for example, the *Saturday Evening Post*, were also conservative. But many of them, particularly those aimed at women, rarely touched controversial issues. Instead, they printed lively short stories or tales of real-life exciting adventures. *TIME*, a weekly news magazine, was well-written and well-edited. However, in retrospect, it may have sullied itself somewhat by choosing Adolf Hitler as its 1938 "Man of the Year" (although the selection process was based on an individual's prominence rather than his morality}.

Business-oriented *Fortune* magazine was undeniably

conservative, but it also contained a great deal of factual material that historians can profitably utilize in their research on the thirties. The great success of *Reader's Digest* proved that people liked to save time through reading condensed and simplified articles. And the rise of heavily illustrated magazines, led by *LIFE* (see Chapter 11), showed that photographers were up to pleasing a public that had always liked pictures.[9]

Notes: Chapter 13

1 Richard Wright, *Early Works. Lawd Today! Uncle Tom's Children. Native Son.* New York: Harper Collins Publishers, 1991, 239-406.

2 James D. Horan, *The Desperate Years. A Pictorial History of the Thirties.* New York: Crown Publishers, Inc., 1962, 252.

3 Burns Mantle, ed., *The Best Plays of 1937-38. And the Year Book of the Drama in America.* New York: Arno Press. A New York Times Company, 1978 (reprint), 31, 67, 71.

4 Burns Mantle, ed., *The Best Plays of 1938-39 and the Year Book of the Drama in America.* New York: Dodd, Mead and Co., 1939, 31-32, 75-76.

5 *Ibid.*, 429, 441; *NYT,* Dec. 14, 1938, X, 4. A future Broadway star, Mary Martin, debuted in Nov. 1938 in Cole Porter's *Leave It to Me* – she sang "My Heart Belongs to Daddy."

6 Frederick Lewis Allen, *Since Yesterday. The 1930s in America. September 3, 1929 -- September 3, 1939.* New York: Harper & Row, Publishers, 1939-40, 253-254.

7 *Ibid.*, 254.

8 *Ibid.*, 272.

9 *Ibid.*, 274-275.

CHAPTER 14

Mass Entertainment: The Movies and Radio

I f escapism dominated much of the 1930's written word, there was even more of it in the movies and radio. In the view of Frederick Lewis Allen, "the movies took one to a never-never land of adventures and romance uncomplicated by thought."[1] Millions of people a week, paying an average admission price of twenty-five cents (ten cents for kids), enjoyed double or even triple features. Various door prizes were yet an additional attraction; and throughout the nation, Shirley Temple dolls and other movie icons sold in the millions.[2]

Dour conservative columnist Westbrook Pegler excitedly praised *Snow White*, a cartoon fantasy that debuted in January 1938, as "the happiest thing that has happened in this world since the Armistice" (in 1918). Adults as well as children sang, hummed, or whistled two of the film's songs, "Heigh Ho" and "Whistle While You Work." During the early part of the year, when the recession of 1938 was at its worst, the Sieberling latex plant in Ohio was three weeks behind schedule, after running twenty-four hours a day for months making rubber dolls of Dopey and the other six dwarfs.[3]

Hollywood robbed the stage of some of its most gifted performers and playwrights, who could not resist its princely salaries. They often responded with good acting and decent screenplays. But though many of these newcomers were leftists. few films dealt with the real issues facing America. The cinematic world was largely devoid of poverty, discontent, conflicts of interest, ideological ferment and, after 1934, of realistic sexuality. In that year the country's Catholic bishops founded the National League of Decency, and Hollywood collaborated with it by implementing a long list of taboos. Banned were lengthy kisses, adultery, double beds, naked babies, and mild curse words such as "damn" and "hell" (Clark Gable's use of the former in *Gone With the Wind* caused a sensation). Along with the sexually frank Mae West, the crime film craze of the early thirties was fading by 1938 because of a League of Decency ruling that criminals should not be allowed to triumph over decent citizens.[4]

Musicals were among the most unreal of all Hollywood productions, including those featuring the teams of Nelson Eddy-Jeanette MacDonald and Fred Astaire-Ginger Rogers. The former were soporific operettas, while the latter had repetitious plots over the course of eight 1930's hits, which included 1938's *Carefree*. Indeed, most of these movies *were* box office winners. Astaire and Rogers, for their part, easily overcame the tepid plots through their magnificent dancing to the music of Cole Porter and other era geniuses.[5]

A lack of realism did not necessarily mean an absence of entertainment value. *Love Finds Andy Hardy* (1938), part of the "Andy Hardy" series, demonstrates this point. Well played by the diminutive teenage actor Mickey Rooney, "Andy" was a romanticized version of the typical American boy. He lived in the mythical town of Carvel, but many movie fans seemed to see him as the kid who lived just down the block. The plot centered around "Andy's" indecisiveness about which of three girls should become his steady date. Incidentally, the film was (successfully) showcasing the actresses playing the girls: Judy Garland, Lana

Turner, and Ann Rutherford. By 1939-40 Mickey Rooney had become Hollywood's number one box-office attraction.[6]

Love Finds Andy Hardy was not the highest grossing film of 1938. That distinction belonged to *Alexander's Ragtime Band* (at $3.5 million). This musical followed the career of the fictional Alexander, played by Tyrone Power, who had been trained as a classical violinist but found his fulfillment playing and conducting the Ragtime music popular during the early twentieth century. The cast included Alice Fay, Don Ameche, and Ethel Merman, along with twenty-eight Irving Berlin songs.

Second in earnings was *Boys Town*, starring Spencer Tracy as the real-life Father Edward Flanagan who brought orphans and delinquents to the Boys Town facility that he had created near Omaha, Nebraska. Showing his versatility, Mickey Rooney played one of the toughest delinquents whom the priest ultimately succeeded in reforming. The role of Flanagan earned Tracy the 1938 Academy Award (although the engraver carved the name on the Oscar as Dick Tracy, the detective of comic pages fame).[7]

Other Academy Awards for 1938 were *You Can't Take It With You* (Best Picture), Bette Davis (Best Actress for *Jezebel*), Walter Brennan (Best Supporting Actor for *Kentucky*), and Fay Bainter (Best Supporting Actress for *Jezebel*). The roster of leading performers in that year had names already familiar to movie fans: Gary Cooper, James Cagney, Humphrey Bogart, Cary Grant, Katharine Hepburn, Shirley Temple, Charles Boyer, and Hedy Lamar, among others. Nineteen twenties' comic actor Harold Lloyd was still making pictures, as were the Marx Brothers (Groucho would have a later career playing himself on the radio and TV quiz show, *You Bet Your Life)*. Chinese American actress Anna May Wong was still there on screen in Chinese roles, but white American Sidney Toler, (poorly) made up to look Asian, was in *Charlie Chan In Hawaii*. Also in 1938, Jewish refugee from Nazism Peter Lorre was the Japanese sleuth in *Mr. Moto's Gamble.* A number of later stars debuted in 1938. They were Eddie Albert, John Garfield, William Holden, June Lockhart, Maureen O'Hara, and Vincent Price.

The 1938 newspapers published a number of interesting stories relating to the movies, especially concerning *The Wizard of Oz.* January editions announced that Judy Garland would be cast in the role of Dorothy, Ray Bolger would play the Tim Man, and Buddy Ebsen the Scarecrow. Bolger and Ebsen subsequently switched roles at the former's insistence. Bert Lahr would be the Cowardly Lion. Lyricist Edgar "Yip" Harburg and composer Harold Arlen signed to work on the score.

Several serious accidents soon followed the filming process that began on October 13th. On October 21st Buddy Ebsen had a severe allergic reaction to the aluminum dust used in his Tin Man makeup, which led to his replacement by Jack Haley. Two months later Margaret Hamilton, who played the Wicked Witch of the West, was badly burned during an accident on the set and had to take a leave of absence for six weeks.

Finally released on August 25th, 1939, *The Wizard of Oz* won huge acclaim for its screenplay, musical score, acting, and technical excellence (it was shot mostly in color, then still a relative novelty). Later re-released in the theaters and on television, it became one of the most popular movies ever made.

◆

"The big box in the living room" – radio – was the other mass entertainment medium in 1938. It provided millions with access to adventure, laughter, various types of music, and romance. Later nicknamed *soap operas* because of their sponsors, serial dramas furnished the romance. They started in the morning and kept housewives tuned in through the afternoon. Late afternoon and early evening were a time for children's shows and news programs, followed by an evening schedule of variety shows, mysteries, dramas, quiz shows, and music.[8]

The schedule for the week of June 5th, 1938 illustrates the specifics of evening programming. For example, the seven in the evening slot on Sunday – on the NBC Red Network – listed the JELL-O Program, starring comedian Jack Benny, assisted by Mary Livingstone, Don Wilson, and Phil Harris (all of whom stayed with what would become the Jack Benny Show into the 1950s). Sunday's eight in the evening slot had The Chase and Sanborn Program, with ventriloquist Edgar Bergen (and Charlie McCarthy) on the NBC Red Network – guests were Don Ameche, Dorothy Lamour, and others. The NBC Blue Network had Spy at Large, a dramatic serial, and CBS had the music show St. Louis Blues. The nine in the evening slot on NBC Blue was broadcasting the Hollywood Players, with host Tyrone Power, and CBS had the Ford Sunday Evening Hour, which featured classical music. At half past nine NBC Blue carried the Jergens Program, with the already famous news commentator Walter Winchell.[9]

Variety shows, such as Jack Benny's, with humorous dialogue and light music, were extremely popular. Besides Benny, favorite hosts included Rudy Vallee, Fred Allen, George Burns and Gracie Allen, Bergen-McCarthy, and Bing Crosby. Serial stories were next in popularity. Amos n' Andy would later become controversial because two white former vaudevillians played its black characters – feasible on the radio – and played them as being somewhat oafish. But in 1938 the show was still going strong and had been since 1930. The Lone Ranger went on the air in 1933 and rose in public esteem until by 1939 it was on three times a week and heard by audiences of twenty million who received it on 140 stations throughout the country.[10]

These shows, and many others on radio, obviously had little relation to reality. There were no unemployed, no budget deficits, no raging dictators, and no racism. But racism was certainly there anyway, and not only on Amos n' Andy. For instance, why did Tonto, the Lone Ranger's "faithful Indian companion" who certainly seemed bright, have to speak in pidgin English (as did the movies' brilliant Chinese-American detective Charlie Chan)?

In this writer's childhood memory, The Lone Ranger was a tremendously exciting thirty-minute experience. That excitement certainly included the program's musical theme taken from Rossini's *William Tell Overture*. Classical music, in fact, had grown in popularity by the late thirties, a status that it owed mostly to radio concerts by American symphony orchestras. There had been only seventeen of them in the U. S. in 1915, but that number had expanded to 270 by 1938-39. And the combined radio audiences for the Metropolitan Opera on Saturday afternoon, the NBC Symphony on Saturday evening, and the New York Philharmonic and the Ford Hour on Sunday numbered about 10,230,000 families each week. The Ford Sunday Evening Hour, featuring the Detroit Symphony Orchestra, was 118 percent larger in 1937 than it had been in 1935. By 1938 it was fifth in popularity among all radio programs, exceeded only by the news broadcasts and three commercial shows.[11]

During 1938 broadcasts of symphony orchestras and grand operas were heard on both NBC networks at a rate that averaged more than an hour a day. The growing number of listeners to New York City's independent station WQXR, which had a classical format, and the large audiences at summer festivals in the Berkshire Mountains of Massachusetts were further signs of the ascent of classical music.[12]

Technical advances also marked radio's development in 1938. The coast-to-coast networks continued to acquire new member stations, with the combined NBC hook-up reaching 153 links, while CBS had 114 and the Mutual Broadcasting System had seventy-seven. New modern studios opened too, with KNX's $1,750,000 layout in Hollywood and WGY's streamlined headquarters in Schenectady, New York heading the list.

For listeners there were newly designed radios equipped with push-button tuning and greater numbers of radio-phonograph combinations. Also available were all-wave tuners designed to search the wave lengths of the world and capture foreign broadcasts, which could be transmitted with the volume and clarity of domestic programs.[13]

Notes: Chapter 14

1   Allen, *op. cit.*, 278.
2   Ezra Brown and May Y. Steinbauer, eds., *The Fabulous Century. Sixty Years of American Life.* Vol. IX 1930-1940. New York: TIMES-LIFE Books, 1971, 180.
3   Allen, *op. cit.*, 278-279.
4   *The Fabulous Century, op. cit.*, 180.
5   *Ibid.*, 188. See also *NYT*, July 24, 1938, IX, 4.
6   *The Fabulous Century, op. cit.*, 194.
7   Boardman, *op. cit.*, 219.
8   *The Fabulous Century, op. cit.*, 30.
9   *Ibid.*, 32-33.
10 Allen, *op. cit.*, 276.
11 *Ibid.*, 268-270.
12 *Ibid.*, 271.
13 *NYT*, July 3, 1938, X, 10.

CHAPTER 15

A Depression Within a Depression: The Recession of 1937-38

Many Americans had the wherewithal to divert themselves by reading for pleasure, seeing movies and plays, and listening to the radio. But others were overwhelmed by "a depression within a depression," also known as the Recession of 1937-38. A genuine if limited recovery – since 1933 – had occurred by May of 1937. Nineteen twenty-nine, the last year of prosperity, should have been the benchmark. Real income of farmers had risen to the (unsatisfactory) 1929 level. Industrial production was only seven and a half percent lower, stock dividends were within ninety percent, and real wages were actually ten percent higher.

Yet there were less favorable signs too. National income was well below that of 1929, as were construction projects and new issues of stocks and bonds. The unemployment rate was still high at eleven percent, and there were 4.5 million families on relief.[1]

The 1937-38 recession was a surprise to most Americans, including President Roosevelt and most members of his Administration. But there were a few pessimists. For example, Leon Henderson of the Commerce Department circulated a memorandum that described the current prosperity as uncomfortably similar to that of 1929 in that prices were rising too rapidly for purchasing power to keep pace. Unlike Henderson, however, the optimists were focusing on the years since 1933, not on 1929.[2]

By the end of August 1937, it was becoming increasingly clear that things were trending downward. Still, the president continued to express confidence that the movement was simply a normal "correction." Then, from September 1937 to March 1938, the economy sank to a level that seemed headed back to the depths of the Great Depression. October 19th, 1937 saw a stock market crash reminiscent of the 1929 original, and by the following spring the market had lost forty-eight percent of its value. The ranks of the unemployed during this period grew by four million. Industrial production dropped by forty percent, corporate profits by seventy-eight percent, and national income by thirteen percent. These declines were much more rapid than those of 1929-30. In fact, the 1937-38 losses were more remarkable because they were *the swiftest in the history of U. S. business and finance!*[3]

Human misery also grew apace. For instance, 100,000 demonstrated on the streets of Detroit for increased relief payments; and three thousand high school age people marched in Washington, D. C. to demand a "youth act" that would provide them with part time jobs. Many Americans came close to starvation, as reflected by children in Chicago rummaging through garbage cans and adults in Cleveland fighting in the streets over rotten vegetables.[4]

What were the causes of what political enemies of the New Deal were soon calling "the Roosevelt Recession." There was some truth in the president's counterattacks that the recession was a normal part of the business cycle after four good years, and also due in part to rising prices, especially in the several months before October 1937. But FDR certainly shared a good part of the blame. In June 1937 he had submitted major cuts to the budgets of WPA, PWA, and other work relief agencies which, passed by Congress, sharply reduced the income of some of the nation's poorest citizens. Secretary of the Treasury Henry Morgenthau and other Administration budget hawks advocated even further cuts. These, they believed, could lessen the threat of inflation by removing money from circulation, as well as building business confidence.[5]

Through most of the years of his presidency (1933-45), FDR continued to believe in the benefits of eliminating deficits whenever possible. His attacks on Herbert Hoover during the 1932 presidential election campaign for excessive government spending were genuine, not electioneering rhetoric; and throughout the 1936 race he spoke about the need for a balanced budget. Among the reasons he advanced was that the end of deficit spending would be a sign that the emergency was over – that the Great Depression had been vanquished. The continuation of deficits, on the other hand, could be interpreted as a contradiction of the New Deal's claims.[6]

As late as December 1937, FDR was still mulling over the idea of a balanced budget, this time for the 1939 fiscal year (July 1938-June 1939). He also insisted, privately, that the economy was really not so bad and would soon recover (these remarks were private because otherwise he would seem to be echoing President Hoover's clearly misdirected optimism during the dismal days of the early thirties).[7]

The first three months of 1938 found the president at a loss over what actions he should take to stimulate the economy. Secretary Morgenthau argued that the key to any stable recovery was an expansion of production through private investment. Indeed, such investment had remained sluggish throughout the years of the New Deal, and most of what had occurred had gone into replacement of existing facilities. Business leaders laid the blame entirely on what they deemed the Administration's anti-business attitudes and policies. Winthrop Aldrich, chairman of Chase National Bank, listed them in a speech to business associates. Included were "punitive" tax provisions targeting profits from investments; "unreasonable" restrictions by the Securities and Exchange Commission on speculative investments; the pro-collective bargaining Wagner Act (of 1935) that encouraged labor unrest and raised labor costs; the federal deficits and the ensuing inflation they portended; and a general atmosphere of government hostility toward the corporate world. Potential investors consequently were uneasy and defensive. The solution, Aldrich asserted, was a dismantling of the anti-business elements of the New Deal and a return to a federal government that occasionally assisted but seldom restricted private enterprise.[8]

At first Roosevelt seemed poised to follow the advice of Morgenthau and former New Dealers, such as Adolf Berle, to conciliate business interests. There were several meetings early in 1938 between government officials and businessmen. And in his public remarks the president spoke warmly of a majority of the latter as well-intentioned, as opposed to a small minority who were not. It was accurate that business leaders did not have uniform views, except perhaps in their continued reluctance to increase investments and their general, and long-term, disdain for the New Deal.

By the end of February 1938, what was sometimes referred to as the Administration's "appeasement" of business was a clear failure. It was obvious in March, moreover, that the economic situation was deteriorating even more rapidly. Factory production and farm prices, for example, were sinking to levels close to those of 1933, national income was falling at a rate of $800 million a month, and the stock market had again dropped precipitously.[9]

Against this backdrop, left-leaning figures from the middle ranks of the Administration were making their views known. Most of them were *protégés* of Harvard Law professor Felix

Frankfurter, and they also enjoyed the patronage of Secretary of the Interior Ickes, Secretary of Agriculture Henry Wallace, and Secretary of Labor Frances Perkins. This group became known simply as the "New Dealers." It included Thomas G. Corcoran of the Reconstruction Finance Corporation, Benjamin V. Cohen at the National Power Committee in the Interior Department, Jerome Frank at the Securities and Exchange Commission, and Leon Henderson, now at the WPA. Corcoran, a gifted speech writer and legislative draftsman, was basically their leader; and they often met at his home in Georgetown (that political foes maliciously designated as "the Little Red House").[10]

Closely associated with the "New Dealers" but higher in governmental rank were Robert Jackson, Marriner Eccles, and Lauchlin Currie. An upstate New York lawyer Jackson, in quick succession, became head of the Antitrust Division of the Justice Department, solicitor general, attorney general, and Supreme Court justice. He characterized the disinclination of businessmen to invest as a "capital strike" designed to wreck the economy which, they hoped, would result in the political demise of the New Deal. Eccles, from a conservative Utah Mormon background, became a liberal over time and an FDR-appointee to the chairmanship of the Federal Reserve Board. He viewed deficit spending as a long-term antidote to a sick economy. Lauchlin Currie, a Harvard economist and subsequently Eccles's special assistant at the Fed, was another important "New Dealer."[11]

All "New Dealers" harbored a deep suspicion of big business and a strong faith in government as the agency of justice and progress. Above all, they were particularly enthusiastic about the teachings of British economist John Maynard Keynes. Author of the 1936 scholarly landmark – *The General Theory of Employment, Interest, and Money* – Keynes was a strong advocate of deficit spending which, he believed, would spark consumption and lead to long-term economic growth.[12]

By March 1938, given the sense of urgency, the spending argument was becoming more powerful. Pressure for it was emerging from non-government sources, especially from the labor movement, farm organizations, and consumer advocate groups. Even Administration conservatives – Postmaster General James Farley, for one – saw a fiscal response to the recession as acceptable. Public opinion polls taken in March showed a rise in those who blamed Roosevelt for the recession. The spread of fascism in Europe and even in the United States (see Chapter 7) convinced Marriner Eccles that faith in democracy's ability to get things done was rapidly waning. He shared this thought with the president, urging him to provide leadership in making democratic government function better. In a memorandum to FDR-adviser Harry Hopkins, Leon Henderson used American history to furnish examples of how past government spending had spurred prosperity: land grants to railroad companies, homesteads to western settlers, and the opening of gold fields to private miners were among his examples.[13]

In the midst of the worsening economic crisis, Roosevelt left Washington in late March for his vacation home in Warm Springs, Georgia. A few days later Henderson and Hopkins, joined by a few lesser "New Dealers," converged on Warm Springs. Historian Alan Brinkley succinctly observed: "All were there for only one reason: to persuade the president to recommend a major increase in public spending."[14]

On April 2nd FDR told Hopkins that he would support a substantial spending program. The meetings at Warm Springs evidently convinced him to act. Specifically, it was likely that the worsening economic situation, the political damage that it was causing him, and the reassurance he received from Hopkins and Henderson that major peacetime spending could be historically justified all played a role. But more decisive may have been what the New Deal itself had taught him – that in the time of a major economic downturn, pump priming worked in real terms as well as psychologically. In a variation of the same thought, on the way back to Washington, he looked out the train window at nondescript people waiting to see him, then remarked to an aide: "They understand what we're trying to do."[15]

On April 14th Roosevelt sent Congress a set of recommendations to stimulate recovery. The package included appropriations for WPA and other public works agencies as well as a variety of federal loans, an infusion of $6.5 billion into the economy. It was an enormous sum by 1938 standards. Congress would approve the program by mid-June, and it went into effect quickly.[16]

Economic conditions over the next few months improved slowly but noticeably. Yet though the recession abated, it did not end. The amounts added to the federal budget -- a nearly twenty-five percent increase – were not insignificant, but they were not enough to stimulate *long-term* prosperity. The economy sputtered on, not reaching the level of May 1937 (the heyday of New Deal prosperity) until 1941 when the threat of war, not New Deal reform policies, compelled government expenditures at levels previously unimaginable.

The president did pay a price for the "Roosevelt Recession," and also for his abortive attempt in 1937 to pack the Supreme Court. Democrats lost eighty seats in the House of Representatives and eight in the Senate in the 1938 elections, which meant that liberals no longer had effective control of Congress. Harry Hopkins observed that America had become "bored with the poor, the unemployed, and the insecure."[17] FDR himself knew that half-way through his second term, eight to nine million people were unemployed, still living in shanties or tenements, and often on the verge of starvation. He had lamented this in his 1937 inaugural address. But now the dangers emanating from international developments were beginning to overshadow everything else.

Notes: Chapter 15

1   Freidel, *op. cit.*, 248.
2   Alan Brinkley, *The End of Reform. New Deal Liberalism in Recession and War.* New York: Vintage Books, 1996, 23-24.
3   *Ibid.*, 26, 29.
4   James MacGregor Burns, *Roosevelt: The Lion and the Fox.* Norwalk, CT: The Easton Press, 1956, 325; Robert Goldston, *The Great Depression. The United States in the Thirties.* Indianapolis, New York: The Bobbs-Merrill Co., 1968, 182.
5   Brinkley, *op. cit.*, 49; Goldston, *op. cit.*, 181; David Kennedy, *Freedom From Fear. The American People in Depression and War.* New York and Oxford: Oxford University Press, 1999, 351.
6   Brinkley, *op. cit.*, 25.
7   *Ibid.*, 29; Burns, *op. cit.*, 320.
8   Brinkley, *op. cit.*, 32.
9   Freidel, *op. cit.*, 254. FDR never ceased to hope for the cooperation of businessmen. He was bemoaning this failure at a White House supper in May 1939, wondering why they lacked confidence in the economy, when Mrs. Roosevelt spoke up: "They are afraid of you." See Freidel, 257.
10 Kennedy, *op. cit.*, 56-57.
11 Brinkley, *op. cit.*, 57, 82, 95.
12 Kennedy, *op. cit.*, 354.
13 Brinkley, *op. cit.*, 98-99.
14 *Ibid.*, 98.
15 Burns, *op. cit.*, 328; Brinkley, *op. cit.*, 99; Freidel, *op. cit.*, 255.
16 Freidel, *op. cit.*, 256; Brinkley, *op. cit.*, 100-101.
17 Quoted in Goldston, *op. cit.*, 185.

CHAPTER 16

A Few Notables of the 1930s

This book contains the names of many noteworthy people of the 1930s. The next few chapters will delve a bit further into the careers of some of them.

Fiorello H. La Guardia:

Franklin D. Roosevelt was unquestionably the most prominent American political figure during the twelve years and three months that he served as president. Second place arguably belongs to Fiorello H. La Guardia. The two men were physical opposites. FDR stood (when he could stand) at six feet, two inches and spoke in a powerful baritone. La Guardia barely reached five feet, two inches and had a high-pitched voice that one historian characterized as falsetto.[1] The president was a scion of the colonial aristocracy, while the latter's parents were Italian immigrants: a lapsed Catholic father and a Jewish mother. On the other hand, their life spans and time in office were similar. FDR (1882-1945) won election four times (1932, 1936, 1940, 1944) but died in the third month of his fourth term, while La Guardia (1882-1947) served three full terms (1934-46) as mayor of New York City.

La Guardia's life was eventful long before his election as mayor. Though born in New York, he spent much of his childhood in Prescott, Arizona where his father was bandmaster at the

Fort Whipple army garrison. The long-term western influence was apparent in Fiorello's favorite headgear — a broad Stetson – and in one of his frequent execrations for alleged scoundrels, whom he termed "tinhorns." With his father's illness and medical discharge, the family headed back to Europe in search of better prospects. They settled in Fiume, then an Austro-Hungarian port on the Adriatic Sea, where Fiorello eventually became an assistant at the U. S. consulate. These few years increased his knowledge of languages. Returning to New York, he became an interpreter at Ellis Island, while also attending classes at New York University's Evening Law School.

After earning his law degree, La Guardia left the Immigration Service to open up his own legal practice. He also began electioneering work for the Republican Party, a choice dictated by his hatred of the corrupt Democratic machine known as Tammany Hall. Unlike most of his Republican associates, however, he was an enthusiastic supporter of labor unions, especially the International Ladies Garment Workers' Union.

La Guardia's political ambitions dated back to his return to New York. His Republican activism helped him secure the party's 1914 nomination for a congressional seat representing a lower Manhattan district. He lost that contest to the Democrats. But in 1916 he defeated the same opponent by attracting the support of local Italians, Jews, Germans, Irish, and even the alcoholic residents of flop houses. He ran not only as a Republican but on a fusion ticket that included Progressives. Yet when the country entered the First World War in 1917, unlike his Progressive allies, he supported the move. American participation, he asserted, was not only inescapable self-defense but a critical intervention on behalf of democratic ideals. He did join Progressives in opposing the Espionage Act and other legislation that he correctly perceived would stifle freedom of expression.[2]

In October 1917 La Guardia took a leave of absence from

Congress to help lead a unit of the Army Air Corps that had been organized to train Italian military personnel. He ended up at Camp Foggia which, by chance, was very near the Adriatic coastal area where his father had been born. Soon promoted to major, his duties included training pilots, flying combat missions, and disseminating Allied propaganda in various Italian cities. In a flagrantly illegal action, several comrades and he smuggled steel from neutral Spain to Italy where it was desperately needed to manufacture planes. La Guardia returned home in October 1918 to run for re-election to his congressional seat. He easily defeated Socialist candidate Scott Nearing, his main opponent, by a margin of 14,523-6,214.[3]

Within a year, though, La Guardia had tired of his subordinate status in Congress. He not only lacked seniority, the path to advancement, but was decisively outnumbered by conservatives of both major parties. In 1919, with his ambition now focused on the New York mayor's office, he ran for President of the City Board of Aldermen, part of the municipal legislative branch whose presidency was seen as a stepping stone to becoming mayor. His victory was largely due to Italian and Irish voters angry at Democratic President Woodrow Wilson's actions at the Paris Peace Conference. They resented his decisions not to award Fiume to Italy or to support Irish independence from Britain.

La Guardia lost the 1921 mayoralty race, mostly because of Republican unhappiness with his open opposition to ultra-conservative Governor Nathan Miller. Miller hated New York City, immigrants and first-generation Americans, while enthusiastically supporting the adoption of Prohibition. La Guardia also suffered the tragic loss that year of his baby daughter and wife to tuberculosis. In 1922 he returned to Congress but from a different district, the 20th, which encompassed East Harlem. He ran on a very progressive platform and was backed by its largely Italian and Jewish voters.

Although technically he remained a Republican – and home

town Republicans usually backed him because he could win elections – La Guardia's next ten years in Congress (1923-33) were the epitome of progressive politics. For example, as already indicated he adamantly denounced Prohibition while backing various labor causes, including the struggles of coal miners in Pennsylvania, West Virginia, and Kentucky (he even advocated nationalization of the mines). Together with Nebraska progressive Republican Senator George Norris, he prevented the development of the Tennessee Valley from falling into private hands, particularly those of Henry Ford.

La Guardia fought unsuccessfully against the Johnson-Reed Immigration Bill of 1924 that was designed, through a quota system, to drastically curtail the "New Immigration" from southern and eastern Europe and to end all immigration from Asia. On this issue, and that of race, he differed from western progressive Republicans. He had the distinction of being the only House member who agreed to allow Oscar De Priest, a new black member of Congress, to occupy office space next to his.[4]

In 1931 La Guardia became one of the leaders of the Progressive coalition in Congress. Critics called it the "Sons of the Wild Jackass" because most of its members were from western states. La Guardia's proposals clearly anticipated much of the later New Deal: a five-day work week; large public works projects; government-backed insurance for savings accounts; and tighter regulation of the stock market. Progressives gave the Democrats an advantage in a Congress where the vote was close. As the Depression worsened, public opinion was catching up to the idea that government should help the poor fight the powerful. The courts were clearly anti-labor and often issued injunctions against striking unions. For years La Guardia had introduced anti-injunction legislation that had always been tabled or defeated. But on January 5th, 1932 Senator Norris joined him in sponsoring similar legislation. The Norris-La Guardia Bill easily passed Congress and was signed by President

Hoover. It was a direct precursor of the more sweeping Wagner Act of 1935.

Having lost two mayoral races – in 1921 and 1929 – La Guardia ran for a third time in 1933; and this time he won easily. His first term (1934-38) and the first two years of his second term constituted a period of activity unprecedented in the history of New York City.

La Guardia envisioned a grand program of new bridges, airports, playgrounds, roadways, schools, parks, public housing projects, and beaches. In addition, he wanted the city to be more beautiful and to lift spirits through increased access to fine art and music. Along these lines, his efforts included the construction of the first municipally-owned art gallery in the United States and the High School of Music and Art (later named after him), where students could major in the performing arts. He also fought crime, perhaps most dramatically by personally chopping up slot machines that were previously ubiquitous in candy stores, diners, and other locales. Somewhat related targets were racy magazines and strip shows.[5]

Obviously La Guardia's efforts required a great deal of financing, which was beyond the city's means during these depression years. The mayor therefore reached out to the Federal government, circumventing state authority and establishing excellent relations with President Roosevelt and with the officials who administered the relief agencies' flow of cash – principally Harold Ickes at PWA and Harry Hopkins at WPA. La Guardia accepted cash but still managed to keep a considerable amount of control over the projects. In effect, Washington was treating the city as the forty-ninth state.[6]

The Williamsburg neighborhood in the Borough of Brooklyn represented the most comprehensive slum clearance and low-rent housing project ever attempted up to then in the entire country. On September 30th, 1937, two years after construction began, six of the twenty buildings opened for occupancy. Monthly rents were a modest seven dollars a room.

In 1935 the mayors of twenty-five cities elected La Guardia president of the U. S. Conference of Mayors, a post he would hold for ten years. They benefited from his experience in dealing with Washington, although they could not match New York's success in procuring funds, especially with respect to WPA programs. Examples of these included the following: the East River Drive (later re-named the FDR Drive); the Triborough Bridge; the Lincoln Tunnel; the Queens-Midtown Tunnel; Brooklyn and Hunter Colleges (La Guardia kept all city colleges tuition-free); public schools; subway extentions; garbage treatment plants; swimming pools; parks; and many miles of repaved streets. These numerous projects created thousands of new jobs, stimulated dormant industries, and enriched the quality of life.[7]

Nor did the mayor ignore the needs of women and blacks. He appointed more women to responsible city posts than any of his predecessors and helped calm the Harlem riots of 1935 by personally talking to people on the streets. During the next four years, besides the Harlem River Homes he built the Central Harlem Health Center, a new Women's Pavilion for Harlem Hospital, and two new schools. He also integrated the all-white staffs of city hospitals, expanded civil service opportunities for blacks in the Fire and Sanitation Departments and in the offices of the District Attorney and Corporation Counsel.[8]

La Guardia's pro-labor sentiments manifested themselves in his interventions to settle disputes, usually by putting pressure on employers. For instance, he threatened to turn off a commercial laundry's hot water unless the company settled, and he pressured hotels by sending city health inspectors to investigate their premises. More dramatic interventions saw him racing to the sites of fires where he rendered advice, aid, and comfort to Fire Department personnel. Occasionally he also donned judicial robes to hear cases, which he was legally entitled to do.

La Guardia ran for a second term in 1937, backed by labor elements (concentrated in the American Labor Party), the Progressive Party, the Socialist Party, and the more liberal Republicans. His opponent was a locally prominent New Deal Democrat, Jeremiah T. Mahoney, a New York Supreme Court justice and former state counsel for the American Federation of Labor. He had also been president of the American Athletic Union in 1936 when he had opposed participation in the Olympic Games in Nazi Germany. Notwithstanding these liberal credentials, La Guardia still won easily: 1,344,016 to 889,591. Quietly backing him against the Democratic machine was none other than FDR.[9]

Among La Guardia's most fervent supporters were Jews and Italians, New York City's largest ethnic groups. Although he seldom mentioned his mother's Jewish background, most Jews loved him because of his caustic comments about Hitler and the Nazis (see Chapter 8). Italians were equally fond of La Guardia whom they had lionized in Congress and later over his becoming New York's first Italian mayor. His fear of offending them kept him quiet about Mussolini's fascist regime and its brutal aggression against Ethiopia.

What was probably La Guardia's favorite project reached completion during his second term. He longed to make New York the air capital of America, if not the world. A few years back – in 1934 – upon arriving at Newark Airport, he refused to disembark, insisting that his ticket read "Chicago to *New York*" (italics mine). Eventually, before being shuttled to Floyd Bennett Field in Brooklyn, he remarked to reporters: "And remember, Newark is not New York!"

La Guardia's relentless pressure ultimately succeeded. The Federal government contributed $27 million, out of a total estimated cost of $40 million, to build a new airport on the site of the former Glenn Curtiss Field at North Beach on the north shore of the Borough of Queens, where wealthy fliers had once cavorted.

It took nearly two years to complete the job, with a force of five thousand men divided into three shifts and working six days a week. The formal dedication took place on October 15th, 1939 before a crowd of 325,000. North Beach, later (in 1947) renamed La Guardia, soon became the busiest airport in the world, handling an average of two hundred flights a day. La Guardia had a vision for another major airport and got the Board of Estimate to purchase Idelwild, a polluted beach on the south shore of Queens. Completed in 1948, it eventually became JFK International Airport.[10]

The airport, the preparations for the New York World's Fair, and numerous other issues certainly kept La Guardia busy. But he was also eagerly looking forward to a new career, in fact, to the highest one possible in America. Assuming that Roosevelt would not run in 1940 for a third term, he contemplated a race of his own for the presidency. Exploration efforts included two 1938 trips to the West and Midwest. His speeches were highly successful, with subjects ranging from the dangers of fascism to the depressed conditions facing the American farmer. As befitting a future presidential candidate, who would need a broad appeal, he became less liberal. For example, he refused to allow City College to confer a chair in philosophy on radical British intellectual Bertrand Russell. Unfortunately for La Guardia, and against most expectations. FDR would run and win again in 1940.[11]

La Guardia supported the president in 1940 and hoped to be rewarded with a cabinet appointment. He thought his World War experience more than qualified him to be Secretary of War. However, FDR's advisers thought the mayor's explosive temper disqualified him for *any* cabinet post; and his only immediate appointment was to the sub-cabinet U. S. – Canadian Joint

Permanent Defense Board. It hardly ever met. But Roosevelt's genuine esteem and respect for his fellow New Yorker soon (in December 1941) led to a subsequent appointment as Director of the Office of Civilian Defense. La Guardia accepted it, even though he had just gotten himself re-elected to a third term as New York's mayor. He defeated Brooklyn D. A. William O'Dwyer but by the closest margin thus far.

La Guardia gave up his Civilian Defense post on February 10th, 1942. Working two full-time jobs was simply too exhausting. There were the bi-weekly commutes, complaints from New York constituents about the mayor's subpar performance, and from governors antagonized by his abrasiveness. In fact, he would only become more abrasive and less liberal. For instance, when asked by the press, he agreed that southern blacks arrested for sexual crimes should be beaten at the discretion of the police. While he argued that German and Italian aliens should be able to lead normal lives during the war, he was much less understanding toward people of Japanese ancestry, whether they were aliens or U. S. citizens.

In 1944 the government began releasing a number of Japanese internees. They were relocated, and several hundred of them ended up in New York City. La Guardia not only protested their presence but dispatched the police to act as watchdogs. He also publicly referred to them as "monkeys."[12]

At the same time, La Guardia was slower to react against anti-Semitism than during his earlier years in office. The Jewish situation was dire anywhere in Nazi-dominated Europe, but the mayor was not enthusiastic about the U. S. opening its doors to potential refugees before other countries opened theirs. Still desirous of leaving City Hall for a federal position more worthy of his talents, he chose to avoid raising the sensitive subject of the refugees with the president. In fact, FDR did consider making him a brigadier general but dropped the subject when protests arose from Generals Marshall and Eisenhower and from War Secretary Stimson. While praising his patriotism, the president informed the devastated mayor that no position in the Army could be found for him.[13]

The old La Guardia did not vanish entirely during his third term. His public outreach included a weekly radio program, launched January 18th, 1942 on the city-owned station WNYC. It received good reviews, probably because New Yorkers appreciated the head of their local government communicating directly with them. La Guardia also used radio to address the people of Italy and helped Italians in American-controlled areas of the country get food and other desperately needed aid. During a newspaper strike in the summer of 1945, his broadcasts on WNYC kept children updated on the comic page features of "Dick Tracy," "Little Orphan Annie," and other favorites.[14] He also boosted the new City Center for the Performing Arts as a fulfillment of his idea of great classical music at affordable prices.[15]

La Guardia's third term expired at the end of 1945, but he kept busy with a newspaper column in the *New York PM* and a radio program on the ABC Network. In March 1946 President Truman nominated him to the post of Director General of the United Nations Relief and Rehabilitation Administration (UNRRA). He was immensely shocked by the tremendous destruction, starvation, illness, and death left by the war, more so than by any other situation he had ever encountered. He was especially outspoken about the emerging U. S. policy aimed at making Germany, whom he blamed for the death and destruction, an ally against the Soviet Union. He found it particularly lamentable that the U. S. Army was employing armed German guards at the displaced persons' camps for Jewish survivors of the Holocaust.

La Guardia resigned from UNRRA in the spring of 1947, having aged a great deal since the end of his mayoral term. He had returned to his liberal roots, not only through his UN work but in his writings and radio broadcasts. But he was deathly ill – what was initially diagnosed as a kidney stone turned out to be metastasized cancer of the pancreas. He died on September 20th, 1947. President Truman summed up his essence in a telegram to La Guardia's family: "The greatest mayor in the history of New York is dead." The 45,000 New Yorkers filing past his casket reaffirmed this sentiment.[18]

William E. Borah:

Somewhat similar to La Guardia in his Republican progressivism, William Edgar Borah was a long-time figure in the United States Senate (1907-40). Borah's resemblance to his New York counterpart cannot be overdrawn, however. He was born on June 29th, 1865 near Fairfield, Illinois, the son of a farmer, attended high school and college in Kansas (three years at the University of Kansas), and read law – also in Kansas. To further his career, he moved west in 1890, settling in Boise, Idaho, which was as far west as his train fare permitted him to travel. Idaho was a predominantly agricultural and mining state. Unlike La Guardia, the son of immigrants, he could trace his family's settlement in America (from Germany) to the 1760s.

After supporting Democrat-Populist William Jennings Bryan's "Free Silver" presidential campaigns of 1896 and 1900, Borah returned to his roots and was elected to the U. S. Senate in 1906. But progressivism would always constitute a strong part of his political outlook. His first term, for example, saw him oppose the high Payne-Aldrich Tariff that was favored by conservatives, including President William H. Taft. It passed but so did the progressive sixteenth and seventeenth Amendments to the Constitution, for which Borah voted. The former created a federal income tax, and the latter introduced direct election of U. S. senators (formerly chosen by state legislatures). On another issue, the Idaho progressive would criticize President Woodrow Wilson's intervention in Latin American affairs, particularly with respect to the Huerta regime in Mexico. Borah disliked the dictatorial Huerta but argued that Mexicans alone should determine their political future.

A strong supporter of American neutrality during the first three years of the World War, Borah reluctantly changed his mind to vote for a declaration of war when Germany resumed unrestricted submarine warfare in early 1917. Yet he insisted that the U. S. should basically confine itself to self-defense and disavow expansionist policies associated with the Allies. His progressivism was still evident too in his opposition to the draft and to the repressive Espionage Act.

Borah broke completely with the Wilson Administration during the war's aftermath. Negotiating with the Allies in France, the president had persuaded them to include a provision for a peace-keeping body in the draft treaty – it would be called the League of Nations. Strongly isolationist, the senator feared that America's membership in the League could involve the country in another conflict, without its permission and in which it had no interest at stake. As a member of the Senate Foreign Relations Committee, he became one of the strongest voices among the "Irreconcilables" – those who opposed any compromise on this issue. With their majority, the Republicans were able to defeat Senate ratification of the Treaty of Versailles. Consequently the U. S. neither ratified the Treaty nor joined the League.[17]

Borah remained a maverick during the "Republican Era" (1921-33), criticizing agendas associated with Presidents Harding, Coolidge, and Hoover. Among the exceptions were prohibition, restrictive immigration legislation, and the "Wet," Catholic, Tammany Hall-affiliated Alfred E. Smith, the 1928 Democratic candidate for the presidency. Borah himself had presidential ambitions in 1928 but had no chance of being nominated by the conservative majority in his party. The nomination went to Hoover, who won in a landslide. Borah belatedly endorsed him, but once the depression worsened, he would advocate relief legislation to the reluctant Republican

Administration. He was also angered when, in 1932, Hoover ordered army troops to disperse the so-called Bonus Army. It consisted of thousands of World War veterans who had encamped in Washington to demand early disbursement of their pensions.

Borah was attracted to many of new Democratic President Roosevelt's liberal policies, such as the Glass-Steagall Act of June 1933. Glass-Steagall separated commercial from investment banking, intending thereby to make the former safer. Many bank failures had been caused by the risky stock speculation of commercial bankers. The safety of deposits was further enhanced by the Act's creation of the Federal Deposit Insurance Corporation, which insured a considerable proportion of customers' deposits. Borah's fifteen-year campaign for U. S. diplomatic recognition of the Soviet Union also came to fruition under the Roosevelt Administration. By 1936 he had supported eleven of seventeen major New Deal measures. The Agricultural Adjustment Act of 1933 was one of those he opposed. One of its provisions called for the destruction of surplus crops as a means of exerting upward pressure on farm prices; and this farmer's son could not comprehend such action in the midst of widespread hunger.[18]

Borah's presidential itch returned in 1936, and he became the first Republican candidate to declare himself. A westerner seemed in order, particularly a progressive one. Yet though he won a few primaries, this would not be enough to surpass more conservative Republican contenders. One of them, Kansas Governor Alf Landon, won the nomination. The disappointed Borah made no speeches on behalf of Landon, whom FDR defeated in one of the largest landslides in American history. Meanwhile, in Idaho, the longtime senator defeated his Democratic rival by a margin of nearly two to one.[19]

Although he personally liked the president, Borah's isolationism increasingly separated the two men. For example, he joined fellow Senate isolationists Burton Wheeler and Gerald Nye in characterizing FDR's so-called Quarantine Speech of October 5th, 1937 as "warmongering." A relatively mild condemnation of the aggressive behavior of Japan, Germany, and Italy, the speech refrained from naming its targets. Responding to the *Panay* incident of December 1937, in which Japanese planes sank a U. S. Navy gunboat on China's Yangtze River, Borah warned against strong retaliatory action (see Chapter 2).

Borah's attitude toward Germany was equivocal. At first, he was attracted to Hitler because of the *Fuhrer's* repudiation of the Versailles peace settlement and by efforts to improve the national economy. He was privately appalled by Nazi anti-Semitism but, as with many in Congress and in the State Department he refused to speak out against what he characterized as an "internal affair." Eventually, he did censure Hitler for the persecution – while defending Germany's March 1938 annexation of Austria as "perfectly natural" in light of their shared language and culture. Borah joined a majority of Americans in opposing liberalization of the country's immigration laws on behalf of Jewish refugees from Germany, fearful of the possible impact on the nation's unemployment situation. In the aftermath of the Munich crisis, he was much harsher on Britain and France for betraying Czechoslovakia than he was on Germany for threatening to launch a European war.[20]

The last chapter in Borah's life occurred after Munich, when he realized that the odds of another world conflict had not really diminished. Envisioning himself as capable of calming Hitler, he suggested a trip to Germany for this purpose. But it never happened, in spite of Berlin's lukewarm willingness to receive him. The Roosevelt Administration was non-cooperative, however, and there was his own growing apprehension that failure was a likely outcome. There was also the reality of his own rapidly declining health; and, indeed, he died of a cerebral hemorrhage on January 19th, 1940.

Notes: Chapter 16

1   Thomas Kessner, Fiorello H. La Guardia and the Making of Modern New York. New York: McGraw-Hill Publishing Co., 1989, *passim*.

2   Ayn Brodsky, *The Great Mayor. Fiorello La Guardia and the Making of New York.* New York: Truman Talley Books. St. Martin's Press, 2003, 75, 86-88.

3   *Ibid.*, 92-94, 114.

4   *Ibid.*, 182, 199-200, 207-208.

5   *Ibid.*, 230-231, 236-239.

6   Kessner, *op. cit.*, 339.

7   *Ibid.*, 341.

8   Brodsky, *op. cit.*, 321. These moves occurred in a city that, in many ways, was as segregated as those in southern states.

9   Brodsky, *op. cit.*, 360, 363; Kessner, *op. cit.*, 419.

10   Brodsky, *op. cit.*, 383-385; Kessner, *op. cit.*, 432-435.

11   Kessner, *op. cit.*, 465, 467, 476. FDR did not believe that La Guardia, with an Italian name, a Jewish mother, and a pushy "New York" personality, could ever win the presidency.

12   Kessner, *op. cit.*, 505, 508-509, 537.

13   *Ibid.*, 522-524, 526.

14   *Ibid.*, 514, 517. 519, 575.

15   *Ibid.*, 551, 553-554.

16   *Ibid.*, 592-593.

17   Borah opposed the Versailles Treaty not only because of its "victors' club" League of Nations but because of its punitive terms against Germany. These terms, he believed, might facilitate the destruction of the Weimar Republic. His sympathy for Germany would persist through the twenties and even into the Nazi era. In 1923, for example, he condemned the French occupation of the Ruhr industrial region intended as punishment for German suspension of reparations payments. These views won him praise from many anti-Versailles European radicals, especially the British organization called the Union of Democratic Control. Founded during the war by E. D. Morel and others, the UDC drew its name from its advocacy of transferring war-making power from the cabinet to Parliament. See, e. g., Sheldon Spear, *E. D. Morel's UDC International*, Peace and Change, Jan. 1981, 97-108.

18 Marion C. McKenna, *Borah*. Ann Arbor, Michigan: The University of Michigan Press, 1961, 308-309, 325.
19 *Ibid.*, 319, 340-341.
20 *Ibid.*, 349, 351-352, 355-356. See also Chapter 8, above. The *Anschluss* was an eventual death sentence for thousands of Austrian Jews.
21 *Ibid.*, 360, 372.

CHAPTER 17

More Notables

<u>John D. Rockefeller, Jr.</u>:

To many Americans and foreigners as well, the name John D. Rockefeller meant unimaginable wealth and monopolistic business practices associated with the Standard Oil Trust. With his only son, John D. Rockefeller, Jr. (1874-1960), it still signified enormous wealth. Yet in his case, it also suggested national parks, medical and other scientific research, and culture for the millions. We will call this Rockefeller *Junior* to distinguish him from his world-famous parent.

Despite his often nefarious business practices, Rockefeller, Sr. considered himself a good Christian – a Baptist – and passed his world view on to his son. Before he was ten, *Junior* had signed a lifelong pledge never to use profanity, tobacco, intoxicating beverages, or even coffee and tea. Later, though converting to a more liberal form of Protestantism, he continued to keep the pledge. In his eighties, for example, he would decline to entertain visitors on Sundays.

Junior enrolled at Brown University in Providence, Rhode Island, a Baptist-affiliated school. Though shy like his father, he still participated in a number of extracurricular activities. He joined the Glee Club, the Mandolin Club, taught Bible classes, and managed the football team. At first he knew little about this last activity but he did well, at least in part because of his frugality (which was unlike that of other rich men's sons). He also learned to dance at Brown, a non-puritanical side of him that lasted a lifetime. Unable to dance in his later years, he still enjoyed watching the Radio City Rockettes.[1]

Junior had what can only be called a very happy family life. In 1901 he married Abigail Greene Aldrich, the daughter of a prominent Republican United States senator. She bore him six children. In the order of their ages, they were young Abby (the only girl), John D. III, Nelson, Laurence, Winthrop, and David. The four younger children were more outgoing than their father, in this respect far closer to their mother who played a major role in raising them. She was also an art connoisseur who donated her money and energies to support the growth of New York's Museum of Modern Art.

Junior outlived Abby Aldrich Rockefeller, who died in 1948. In 1951 he married the widow Martha Baird Allen at Providence City Hall, where he modestly listed his occupation as "real estate investor." He lived long enough to see son Nelson elected Governor of New York and son David earn a Ph. D. in Economics and later become one of the nation's leading bankers.

Junior entered his father's business empire after graduating from Brown in 1897. But the transformative experience of his life took place approximately two thousand miles from Standard Oil's New York corporate headquarters. He owned the largest share of the Colorado Fuel and Iron Company, against whom the United Mine Workers went on strike from September 1913 to December 1914. The most horrific event associated with what was termed the Colorado Coalfield War was the Ludlow Massacre of April 20th, 1914. Elements of the Colorado National Guard, backed by Company police, attacked a group of twelve hundred striking miners and their families near the town of Ludlow. The Guard's use of machine guns helped them kill an estimated twenty-one men, women, and children. Pro-labor spokesmen and much of the press mostly blamed *Junior*, an unpopular Rockefeller clan member, although he was not on the scene and played little role in running the company. His first inclination was to support management, but then he made several visits to the area. Industrial expert William Lyon Mackenzie King, a future prime minister of Canada, had suggested this action. Meetings with the miners in their work environment was the beginning of a major conversion experience for *Junior*, who offered them a package that featured wage scales, a grievance procedure, an eight-hour day for underground workers, and no discrimination against union members. The men accepted the deal by secret ballot.

By the early 1920s, *Junior* had become convinced that big business paternalism was "antagonistic to democracy" and that it was "just as proper … for labor to organize as it was for capitalism." In 1920 he sold his shares of U. S. Steel because the corporation would not abandon the seven-day week, twelve-hour day for steelworkers. He began to use the term "industrial enlightenment" and shocked business leaders by telling them that their attitude toward labor was immoral.[2]

Junior, the new friend of labor, remained a Republican out of loyalty to his father. Yet in terms of his contributions to public welfare he really moved beyond politics. Part of his philanthropic heritage dated all the way back to John D.'s contribution to the Underground Railroad when he was still an impoverished young bookkeeper. By the turn of the twentieth century, father and son were underwriting Negro colleges (while also spending millions on white schools in order to avoid their possible resentment).

In the late twenties *Junior* founded the Dunbar National Bank in Harlem, located within the Paul Lawrence Dunbar Apartments. Dunbar (1872-1906) was an admired African American poet, novelist, and playwright. The bank was unique in employing black tellers, clerks, bookkeepers, as well as managers.[3]

In an essay of this size, it is not feasible to discuss, or even enumerate, *Junior's* contributions to America's cultural life. But among them were developments that eventually became national parks, such as Grand Teton, Mesa Verde, Acadia, and Yosemite. Impressive in another sense were restored eighteenth and nineteenth century habitations. These included the incredible colonial Williamsburg in Virginia and the Sleepy Hollow Restorations in New York's Hudson Valley – Washington Irving's magnificent home on the river was one of them. Further south *Junior* donated the medieval art for the Metropolitan Museum of Art's Cloisters and the land for the adjoining Fort Tryon Park. France benefited by his contributions to restoring chateaus and cathedrals damaged during the First World War. The French government honored him in 1936 with one of its highest decorations: the *Grand-Croix de la Legion d'honneur*.

Two of *Junior's* largest construction projects were Rockefeller Center in midtown Manhattan and the United Nations complex occupying several blocks near the East River. He pressed ahead with Rockefeller Center in the early thirties, after other backers had withdrawn. The project provided employment for a huge workforce who were paid at union rates. Financing the $125,000,000 Center was a feat, even for him.[4]

Another of *Junior's* personal qualities was a deep and genuine modesty. Several incidents can serve to illustrate this point. For instance, in 1927 he drove from Paris to Versailles to view the complex that he had just given $2 million to restore. Finding the visitors' gate locked, he drove back to Paris. He was later flabbergasted when someone suggested that he ought to have identified himself to secure admission. Later on, in the thirties, he gently reproved elevator operators in Rockefeller Center who had offered to ignore other passengers and take him directly to his office on the fifty-sixth floor. One of *Junior's* greatest monuments is found in his own words inscribed on a tablet facing the Center's main gate: "I believe that every right implies a responsibility, every opportunity an obligation, every possession a duty."[5]

Mary McLeod Bethune:

John D. Rockefeller, Jr. (1874-1960) and Mary McLeod Bethune (1875-1955) were close in age and in their beneficence to many people. But their backgrounds – he, a billionaire industrialist's son and she, the fifteenth of seventeen children born to former slaves in the South Carolina back country, were vastly different. While he graduated from the elite Brown University, she attended mission (read *charity*) schools for "colored" students.

In spite of her circumstances and a subsequent broken marriage, Mary McLeod Bethune was determined to achieve something positive for her people and herself. Moving to Florida, in 1904 she founded the Daytona Educational and Industrial School for Negro Girls. It soon merged with the Cookman Institute of Jacksonville. This school in turn developed into the four-year coed Bethune-Cookman College, with Bethune as president – a post she held from 1923 to 1942. She was also president of the Florida Federation of Colored Women's Clubs. Among its achievements was the establishment of a home for delinquent black girls. On a higher level in 1935, she founded the National Council of Negro Women.[6]

Like most black activists, Bethune initially was a Republican, a legacy dating back to the distant days of Emancipation and Reconstruction. By the mid-1930s, however, she had switched to the New Deal and become part of it – as head of the National Youth Administration's Division of Negro Affairs (which made her the highest-paid African American in government. One of her functions was convening the New Deal's mid-level black personnel, nicknamed the "Black Cabinet."

Bethune's work at the NYA was both visible and significant. In the view of historian Elaine M. Smith, she became a driving force in government by enlightening elements of white public opinion, such as First Lady Eleanor Roosevelt, about the level of administrative responsibility that black women could handle. She was very much part of NYA's efforts to assist young people to obtain vocational training, work relief, and job placement, and to help those so inclined to remain in high school or college. Her labors persuaded many blacks that NYA was more evenhanded racially than any other New Deal agency.[7]

Bethune had a dramatic success in 1939 involving NYA's introduction of a Civilian Pilot Training Program. Through her assistance, the black West Virginia State College received a plane from the War Department. She also assisted Tuskegee Institute in its quest for a civilian air program. Some of the students receiving this instruction in peacetime later entered wartime training at Tuskegee as fighter pilots.

By the summer of 1939, NYA funds had helped to push the number of students in black colleges back to 1930-31 levels. Many young black women owed their employment in war industries to NYA-sponsored training and job placement. Bethune's influence also made it possible for approximately ten percent of the first officer class (1942) of the Women's Army Corps (WACs) to be African American. Near the war's end, she persuaded President Roosevelt to order the Navy, Coast Guard, and Navy Nurse Corps to accept a small number of black women (the Marines managed to hold out till 1949). Bethune supported the war effort in other ways too, for example, by leading the National Council of Negro Women's "Buy War Bonds" drive. In 1945 she assisted at the birth of the United Nation' Charter by serving as an associate consultant to the U. S. delegation.[8]

Bethune's popularity in the African American community probably peaked in the 1940s and early 1950s, when she was in her seventies. She had a melodious and authoritative speaking voice, which she used often; and she also wrote weekly columns for the *Pittsburgh Courier* and the *Chicago Defender*. Many ordinary blacks viewed her as a role model and a mother figure, while white progressives deemed her a voice of reason on racial matters. At times, though, she could be tough, such as demonstrating against discriminatory hiring practices and lynching. Associated with the Methodist Episcopal movement, Bethune was deeply religious. Above all, she had a vision that America's principles of democracy and equality would eventually triumph over discrimination based on color, caste, or gender.[9]

John L. Lewis:

John Llewellen Lewis (1880-1969), the son of Welsh immigrants, was one of the most prominent labor leaders of the twentieth century. A biographer, Robert H. Zieger, seizes upon his intelligence, oratorical skills, and lack of a higher education to compare him to Abraham Lincoln. Both of these Midwesterners were born on February 12th and later settled in Springfield, Illinois where today they are buried several yards apart in the same cemetery. This analogy can go only so far, however, because of their very different personalities. Though Lincoln was subject to occasional bouts of depression, he had a delightful sense of humor, whereas Lewis was domineering and irascible. Thomas Lewis, John L.'s father, worked in the coal mines and in a number of other occupations in south-central Iowa. His eldest son was born there and managed to complete three years of high school before also going into the mines. In 1908 John and his new wife, the former Myrta Bell, a physician's daughter, moved to a wealthier area in central Illinois. His entire family followed them there, and soon all the Lewis men found jobs in mining. John's union career grew with his election as president of the United Mine Workers (UMW) local district

The First World War years (1914-18) were good ones for the American Federation of Labor. Its UMW affiliate increased its membership from 250,000 to 500,000, and Lewis's union resume kept pace. He became an organizer for the AFL and an assistant to consecutive UMW presidents who were impressed by his mastery of parliamentary procedure, statistics, and disciplinary skills. He eventually became UMW president in 1920 at the age of thirty-nine, a striking figure with a mass of black hair and bushy dark eyebrows.

The end of wartime mobilization put a major crimp in the demand for coal. This led to decreased employment, which was also affected adversely by the modernization of mining technology and the substitution of petroleum for coal in industry and home heating. In the twenties a cycle of lengthy strikes and protracted negotiations exacerbated this decline. There were stoppages in 1922, 1923, and 1925-26. UMW membership dropped as greater quantities of coal were mined in non-union enterprises in Kentucky and West Virginia. By 1928, in fact, about two-thirds of bituminous came from non-union sources, and by the following year barely 85,000 of the nation's soft coal mineworkers were still in the UMW.

Yet in spite of these problems and growing opposition within the ranks of district organizations, Lewis still succeeded in solidifying his position. He had the assistance of a number of capable and respected underlings and from the less capable, but more obsequious people who controlled the *UMW Journal*. His knowledge of parliamentary procedure allowed him to silence opposition, while brother Dennie Lewis led a group of toughs in intimidating or even assaulting dissenters. John L.'s rich baritone became more formidable after he introduced a loud-speaker system not made available to protesting conference delegates. His voice was also a perfect fit for the relatively new medium of radio.

Lewis's opponents inside and outside the UMW were a mixture of communists, non-communists, and various others. One of these groups – the United Anthracite Miners – had its strength in northeastern Pennsylvania where it waged a rebellion between 1933 and 1935. The UAM perceived Lewis and his local satraps as basically corrupt and working in collusion with the coal companies. When employment declined and uneconomical mines were closed, it went beyond Lewis by calling for job equalization. This meant an equitable distribution of the available work. When the UMW leadership failed to challenge management on this issue, the UAM engaged in wildcat strikes for job equalization and for its recognition as a legitimate bargaining agent. The UMW joined the coal companies in resisting, and the result was widespread violence, including rock throwing, shootings, and bombings. Injuries and deaths numbered at least in the hundreds. Since the UMW and the mine owners had all the power of government and the courts on their side, the rebellion collapsed by 1935.[10]

Although Lewis often used the word democracy, he did not apply it accurately to his leadership style. Specialists in Russian history might be reminded of Stalinism, though a less brutal variety. An old-fashioned urban political boss would be a better match. Certainly, nepotism and favoritism were key components, and loyalty to the chief counted most of all. But as Lewis saw it, "obstructionists" and "wreckers" were objecting to his efforts to create an effective and efficient modern union.[11]

In the early days of the New Deal, Lewis asked the Roosevelt Administration to guarantee the rights of unions and collective bargaining. He maintained that this would increase wages and thereby boost the economy. FDR agreed. On June 16th, 1933 he signed the National Industrial Recovery Act (NIRA) that, among other things, permitted union membership and established minimum wage and maximum hour standards.

The enactment of NIRA facilitated the growth of unionization and this, in turn, led to more collective bargaining and higher wages. The UMW gained the right to help draft the coal industry's code that, among other things, gave the union dues checkoff advantages, local grievance committees, and an end to the operators' arbitrary power.[12]

Lewis's personal status rose in lock-step with that of the UMW. In 1934 he moved the union's headquarters from the somewhat provincial city of Indianapolis to the nation's capital. There his income (not counting expenses) rose to $12,506 – at a time when three fourths of American wage earners were making less than $1,200 annually. He soon acquired a Cadillac and a commodious house in Alexandria, Virginia. Meanwhile wife Myrta was amassing a huge antique collection and successfully pursuing acceptance by Alexandria's elite. Her husband, in turn, socialized with Supreme Court justices and other notables. By 1938 his salary had risen to a princely $25,000, from which he paid three servants, vacation expenses, and the tuition at elite schools for son John, Jr. and daughter Kathryn.[13]

Lewis's most enduring contributions to American life also took place in the late 1930s. He oversaw the establishment of the collective bargaining process in previously non-unionized huge industries, such as steel, rubber, autos, textiles, and others. Urging this expansion on the AFL leadership, he achieved little progress before 1935 (the AFL was a federation of craft unions in which the UMW, essentially an industrial union, was one of the exceptions). Tired of AFL stalling, he vigorously denounced its leadership at the union's convention at Atlantic City in 1935 for not honoring its earlier, if vague, promises. The CIO, or Committee for Industrial Organization, was born on October 20th, one day after the end of the AFL convention. The leaders of the UMW, the Amalgamated Clothing Workers, and the International Ladies Garment Workers each pledged $5,000 to meet expenses, but Lewis was the dominant figure. At first, he opposed independence for the CIO but began to change his mind when the AFL refused to recognize CIO autonomy.

The years 1936-37 saw Lewis assisting nascent industrial unions achieve recognition from corporate giants. Engaging in a sit-down strike and utilizing money and advice from the CIO, Akron-based rubber workers won their struggle in March 1936. The steel industry, with 500,000 employees, was next. Lewis created a Steel Workers Organizing Committee (SWOC) that pledged $1.5 million to bring unionism to steel. The United Auto Workers used the sit-down tactic to help wring settlements from auto makers, most dramatically with General Motors. Nineteen days later, on March 2nd, 1937, SWOC reached an agreement with U. S. Steel containing modest wage and hour gains and a grievance procedure that recognized the union as the sole workers' agent in the operation of the mills.

At the beginning of 1937, the CIO was a small committee of dissident unionists still hoping to avoid the complete alienation of the AFL. But by December of that year, it was an independent mass movement embracing at least two and a half million workers and holding collective bargaining agreements with the likes of GM and U. S. Steel. Almost one-quarter of non-agricultural workers were in unions by the end of 1937, triple the number enrolled in 1933-34.[14]

Using the assets of the UMW to staff and finance the new CIO, Lewis's role was clear. Starting in 1938, however, his image as the country's foremost labor leader began to recede, largely because he became increasingly critical of the "big boss." The lifelong Republican had rendered major financial aid to FDR's 1936 election campaign. Then, in 1937-38, there was the "Roosevelt recession" that Lewis (and many others) blamed on the president's cutting of work relief projects (see Chapter 15). When the country's pre-war mobilization began, he criticized the award of big government contracts to non-union companies. As an isolationist, moreover, he was critical of the Administration's rapidly emerging pro-British policy that he feared would lead to involvement in another European war. He declared: "Labor wants the right to work and live – not the privilege of dying by gunshot or poison gas to sustain the mental errors of current statesmen."[15]

Lewis searched for a way to defeat Roosevelt in the 1940 election. His first thought was the formation of a new progressive coalition uniting labor, farmers, youth groups, minorities, and the elderly. When this idea fizzled, he turned to endorse Herbert Hoover, his favorite politician of the 1920s. Unfortunately, that name was synonymous with depression and failure throughout working class America. Later, in the fall, he endorsed Republican candidate Wendell Willkie, a lawyer for large utility companies whose views on foreign affairs differed little from those of the president.

Shortly after FDR's victory Lewis, as promised, resigned as president of the CIO; and early in 1942 he pulled the UMW out too. He attempted to organize new members for his remaining union from the ranks of the un-affiliated and the AFL. Dairy workers were among the new recruits. They and other newcomers became part of a little known UMW group termed District fifty. Within three years, this entity had faded away. Even most of the dairy workers, at first enthusiastic about having union negotiators, had left. It was now obvious that only coal mining would remain as an arena for Lewis, who basically was at war with the rest of organized labor.

In 1943 Lewis defied the federal government by leading 416,000 soft coal miners in a series of strikes that violated Labor's "No strike pledge." Though vilified by government officials, the media, and millions of fellow citizens, he was actually following the wishes of miners who blamed the National War Labor Board for not creating fair dispute resolution machinery. There was much jealousy over the high wages paid to some big city war industry workers. These wages contributed to higher consumer prices; but because of the "No strike pledge," mineworkers had no lawful means of adjusting their income. They were now demanding a $2 a day increase.

Four separate UMW-authorized strikes took place in 1943. All of them were of short duration – from forty-eight hours to six days. In addition, wildcat strikes broke out periodically. Despite the walkouts, UMW miners still provided 590 million tons of coal in 1943, the greatest amount on record. At no time were coal supplies seriously jeopardized or military production basically affected. Still, the specter of nearly 500,000 men walking out of the mines caused public outrage, with visions of soldiers without weapons, defenseless ships, and freezing cities. FDR periodically placed the mines under the Solid Fuels Administration and warned that continued strikes could lead to induction of the miners, who would be forced to work for (low) military wages.

Harold Ickes was Solid Fuels Administrator as well as Secretary of the Interior, which meant that whenever FDR temporarily replaced the operators Ickes was in charge. Lewis respected him. Eventually the president gave Ickes the right to negotiate with the union, and Lewis and he worked out a deal: a $1.50 a day pay raise, but also overtime pay and longer lunch breaks. This package actually exceeded the union's original $2.00 a day demand. The strikes were over. Of all the government's functionaries, only Ickes seemed to understand the justice of the miners' thinking, which was to stop the steady decline of their living standards. Aside from his frequently sharp condemnation of Lewis and his threat to draft miners, FDR also deserved some of the credit for facilitating a settlement. Above all, he permitted Ickes to negotiate, against the National War Labor Board's rule that a strike could not continue while negotiations were on-going.[16]

Lewis's image as a labor leader continued to fade after the end of the war, but not all at once. Through a series of strikes and negotiations, and despite the steady decline of the industry, by 1950 he was able to obtain union-dominated health care. A chain of UMW-owned hospitals administered much of it. Unfortunately, with no upturn in coal sales, these benefits had mostly vanished by the mid-1960s, including the end of UMW-controlled hospitals.

Lewis's health also declined, due mainly to a series of heart attacks. He retired as president in 1960, although he would still draw a salary of $50,000 as president *emeritus*. Even before his retirement, the union's governance had become highly problematic. For example, the leadership invested UMW assets in questionable corporate investments. Buying out or leasing non-union mines and running them at the expense of UMW members was particularly reprehensible.

John L. Lewis died on June 11th, 1969. He had not had the energy or gumption to train a new union leadership. One of his underlings, W. A. "Tony" Boyle, had adopted the worst of his leader's techniques to preserve power -- information control, shady dealings with operators, and the stifling of intra-union dissent – in addition to which he turned out to be a murderous criminal. Lewis died without ever having commented on the events of these later years.[17]

Walt Disney:

Walter Elias Disney's background was just as modest as John L. Lewis's. His father, Elias Disney, of Irish descent and a socialist by inclination, moved the family around the Midwest seeking a livable wage. Besides Walt, there were three other sons and a daughter. Walt, the second youngest, was born in Chicago on December 6th, 1901. The family moved to the small town of Marceline, Missouri in 1906 and bought a farm just beyond the town limits. The area's layout, especially the presence of the Atchison, Topeka, and the Santa Fe Railroad, stayed with Walt his entire life.[18]

A few years later the family moved to Kansas City, Missouri where Elias bought a newspaper route. Walt and brother Roy, future partners in the film business, also worked on the route, and Walt and sister Ruth graduated from the seventh grade. The next year found the family in Chicago again where Walt completed eighth grade, his highest schooling. He also took classes three nights a week at the Chicago Academy of Fine Arts, which turned out to be his only formal art instruction. Then, at the age of seventeen, he lied about his age to enlist in the American Ambulance Corps for World War duty in France. There, in his few spare moments, he sent cartoons to humor magazines but received only rejection slips in return.[19]

After returning home, Walt moved in with two of his brothers in Kansas City. He worked at a number of advertising jobs. One of them, Kansas City Film Advertising, used cut-out figures that were easily manipulated and meant to be shown on movie theater screens. Though the business was not a long-term success, Walt identified his experience there as the real start of his career in motion pictures.[20]

The future film titan left Kansas City for California in 1923; and within a year he was developing a reputation as a producer of quality animations. Most notable was the *Alice* series, part animation, part real (a four-year-old actress played Alice). *Oswald the Lucky Rabbit* was another of his creations.

The lucky rabbit was not as lucky for Disney's career as another small animated creature. On a train trip from New York City to Los Angeles, he focused his thoughts on a mouse he called *Mortimer.* But his wife Lillian, whom he had married in 1925, convinced him that the name *Mortimer* was too serious, depressing, or both. She suggested *Mickey,* and fortunately he agreed.

The first two Mickey Mouse cartoons were standard, silent short features. The third one, however, was revolutionary: *Steamboat Willie* was the first cartoon with sound effects. The production was an undisguised borrowing from the film *Steamboat Bill, Jr.,* released in May 1928 and starring Buster Keaton. November 18th, 1928 was Mickey's true "birthday," at the Colony Theater in New York. Mickey did not speak but made sounds in reaction to his gruff treatment by the steamboat's captain.[22]

Disney's key insight was that sound, in conjunction with music, would be essential to the success of all subsequent cartoons. He proved it by winning an Academy Award in 1932 that read: "To Walt Disney for the creation of Mickey Mouse." In 1935 the League of Nations awarded him an honor for the goodwill that Mickey had spread around the world.

A California theater, in 1929, began holding Mickey Mouse Club meetings on Saturday afternoons. Soon formalized at theaters across the country, membership soon numbered about one million. The kids elected leaders, sang songs, acted in talent shows, and engaged in yo-yo competitions. The first Mickey Mouse comic strip appeared in 1930 and the first comic book in 1940. Merchandise also became very popular, particularly the Mickey Mouse watch that was introduced at the 1933 Chicago World's Fair. Over the course of the next two years. fans purchased two and a half million of them, during what were dismal depression days.[23]

In 1932 Disney Studios negotiated a contract for the use of Technicolor, and later that year they released *Silly Symphony*, the first cartoon in full color. Another color cartoon, *The Three Little Pigs*, won the 1934 Oscar for Best Short Subject Cartoon, the first year that category existed. Between 1934 and 1937, the Disneys released more *Silly Symphony* and Mickey Mouse cartoons in which Donald Duck, Goofy, and Pluto made their initial appearances.[24]

Audiences loved the color effects which, as early as 1934, prompted Walt Disney to consider making a feature-length film in color. *Snow White and the Seven Dwarfs* would not be solely about color but also examine emotions, attitudes, and motivations. A new type of camera would imitate perspective more realistically.

Snow White premiered in Hollywood on December 21st, 1937, with famous film stars in attendance – these included Marlene Dietrich, Douglas Fairbanks, Jr., Shirley Temple, Clark Gable, and Carole Lombard, among others. It opened at New York's Radio City Music Hall in January 1938 and played there for four months. Possibly it was the most eagerly anticipated film ever because there was uncertainty over whether people who loved Disney's short cartoons would love one ten times as long. But it won universal acclaim because the producer had pioneered new animation techniques. Throughout 1938 *Snow White* was not only in theaters across America but all over the world, with ten foreign language versions. The film won Disney another Academy Award, appropriately represented by one large Oscar and seven little ones. Even Harvard and Yale became involved by conferring honorary Master's degrees on the creator. Disney Studios' income rose from $1.565 million in 1937 to $4.346 million in the first nine months of 1938.[25]

Between the release of *Snow White* and the beginning of U. S. involvement in World War II, Disney produced his best and most famous feature animations. They were: *Pinochio (1940); Fantasia (1940); Dumbo (1941); and Bambi (1942).* Although they all won a modicum of praise, especially *Dumbo* and *Bambi,* none of them approached the popularity of *Snow White.* The large profits of 1938 turned into major losses by 1941, losses that were exacerbated by the impact of war on the European market and the construction of a new studio in Burbank. Disney had to swallow his opposition to the sale of company stock to the general public. The first issue, on April 21st, 1940, would help pay for the new studio. As of February 5th, 1941, the company owed the Bank of America the substantial sum of $2,781,737.

Walt Disney seemingly became more distant from his employees by 1941, which was perhaps related to the sizable growth of the staff during the bonanza year of 1938. He certainly had his favorites – the veteran animators – whom he affectionately nicknamed "the nine old men." A lack of equitable distribution of bonus payments was certainly obvious.

The thirties and early forties were a time of growing unionization, a trend visible even in Hollywood. By late 1940 a truly independent union, the Screen Cartoonists' Guild, wrote to inform Disney that it now represented a majority of his workforce. But even leaders of the "company Union," the Federation of Screen Cartoonists, believed that the boss no longer respected them. A picket line went up on May 28th, 1941, after management had laid off twenty-four union activists.

To Walt Disney the strike was a turning point (despite his father's socialist ideals). He dated his own affiliation with the Republican Party to this period. As he informed conservative columnist Westbrook Pegler, the event was not only a financial catastrophe but a Communist-led abomination (no evidence supports his second point). Although the strike theoretically ended on July 28th, 1941, after the arrival of Stanley White, a top federal mediator, further negotiations were necessary to mediate the studio's efforts to rid itself of "radicals." There were pay raises, improved working conditions, and responsibility guidelines, but the days of a big happy family were over.[26]

As the strike was winding down, Walt Disney, his wife, and a number of (non-striking) employees left for a goodwill tour of Latin America. The State Department sponsored it, basically as part of the "Good Neighbor" policy. The context was the disturbing amount of pro-Nazi sentiment south of the border at a time when a U. S.--German war was a strong likelihood. With the tour a great success, a forty-two-minute film, *Saludos Amigos* (Greetings Friends) followed in 1942. It starred Donald Duck and other Disney characters and was an even greater success than the tour. *The Three Caballeros* (horsemen or cavaliers), a film released in the fall of 1944, was another example of this outreach. Donald Duck, Jose Carioca, a Brazilian parrot, and Panchito Pistoles (Little Pancho Pistols), a Mexican rooster, headlined an animated travelogue mixed with live action.[27]

Nobody yet knew it, but the 1941 strike marked the end of the "Golden Age" of Disney feature animations. By 1943 about one-half of the new footage was live action. The studio ended up making seventy-five films for the U. S. military, many of which were for training purposes. For example, a Navy training film helped sailors identify enemy ships and planes. Other productions were ideological, such as the Donald Duck short entitled *Der Fuhrer's Face*. Released in January 1943, it won the Academy Award for best cartoon. The anti-Nazi title came from the hit song recorded by the unorthodox band of Spike Jones. *Victory Through Air Power*, also released in 1943, the animated version of a 1942 book by Alexander de Severesky, advocated the use of long-range bombers to crush the Axis. President Roosevelt and British Prime Minister Winston Churchill, commanders of scores of bombing squadrons, liked it very much.[28]

Such high-level praise aside, *Victory* lost $450,000. *The Three Caballeros* lost $200,000. The war was a tough time for Disney Studios, partly because theaters preferred to show the flood of more standard propaganda films. Training films were also a losing proposition. The situation improved in 1946-47 with the release of *Song of the South*. Based on Joel Chandler Harris's stories written in the Reconstruction period and narrated by "Uncle" Remus, the production was two-thirds live action and one-third animation. Critics liked the animated parts – with B'rer Rabbit, B'rer Fox, and B'rer Bear – much better than the live action, which many of them found patronizing, if not outright racist toward blacks.[29]

Nevertheless the controversial *Song of the South* earned millions from its initial release and from a re-release in the 1980s. At a time when fans of cartoons were beginning to enjoy *Bugs Bunny* (Warner Brothers) and *Tom and Jerry* (MGM) more than Mickey Mouse and Donald Duck, Disney was concentrating on what he called True Life Adventures (one notable exception was 1950's *Cinderella*). They earned him eight Academy Awards between 1948 and 1960. Nature films, such as *Seal Island*, were among them – it dealt with the life of seals on islands off the coast of Alaska.[30]

Dramatic features included the following: *Treasure Island* (1950); *The Story of Robin Hood and His Merrie Men* (1952); *The Sword and the Rose* (1953); *Rob Roy: The Highland Rogue (1954); Twenty Thousand Leagues Under the Sea* (1954); and *Old Yeller* (1957). Nineteen sixties' releases were *The Absent-minded Professor* (1961), full of special effects, and *Mary Poppins* (1964), a mixture of animation and live action that received thirteen Academy Award nominations, and a Best Actress Oscar for Julie Andrews.[31]

Walt Disney's imaginative thinking and creative story telling was reflected in Disneyland, first inspired by his perception that people requesting tours of the Burbank studios would not find much of interest there. So he bought a 160-acre site in Anaheim, south-east of Los Angeles in Orange County. There he supervised the construction of Disneyland, which he called a theme park. He may have been influenced by the 1893 Columbian Exposition, one of his father's employers in Chicago, and by Henry Ford's Museum and Greenfield Village in Michigan, which he himself had visited.

Realizing the importance of advertising to the success of the venture, Disney first approached the NBC and CBS Television Networks. Rejected there, he succeeded with ABC which agreed to invest $500,000 and co-sign a loan for $4.5 million. In return the network received thirty-five percent of Disneyland's ownership and a weekly show produced at Disney Studios.

The first TV show on ABC, entitled "The Disneyland Story," aired on October 27th, 1954. It described the park's design with its four "worlds:" Adventureland, Tomorrowland, Frontierland, and Fantasyland. In addition, there was Main Street, USA that was closely based on Marceline, Missouri, Walt's most memorable childhood home. Later, in 1955, the TV series introduced *Davy Crockett*, touching off a craze for coonskin caps and other mementos of frontier days. The Mickey Mouse Club, more or less patterned after the 1930s version, began its

TV life on October 3rd, 1955. Opening day at Disneyland was July 17th, 1955, and within a few months one million people had visited the premises. By mid-1956 that number had increased to three million.[32]

Disney was also involved in the 1964-65 New York World's Fair – as a contributor to the State of Illinois' exhibit. In the opinion of this youthful observer, "Great Moments with Mr. Lincoln" was simultaneously impressive and ridiculous. The life-sized Lincoln robot's head had taken a year to perfect, and the entire body was electronically programmed for dozens of different movements. Yet the undeniably bizarre voice emanating from the "Great Emancipator" was choppy and altogether unsuitable.

Thrilled by the success of Disneyland, its creator decided that the east coast should have its own version. Walt Disney worked on the planning of Disneyworld until his health gave out in mid-1966. Lung cancer, the possible result of years of heavy smoking, took his life on December 15th, 1966 at age sixty-five. Brother Roy came out of retirement to carry the project to its completion on October 1st, 1971 – before himself dying within a year.

Disneyworld would become the most visited vacation resort in the world, with an average annual attendance of fifty-eight million. The theme parks and the huge number of other Walt Disney creations constitute a fitting monument to one of the best showmen of twentieth century America.

Notes: Chapter 17

1   William Manchester, *A Rockefeller Family Portrait. From John D. to Nelson.* Boston, Toronto: Little, Brown and Co., 1958, 47, 49, 103.
2   *Ibid.*, 97, 99, 118, 166-167.
3   *Ibid.*,54.
4   *Ibid.*, 118.
5   *Ibid.*, 57.
6   Mary McLeod Bethune, *Building a Better World. Essays and Selected Documents.* Ed. by Audrey Thomas McCluskey and Elaine M. Smith, Bloomington, IN: Indiana University Press, 1999,4-6.
7   *Ibid.*, 144, 200.
8   *Ibid.*, 6, 201-203.
9   *Ibid.*, 13, 15-16. Bethune was the first black woman to have a national monument dedicated to her in the national capital.
10   Sheldon Spear, *Chapters in Northeastern Pennsylvania History. Luzerne, Lackawanna, and Wyoming Counties.* Shavertown, PA.: Jemags and Co., 1999, 75-76.
11   Zieger, op. cit., 49, 51-55.
12   *Ibid.*, 63-64, 66, 68-69.
13   *Ibid.*, 45, 47, 49.
14   *Ibid.*, 85-86, 91-92, 94-96. As discussed earlier (Chapter 7, p. 64), Lewis used experienced Communist and Socialist organizers for CIO work, while keeping them out of the UMW.
15   *Ibid.*, 197.
16   *Ibid.*, 132-133, 135, 140-142, 144-145. Coal strikes were not the only ones during World War II. Some of them occurred at war plants. In fact, the number of strikes rose sharply between 1942 and 1945.
17   *Ibid.*, 174-175, 178-179, 181-183. Joseph "Jock" Yablonski, a former UMW district leader, ran against Boyle for the UMW presidency in December 1969. His support came from miners who wanted greater democracy and local autonomy in the union. Boyle won, but Yablonski asked the U. S. Labor Department to investigate the election for fraud. On December 31, 1969 three killers murdered Yablonski, his wife, and his daughter as they lay sleeping. Four years later a jury convicted Boyle of first-degree murder for hiring the assassins, whose payments came from money Boyle had embezzled from union funds. The court sentenced him to three consecutive

terms of life imprisonment. Still imprisoned, he died of a variety of ailments on May 31, 1985,

18   Michael Barrier, *The Animated Man. A Life of Walt Disney*. Berkeley, Los Angeles, London: University of California Press, 2007, 10, 12.

19   *Ibid.*, 18, 20-21,

20   *Ibid.*, 25.

21   Louise Krasnewicz, *Walt Disney. A Biography*. Santa Barbara, CA; Denver, CO, Oxford, UK: Greenwood, 2010, 33, 35.

22   *Ibid.*,38, 43-46; see also Barrier, op. cit., 58. When Mickey began to speak in later cartoons, the (high) voice was Disney's until 1947.

23   Krasnewicz, *op. cit.*, 51-53, 55.

24   *Ibid.*, 62-63, 65. See also Chapter 14 above.

25   *Ibid.*, 68-70; Barrier, op. cit., 131.

26   Barrier, *op. cit.*, 165, 169-173; Krasnewicz, *op. cit.*, 80-81, 83.

27   Barrier, *op. cit.*, 184, 187; Krasnewicz, *op. cit.*, 87, 97.

28   Barrier, *op. cit.*, 91-93, 96.

29   Barrier, *op. cit.*, 185, 187, 192-193.

30   *Ibid.*, 198.

31   Krasnewicz, *op. cit.*, 112, 114-115.

32   *Ibid.*, 124, 126-128, 131.

33   *Ibid.*, 134, 137.

CHAPTER 18

Still More Notables: Female Flyers in the "Golden Age of Aviation"

C hapter Five of this book dealt with several male aviation heroes. For the sake of fairness, Chapter 18 will discuss female aviators – some of their achievements as well as the undeniable injustices they endured. These women were indeed "notables" during what is sometimes called the "Golden Age of Aviation" (roughly from 1927 to 1937).

Amelia Earhart (1897-1937) certainly attracted the most attention, though one could argue that her achievements were equaled by others, most especially by Louise Thaden and Ruth Nichols. Born in Achison, Kansas, Earhart eventually moved with her mother and sister to Medford, Massachusetts, a suburb of Boston where she became a social worker. She began flying in earnest during the late twenties, her career enhanced by excellent communication skills. Also contributing was publisher George Palmer Putnam, her boyfriend and later husband whose wealth and connections were invaluable. Nor did it hurt that her physical characteristics – she was tall, slim, and blond – bore a striking resemblance to those of Charles Lindbergh, the greatest aviation hero of the day.

Several women pilots aspired to match Lindy's transatlantic crossing. Earhart accomplished this twice. On her first effort, in

1928, her plane barely managed to lift off from Newfoundland, then crossed the ocean and flew over Ireland before ultimately setting down in waters just off the coast of Wales. No crowds, celebrations, or photographers awaited her. Yet when she returned home, 20,000 people lined the streets of Boston and another 20,000 turned out in her adopted home town of Medford. Earhart became a global commodity, but the adventure was a bit tarnished. The actual pilot was Wilmer Stultz, while another man was on board as a mechanic. The claim could be made, and was indeed put forward, that Earhart was the first woman to cross the Atlantic in a plane. But as she herself admitted, she was stuck behind the two men as little more than a piece of human baggage!

"Lady Lindy" could not forget what she considered a humiliation and secretly planned a solo transatlantic flight. On May 20th, 1932 at twenty minutes past seven in the evening, exactly five years since Lindbergh had taken off from Long Island's Roosevelt Field, Earhart's plane left Newfoundland. Her destination was Paris. But although her luck just barely held out, a variety of problems made Paris unthinkable. At approximately half past nine in the morning on May 21st, she landed on a farmer's field in Northern Ireland, covered with oil leakage and almost deaf from the plane's engine. She was the fourteenth person to fly across the Atlantic and the first female to do so. In fact, hers was the first solo flight since Lindbergh's.

Earhart's aerial achievements were numerous during her later years. For example, her 1934 flight from Hawaii to the San Francisco Bay area was 2,400 miles, which was actually more than three hundred miles longer than her Atlantic crossing of two years earlier. Less spectacular but still impressive was a 1935 flight from Mexico City to Newark, New Jersey. She often combined flying with lecture tours during which she defended the competence of women against the often-withering attacks of male pilots and journalists.[1]

Louise Thaden (nee McPhetridge – 1905-79} was another outstanding female aviator. Born in Arkansas, she moved with her parents to Wichita, Kansas where she became attracted to airplanes, particularly to those manufactured locally by the Walter Beech Company. With his support she moved to Oakland, California, honing her flying skills and also becoming the only female manager of an airplane distributorship in the United States. In 1928, at the age of twenty-two, Thaden obtained America's 1,943rd flying license (which was signed by Orville Wright, one of two ultimate aviation pioneers.

Thaden broke a number of records during the following year. Flying over Oakland and other California sites, she broke the altitude record for women. It had been 17,000 feet; she was credited with 20,260 feet. Four months later, in March 1929, she claimed her second record – for endurance—by flying non-stop over Oakland for twenty-two hours and three minutes, almost five hours longer than any female pilot had done. She set still a third record in April – for speed – hitting 175 mph and a maintained record of 156 mph – faster than any woman had previously flown.

Later, in 1933, Thaden and another pilot, Frances Marsalis, broke an endurance record by flying their plane over Long Island for 196 consecutive hours. Yet neither they nor any other aviatrix threatened men's records, most of which were set by military pilots supported by full crews.[2]

Thaden's marriage to aeronautical engineer Herbert Thaden was a happy one that produced two children. Incidentally, he was one of the first individuals to discern that metal would be a much safer construction material for aircraft than wood and cloth. Though a conscientious wife and mother, Louise's flying *couture* was reasonably fashionable. Besides goggles it consisted of high boots, trousers, a silk shirt, a jacket, and colorful bandanas around her neck.

Few aviatrixes, however, eclipsed the natural beauty and

glamour of Ruth Elder (1902-77). This "Miss America of Aviation" wore tight sweaters, a colorful scarf around her head and neck, ties and male shirts, and a lot of makeup. She spoke in a sexy Alabama accent and ended up marrying five husbands. For a time, not surprisingly, she was the principal center of attention for reporters.[3]

As early as the fall of 1927, Elder and another woman pilot, Frances Wilson Grayson (1892-1927) were preparing to match Lindbergh's feat. The Indiana-born Grayson, a niece of the late President Woodrow Wilson, was decidedly unattractive. This accounts for her nickname: "the flying matron." Both Elder and she would employ male co-pilots.

Elder's plane took off from Roosevelt Field on October 11th. 1927, flying east to Montauk Point before turning northeast to the island of Nantucket. From there she followed, or tried to follow, the common steamship route to Europe. But storms threw the team wildly off their course. Fortunately, they encountered a Dutch oil tanker that informed them that they were 360 miles from the Azores, the nearest land. Lacking the fuel to get there, co-pilot George Haldeman insisted, and Elder soon agreed, that the plane would have to be ditched while a rescue effort was still feasible. The tanker's crew subsequently reeled them in from the sea.

Despite this obvious failure, Elder remained a hero in America and also in France, which she had visited before sailing home. But in France, and ultimately in America too, the good feelings dissipated. Elder's current husband lambasted her for abandoning her homemaking duties, while many former admirers were soon criticizing her risky flight as a dangerous stunt.

Grayson actually took risks exceeding Elder's. Her point of departure was not initially Long Island but the more northerly and more wintry Orchard Beach, Maine. Her destination in Europe, moreover, was Denmark, not exactly known for friendly fall and winter conditions. Indeed, the weather at Orchard Beach during this particular autumn proved impossibly fierce, rendering Grayson's take-offs abortive. She consequently rescheduled the action to Long Island in early December. Although the weather there was also a problem, she managed to take off later that month. She left without her skilled co-pilot Wilmer Stultz who had abandoned her, leaving only the less competent Grayson and Brice Goldsborogh, the plainly nervous navigator. Grayson's plane eventually vanished somewhere off the coast of Newfoundland.[4]

Although she was a far better pilot than cither of them, Ruth Nichols (1901-60) declined to criticize either Elder or Grayson. In fact, she was one of the best female pilots of Aviation's Golden Age or beyond. Born in New York City, Nichols grew up in Rye, New York, the offspring of a wealthy family. She attended a private preparatory institution and subsequently, in 1924, she graduated from Wellesley, an elite college for women near Boston. While still a student, she secretly took flying lessons – secretly because her parents, who watched over her carefully, were only concerned with her marriage prospects. She received her pilot's license shortly after graduation.

Nichols first drew national attention early in 1928 when she accepted the suggestion of her former flying instructor, Harry Rogers, that they co-pilot a single engine seaplane from New York City to Miami, Florida. At twenty-five minutes past seven in the morning on January 4th, 1928, the two of them took off from the waters near Rockaway Beach, and at five minutes past eight in the evening, almost twelve hours after leaving New York, the plane landed in waters off Miami. Nichols won acclaim for being part of an unprecedented flight; and she received a nickname she hated: the "Flying Debutante." More positively, she accepted an offer to sell Fairchild aircraft (the plane she had co-piloted was a Fairchild).

Nichols made a number of record-setting flights during

the 1930s. In December 1930, for example, she flew from Los Angeles to New York in sixteen hours, fifty-nine minutes, faster than any other woman had flown that route. In January 1931 she accomplished another west-east crossing in thirteen hours and twenty-two minutes. This was an hour and a half faster than Lindbergh's fastest transcontinental trip. A little later that year, in March 1931, she flew nearly six miles into the sky (28,743 feet) – in bad wintry weather, setting another female record. Shortly thereafter, over Detroit, she flew at a sustained speed of 210 mph, which was thirty mph faster than Earhart's earlier record at Los Angeles. Nichols also had her share of crashes, one of which incapacitated her for six months.[5]

Of all the female aviation careers, in some ways the most spectacular (if short-lived) of all was that of Florence Klingensmith (nee Gunderson –1904-33). Half-Norwegian, half-Swedish by background, she grew up in poverty in rural and small-town Minnesota and North Dakota. An excellent athlete, skilled in skiing and other sports, she was also a beautiful blue-eyed blond. She held various blue-collar jobs after dropping out of high school but decided to take up aviation after a disappointing encounter with Lindbergh during his 1927 goodwill stop in Fargo, North Dakota. His *sin* was neglecting to wave back at her while being driven through Fargo. Of course, there was no way he could return all the waves directed his way, but Klingensmith took the omission as a slight. Lindy would learn from her forthcoming career, she told friends, that he was not the only pilot who could master the skies.

Lacking the money to buy or rent a plane, Klingensmith began as a stunt girl who parachuted from a plane or waved from its wings clad only in a bathing suit. She also took flying lessons that resulted in her becoming the first woman pilot in North Dakota. Meanwhile her persistence with Fargo businessmen led to grants amounting to $3,000 that would enable her to buy her own plane. Her career continued as she set new records for aerial loops and won $4,300 for her victory in a 1931 race in Cleveland.[6]

Klingensmith entered the Phillips Trophy Race in Chicago in September 1933. The model of her plane, a Gee Bee, was known for its speed but also for several recent fatal accidents. Besides her, there were six male pilots competing in the Chicago race.

Klingensmith made an excellent take-off, then zoomed to third place behind two of her competitors. Flying expertly at 220 mph, her skills were impressing spectators gathered below. Then catastrophe intervened: the wind shredded one of the Gee Bee's cloth wings, causing a loss of control over the aircraft. Klingensmith was able to fly clear of the crowd on the ground and climb to a height safe enough for parachuting. But then the plane nose-dived directly into the ground. With broken bones in virtually every part of her body, Kliingensmith was dead before the ambulance reached the hospital.[7]

Air accidents in the "Golden Age" were obviously frequent, often fatal, and affected men and women on a more-or-less equal basis. But much of the public took the crashes involving the latter as a reason to exclude them from air races. Among numerous others, Lindbergh gave them no support on this issue. The women in turn, particularly Thaden and Earhart, were furious at being belittled. One of the worst offenders, in their opinion, was organizer Clifford Henderson, who previously had allowed female pilots to participate in his races. The horrific death of Florence Klingensmith was the principal reason for his change of heart. But in 1935, two years after her death, he reversed himself again, apparently because of the loss of a number of men in a race over New Orleans.[8]

Meanwhile, women were not finding much work related to aviation. Thaden and her husband were nearly broke in 1935 before she got a job as an air marking pilot (one of the few jobs open to women). To prevent other pilots from getting lost, a frequent occurrence, the air marking pilot located tall, wide structures, and the United States Department of Commerce printed large letters on their roofs indicating the nearest town. Ruth Nichols was somewhat more fortunate in finding employment. She became a co-pilot on a new Curtiss Condor, a passenger plane with a ninety-three-foot wingspan and seats for twenty-eight people. For the first time in almost two years, she was flying again, mostly on promotional tours to generate interest in the new plane.[9]

Among the sister pilots, Earhart was really the only one doing well – through her numerous flights, lectures, books (about herself), and teaching assignments at Purdue University. Her lectures, incidentally, revealed that she was not only a feminist but a pacifist as well. For instance, she advocated that a future draft should include women and that they should be assigned to combat units and other tough work. Having them in the military, she half-joked, might discourage the nation's male leadership from entering wars they seemed to relish.[10]

Earhart was secretly contemplating what might prove to be the greatest feat of her career: a circumnavigation of the globe. She announced the plan in January 1937. The two engine Lockheed, a state-of-the-art aircraft, would begin the first leg of the journey by flying from Oakland to Hawaii. However, while taking off from Honolulu to points west, the Lockheed crashed. Injuries were avoided, but serious damage would require months to repair.

Earhart returned to California by ship, and two months later she and her new navigator, Fred Noonan, were ready to start anew. Only this time they would be flying east, not west, to take advantage of better weather patterns. During their first month, Earhart and Noonan flew successfully for twenty-two thousand miles, from Oakland to Miami, Brazil to Senegal, Sudan to India, Burma to Australia, and finally to Lae, New Guinea. Their next stop would be Howland Island, 2,556 miles to the east, a tiny coral and sand-covered speck in the Pacific. The two-person crew took off on July 2nd, 1937, hoping to reach Howland in approximately twenty hours. The U. S. Coast Guard Cutter *Itasca* would be waiting to provide any necessary guidance or assistance.

Then, unfortunately, the Lockheed entered the vicinity, where Howland was supposed to be, without finding it, while the plane's fuel supply was becoming dangerously low. Nor could the *Itasca* see the plane. After a short time, radio contact between air and sea ended abruptly. A massive search then began involving the Coast Guard cutter and the U. S. Navy. But a total of three thousand personnel in 102 planes and ten ships could not find the lost plane or its possibly grounded crew. On July 18th – more than two weeks after Earhart and Noonan disappeared – the U. S. government ended its search.

After pursuing various fruitless leads for a year and a half, Earhart's husband petitioned a federal court to declare his wife dead. For many years, however, tales of her survival, or of a bizarre death, lingered on. And even today, Amelia Earhart remains a legendary figure in American history.[12]

The other female pilots discussed above had a variety of experiences in their later years. Louise Thaden's racing career peaked in 1936 when she won the prestigious Bendix Race, which started at Brooklyn's Floyd Bennett Field and finished in Los Angeles. Her flying time was fourteen hours, fifty-five minutes, a new female record. Thaden had beaten her nearest competitor, Laura Ingalls, by twenty-five minutes, the closest man by fifty minutes, and Earhart by about two hours. She won more than $9,000 – $7,000 for first place, and $2,500 for being the first woman to land. There was a lot of journalistic coverage, especially because on the very same day the British aviatrix Beryl Markham flew successfully from England to Nova Scotia. This dual feat seemed to confirm that women had the same flying skills as men. Somewhat surprisingly Thaden, proceeded to retire. She basically devoted the rest of her years to her husband, her son and daughter, and eventually to her grandchildren.[13]

Ruth Nichols undertook a number of charitable activities immediately before and during World War II. In 1939, for example, she headed Relief Wings, a civilian service that performed relief flights of various kinds. After America's entry into the war, she rose to the rank of lieutenant colonel in the Civil Air Patrol. A number of years later, in 1949, she organized a mission of support for the United Nations (UNICEF), including the piloting of a trans-world tour. Yet she experienced frustration in her quest for additional meaningful work. Such moments included the rejection of her applications to fly for major U. S. airlines (in spite of her obvious ability, they regarded her gender as a disqualifier).

Even the consent of the U. S. Airforce, in 1958, to allow Nichols to pilot one of its supersonic jets (when she was age fifty-six and at speeds exceeding 1,000 mph and ten miles high) could not cheer her permanently. In 1959 an Airforce board denied her application to become the first woman in space. Suffering from deep depression, on September 25th, 1960 Nichols committed suicide by taking an overdose of barbituates.[14]

Notes: Chapter 18

1   Keith O'Brien, *Fly Girls. How Five Daring Women Defied All Odds and Made Aviation History.* Boston, New York: Houghton Mifflin Harcourt<, 2018, 13, 15, 62-69, 153. 155-156, 186, 208, 210.
2   *Ibid.,* 82-84, 180.
3   *Ibid.,* 29, 35.
4   *Ibid.,* 38, 40-41, 44-45.
5   *Ibid.,* 128, 130, 137, 139, 149.
6   *Ibid.,* 163-164.
7   *Ibid.,* 174-175.
8   *Ibid.,* 171-172, 175, 178.
9   *Ibid.,* 183, 207.
10 *Ibid.,* 170.
11 *Ibid.,* 248-250.
12 *Ibid.,* 250-252. In the early 1940s, with America at war with Japan, rumors spread that Earhart had crashed in Japanese-held territory in 1937 and that she had been captured and subsequently executed. This theory ignored the fact that Japan had actually assisted in the initial search and that the last thing the Imperial government needed was a major distraction with the U. S. on the verge of a pending war with China.
13 *Ibid.,* 242, 244-245.
14 *Ibid.,* 254. In 1950 Ruth Elder also attempted suicide (by pills and alcohol) but survived. She left her fifth husband for an earlier one and lived happily until her death in 1977.

CHAPTER 19

Philo T. Farnsworth: Founding Father of Television

By Seth D. Chaiken

Biographical Note

At a young age, the author's fascination with the workings of television led him to devour repair manuals and other electronics books. He would often disassemble televisions for parts to use in simple experiments and was also a ham radio operator. After attending Brooklyn Technical High School, he pursued his passion for physics and earned a BS from Cooper Union in 1973, followed by a Ph.D. in Applied Mathematics from MIT in 1980. His doctoral work focused on discrete mathematics and computer science.

Until his retirement in 2015, he continued to pursue his interests in systems and taught a diverse range of theoretical and applied subjects as a faculty member in the Computer Science Department at the State University of New York's University at Albany. He currently judges competitions at Junior Science and Humanities Symposia https://jshs.org/ and has a long-term research interest in the mathematical principles that underlie the design and function of physical systems like electronic circuits. This writing project has allowed him to revisit his old interests and learn new aspects of physics and engineering while also exploring new avenues of scholarship.

The author is joined by his wife, son, and a cat to round out his family. He expresses his gratitude for their unwavering love, encouragement, and advice. He also thanks his friends Franklin Abrams, Lance Nevard, William Rennie, and Jay Sulzberger for their invaluable assistance, as well as Paul Schatzkin for his correspondence. Assistance is acknowledged from the University of Utah J. Willard Marriott Library, the National Archives at Kansas City, Arizona State University Special Collections, the US Patent Office, and library resources of the University at Albany.

Introduction

Philo Farnsworth was a brilliant self-taught inventor who hailed from a dirt-poor farming family. He demonstrated his exceptional talent from an early age, inventing the modern television system at the age of fifteen and doggedly pursuing his dream of making television a practical reality. By the age of twenty-five, he had developed the only working electronic television camera in the world and had secured dozens of patents for virtually all the subsystems required to commercialize television.

During the 1930s, a fierce battle unfolded between Farnsworth and RCA in the race to develop television. While Farnsworth sought to lead a company that would finance inventing from patent royalties, RCA aimed to consolidate its corporate dominance in electronics and broadcasting. RCA relentlessly attacked Farnsworth's business, overwhelming it with assaults on previous and developing patents. Despite winning a legal victory in 1938, Farnsworth became dispirited, and his new 1939 Corporation was too small to compete after RCA proclaimed itself the provider of commercial television to Americans at the opening of the 1939 World's Fair. Commercial development by Farnsworth was impeded, while, with the help of corporate espionage and patent infringements, it continued at RCA.

Although the patent office ultimately ruled in Farnsworth's favor in 1938, RCA's financial and commercial dominance, coupled with the delay caused by the wartime suspension of television and the subsequent expiration of Farnsworth's patents, enabled RCA to establish a dominant position in the commercial television market. Farnsworth became disillusioned with television but continued to invent prolifically and remained a high technology industry leader. In recent decades, his reputation as the inventor of television, as well as his contributions to other important technologies, has been revived. His story serves as an inspiration to young people with a passion for science and technology and can guide them on the path to fulfillment.

A False Dawn

The 1930s were an exciting time for science, with scientists perfecting and connecting the revolutionary theories and discoveries of the previous fifty years, particularly in modern physics. This led to history-making applications in the next decade, such as rockets, nuclear weapons, and radar-capable electronics. The year 1939 could have been the start of commercial television if not for World War II. Historian Donald Godfrey called this period a "false dawn," as great modern technologies take time to develop from conception to everyday use.

Workable ideas for television had been gathering for about twenty years, and the 1930s were the culmination of this preparatory time. The most significant inventions that led to commercial-quality television were due to Philo Taylor Farnsworth, an ingenious young man born in 1906 into a poor Mormon farming family. Farnsworth began his single-minded mission to invent a television system with sufficient quality for commercialization and conveying great social benefits at the age of fifteen. While guiding a plow over a potato field, he got the idea that resulted in the very first television camera device with the requisite image quality, which he called the Image Dissector. In 1927, Farnsworth applied for his Image Dissector and three other television system patents. Over one hundred patents were awarded from then through the 1930s, money was raised, and Farnsworth led his colleagues in a succession of companies.

Farnsworth won a key patent interference case in 1938, for which his attorney Lippincott filed in a brief: "Of course, if we are considering probabilities only, it is extremely improbable that a boy of twenty, whose formal education ceased with the completion of his first year in college, should have filed the application on the Farnsworth device and been granted a patent therefor. No other person out of one hundred and twenty millions in the country at the time did so, but in spite of this improbability the fact remains that the patent was issued. In order that this might be the case, it was necessary that the invention be conceived; …"

He patented and painstakingly engineered all the dozens of different essential components or subsystems needed for television, showing the way to completely electronic television to his overwhelmingly larger rival RCA. From 1927 to 1931, Farnsworth had the only working completely electronic television system in the world. In August 1934, he made the very first public demonstration of electronic television at Philadelphia's Franklin Institute. His system ran two 1930s American experimental television stations, and both Farnsworth's and RCA's systems were used by German and British affiliates to televise the 1936 Berlin Olympics.

Farnsworth received some public accolades but then slipped into public obscurity and personal hardship and disillusionment, while continuing to innovate as a well-respected defense industry leader. In recent decades, Farnsworth's public reputation has been revived. He was inducted into the National Inventors Hall of Fame in 1984 and the Television Academy Hall of Fame in 2013. The Television Academy set up its Corporate Achievement Engineering Award in his name in 1993, and his statue was placed in the US Capitol in 1990 to honor a citizen of Utah. Opening on Broadway in 2007, Aaron Sorkin's stage play "The Farnsworth Invention" unfortunately omits Farnsworth's successes in both his patent disputes and other technological achievements, containing historical inaccuracies. Image Dissectors were used through the early space age. Today, research continues to develop fusion-based neutron sources for radiography, medicine, etc., based on his electrostatic inertial confinement "fusor" idea, and this is still sometimes considered as an energy source. He died in 1971.

David Sarnoff of the Radio Corporation of America, another self-made man, presided over two events at the 1939 World's Fair. At the televised dedication of RCA's pavilion on April 20th, New Yorkers heard: "I come to this moment of announcing the birth in this country of a new art..." *The New York Times* reported: "Lined up in ... the RCA Building were the new television receivers, which dealers were invited to inspect ... for the first time. The sets will be on the market May 1st when NBC begins a telecast schedule." The Fair's April 30th opening was a bigger RCA television publicity splash. Sarnoff spoke again, as did FDR—the first televised president—as well as Albert Einstein and other celebrities. Sarnoff did not mention the contributions of individual inventors to television technology, including Farnsworth and RCA's own Vladimir Zworykin. Instead, RCA showcased their TRK-12 model at the World's Fair, which was a cabinet with an upright picture tube that faced a mirror for viewing. One of the cabinets on display was made transparent, allowing visitors to see that there were no hidden tricks involved.

In 1930, David Sarnoff assumed the presidency and

chairmanship of RCA amidst challenges posed by the depression and government anti-trust action against the corporation. RCA had monopolized broadcast radio infrastructure in the United States since the early 1920s, but now faced a new opportunity - the development of television in the US. Sarnoff saw this as a way to enhance commercial broadcasting's benefits to society and earn greater fortunes for RCA officers and shareholders. Although Sarnoff likely had his eye on television for some time, his call to action was prompted by news coverage and his investigations of Philo Farnsworth and his San Francisco laboratory.

The key difference between RCA's and Farnsworth's objectives was that RCA sought to establish itself as the dominant supplier of the entire television industry in the United States, while Farnsworth aimed to run a visionary electronic research and development laboratory for television and future technologies, with patent royalty money and some manufacturing, sales, and commercial broadcasting to provide practical experience to its developers. Farnsworth sought to license its television inventions to competing businesses for public use as soon as possible, while RCA sought to delay for the purpose of establishing a monopoly position using its larger corporate wealth. However, Farnsworth companies developed, owned, and ultimately won most disputes over the large body of patents behind television.

In 1930, there was excitement about the promise of television, but radio companies and owners were alarmed. Farnsworth responded that his new electronic television would be an inexpensive add-on to existing radios. In December, *The New York Times* reported that "a young man ... Farnsworth" had reported to the Federal Radio Commission a tube that "makes commercial television practical at once." However, the chief engineer of NBC believed "television will not be ready to provide public entertainment for several years. ... we are still far short of the perfection of the motion picture film." Farnsworth asserted that he had abandoned the idea of a whirling television disk and that his device could be plugged into the existing broadcast receiver, costing less than $100. The *Times* reporter assured the public that their radio sets would not be made obsolete or scrapped, nor would television "throw the industry or broadcasting into chaos."

Sarnoff had RCA subsidiary Westinghouse's television researcher, Vladimir Zworykin, transferred to RCA's new research lab in Camden, New Jersey. On April 16, 1930, Zworykin was warmly welcomed to Farnsworth's Television Laboratories in San Francisco, where he saw the Image Dissector for the first time. Farnsworth hoped RCA would become a licensee of his patents and an investor. Instead, Zworykin sent a six-hundred-word telegram to the Westinghouse engineers so they could build a replica Image Dissector while Zworykin traveled back east. He had this device with him when he joined the Camden lab. The RCA research lab was able to replace its mechanical scanning disk image sources with electronic cameras only after copying Farnsworth's Image Dissector. Sarnoff himself visited Farnsworth's lab a year later and subsequently offered to buy the patents for $100,000 and employ Farnsworth, but was refused. RCA was ahead in picture tubes with Zworykin's kinescope but had no satisfactory electronic camera tubes. Farnsworth's inventions prompted Zworykin and other RCA scientists to build and improve Image Dissectors, which they then used to make more sensitive Iconoscopes that they demonstrated in 1933.

Sarnoff decided not to start a television service in the US since it would harm RCA's radio business, and so he kept the television research out of the public eye. Farnsworth, who was always short of money, publicized his ongoing Image Dissector improvements to attract paying licensees. However, better-funded entrepreneurial inventors, like Dean Kamen, have been more secretive. In 1938, the patent office appeals officials finally ruled in favor of Farnsworth's priority.

RCA's dramatic debut of television broadcasting in 1939 forced it to resolve ten years of conflict with Farnsworth. Throughout the 1930s, RCA's publicity claimed that commercial television was not yet ready, while it worked to invent around Farnsworth's patents and legally dispute their priority. Its clandestine task force was informally known as "the Get-Around-Farnsworth Department," as revealed when a top RCA scientist joined Farnsworth. One report shows RCA spending over $2,000,000 in legal expenses and $7,000,000 in equipment development, while another says RCA spent over $10,000,000 by 1938 for no essential patents, while Farnsworth got them all with less than $1,000,000. RCA also lobbied the new Federal Communications Commission (FCC) to delay technical standardization and commercial station licensing.

Whether a television industry would take off in 1939 was a question of such notoriety that Fortune Magazine published a two-part article emphasizing the financial challenges. Technology was addressed in the first part, and programming, marketing, and advertising were addressed in the second. The article reported that "a cross-licensing agreement between RCA and Farnsworth is imminent," but it omits that Farnsworth had already licensed RCA's patents indirectly.

There is a legend from the Farnsworth side that in October 1939, RCA's vice-president in charge of patents, Otto Schairer, had tears in his eyes when he signed a non-exclusive contract for RCA to pay $1,000,000 in royalties on Farnsworth's patents. It was the first and only time RCA ever paid royalties to another company to license patents rather than acquire them. News media reported Farnsworth's ingenuity and achievements, and he was named one of "America's Top Ten Young Men." One can speculate over what drove RCA management to refuse a more productive and equal business relationship with Farnsworth.

Clearly, his personal nature explains why Farnsworth insisted on being, as Waldrop and Borkin put it in 1938, an independent "zealot" rather than a productive "captive inventor. The fiery-eyed zealot who starves himself and pawns his wife's wedding ring while working furiously in a garret, appears to bring out more novel ideas than the well-fed researcher in the corporate laboratory."

Farnsworth's tight-fisted backers enabled him to succeed but with enormous energy and struggle. Yet in the end, when a favorable agreement with RCA was in sight, Farnsworth testified at a In January 1939 at a Federal hearing on patents and monopoly. He was in favor of commercialization of television being delayed because technology and standards had to be perfected, instead of allowing a single company to «police the industry."

In 1939, Farnsworth reached the peak of his success, but his potential fortune was marred by setbacks of the previous decade. The Great Depression had frustrated his objectives of improving and licensing television technology, launching commercial stations, and establishing factories for transmitters and receivers. Corporate backers, who prioritized returns over long-term investment, caused conflicts, including leading backer McCargar, who opposed Farnsworth's strong personality and leadership qualities. Despite this, Farnsworth continued to build a close-knit team of engineers and adopted a philosophy of "building men, not gadgets."

Everson was the moderator; his book describes the positives and negatives of his good friend's personality. McCargar would come to the lab and fire engineers when funds were short. When royalties finally came in from European companies, McCargar refused to use them to build a Farnsworth experimental station. Farnsworth built one anyway, which ran from 1936-1938, with a more sympathetic investor's backing.

As licensing agreements were made with companies

besides RCA, research expenditures grew, and disagreements with McCargar intensified. Television Laboratories was reorganized, and Edwin A. Nicholas, formerly of RCA, was recruited as president. The corporation had many patents and had concluded licensing with all the other television companies, netting $3,000,000 from stock sales. McCargar left management, and the Corporation relocated to Ft. Wayne, Indiana, with a factory under construction.

If the Farnsworth Television and Radio Corporation had participated in the 1939-1940 New York World's Fair, television history might have been different, but they were too busy setting up a new organization and factories. They instead resorted to publicizing themselves with touring vans. One day after the stock sale and Corporation's organization was complete, Hitler invaded Czechoslovakia, which likely would have canceled the stock sale if it took place one day later.

Farnsworth's health deteriorated due to the immense strain of his work in the preceding decade, which involved not just invention and research but also factory management. The outbreak of World War II led the U.S. government to impose the cessation of all commercial manufacturing and development of television. Nevertheless, Farnsworth continued to contribute to his new Ft. Wayne Corporation's defense work from his lab in Maine. After the war, the corporation briefly resumed work in television, but it was eventually bought out by ITT in 1949. Building on Farnsworth's legacy, ITT focused on engineering industrial and defense imaging technologies, such as missile guidance systems, which paved the way for the space age.

Farnsworth's son Kent once quoted his father's opinion on television: "There's nothing worthwhile on it, and we're not going to watch it in this household or have it in our intellectual diet."

It Began in a Farm Cradle

The following paragraphs aim to delve into Philo Farnsworth's earliest thoughts on television theories, his efforts in organizing and funding companies to bring those theories to life, and the successes he achieved up until the early 1930s.

In the summer of 1921, when Philo was just fourteen years old, he was plowing a potato field when the solution for television began to take shape in his mind. He imagined that a visible image, cast by a camera lens, could produce an "electrical image" made up of electrons on a target surface. A "prism" (as Farnsworth put it) of electrons, those sprightly little particles, (half) the stuff of electricity, would be pulled away from the target by a static electric field (which makes dry laundry cling), and then be focused and swept by electromagnets across a tiny receptor that sends them into an electric wire. The resulting electrical signal could then be transmitted through wires or radio waves, and when it reached the receiver, it could be transformed back into a visible light image by a beam of electrons that were swept in synchrony with the camera's sweep. A picture is formed when the electrons energize a florescent coating inside the picture tube. At the boundary where the electron image in the camera reaches the receptor, the beam is steered to the next row in a similar way a plow is worked to get to the next furrow. This fully electronic television, unlike spinning disk or other mechanical televisions, could usher in a new age for humanity. Philo was eager to bring this new age himself.

Philo T. Farnsworth was born in 1906, and his parents first noticed his talent when he was just three years old and drew a detailed picture of a steam locomotive after seeing one for the first time. At age six, he decided to become an inventor after learning that telephones and phonographs were the creations of inventors. When he was eleven, he moved to his uncle's farm in Rigby, Idaho, where he first encountered the marvels of urban technology in Salt Lake City. The sight of the farm's electric wiring gave him a thrill, and he began reading science and technology magazines daily at four in the morning.

It was there that he likely learned about James Clerk Maxwell's electromagnetism theory that electrical and magnetic forces are two aspects of the same physical thing which make electrical generators and motors work. He also learned that vibrating electrical and magnetic fields sustained each other, the phenomenon that results in radio and light waves as Maxwell's theory predicts. He learned these physics principles in practice from the farm's electric generator repairman's expensive visits. In fact, Philo was suspected of breaking the generator on purpose, and he soon took over maintaining it. By age fourteen, Philo had built motors and fixed generators, and he likely knew about Einstein's theory of relativity and of the photoelectric effect. Television relies on this effect which is electrons being dislodged into space when light hits certain substances.

These experiences and knowledge laid the foundation for Philo Farnsworth's groundbreaking work in television, where he would go on to organize and fund companies to bring his theories to life and achieve significant successes in the field up until the early 1930s.

In 1921, the Farnsworth family purchased a farm nearby, which Philo promptly electrified using his knowledge and skills in electronics. To earn money for books and magazines, such as Gernsback's *Science and Invention* and *Radio News*, Philo played his violin. Hugh Gernsback (1884-1967), who was an inventor, science fiction writer, and publisher of extensive technical magazines and books, repeatedly wrote articles extolling the wonder of television and its potential for future inventions.

Philo participated in a *Science and Invention* contest where he invented a magnetized key car ignition lock, met the bank notary, and won $25 and an illustrated newspaper write-up. He paid $200 to an unscrupulous patent attorney to do a search, but the attorney stole his invention.

Radio News was filled with instructions, explanations, and advertisements of parts and kits for enthusiasts to build, set up and operate their own radios. The magazine also contained accounts of Nipkow's spinning perforated disk television, patented in 1884. Philo's readings in 1921 were centered around building vacuum tube circuits and understanding how they worked. The vacuum tube technology had rapidly advanced during World War I, and Lee de Forest's discovery of the grid-controlled vacuum tube in 1906 marked the beginning of the age of electronics.

Philo understood that the mechanical spinning schemes for television, which were enthusiastically reported in his radio magazines and reproduced by hobbyists in small numbers of commercial sets, could not possibly realize his and other visionary people's dreams for what was then called distant vision. Philo's potato field idea, where the entire electrical image was streamed into the tube's evacuated space and then shifted up and down, right and left, resulted in the first demonstration of a working electronic television camera in about ten years.

During the 1910s, scientists, including the British radiologist Campbell-Swinton, wrote about and tried with no success to deploy a different basic idea for an electronic tube to work more like primitive predecessors, such as the cathode ray picture display tubes common before digital flat-panel displays. A few other scientists had similar ideas. It was only years after Farnsworth achieved success with his original idea that the idea of moving a thin electron beam over a fixed image was finally made to work.

I speculate that Philo's familiarity with Einstein's principle of relativity influenced his thinking. It's possible that he imagined the plow at rest in a reference frame where the potato field did the two-dimensional movements. Additionally, Farnsworth's

1927 system was the first electronic one to work and pick up live images in broad daylight because the Image Dissector scanning technology was easier to implement. This allowed Farnsworth and his team to study and solve the many detailed problems that were necessary to create a complete system. The task was so challenging that only someone like Farnsworth, with his inventive genius and direction, could lead a company to complete it first.

However, Farnsworth's Image Dissector scanning idea would have been useless without solutions to other problems. For example, a glass tube strong enough to withstand a vacuum with an optically flat window had to be fabricated, and the best chemical (cesium oxide) for the photoelectric emitting surface had to be found. Additionally, a delicate process of forming a thin layer of the chemical had to be perfected, and a high enough vacuum had to be made for the electrons to move freely without degrading. Baking the inside parts of the tube allowed the necessary vacuum to be maintained. The pickup for the electrons had to be invented, and the physics of electric and magnetic field generation and actions of those fields on electrons had to be understood and then applied to inventing the deflection system, both for the camera and the display. Electronic circuits for uniform speed (sawtooth) deflection drivers, amplifiers, synchronizers, pulse and other waveform generators, and high voltage power supplies had to be invented as well. Moreover, large, bright, and sharp cathode ray picture tubes were needed. This list of challenges had to be solved first before any of the in-camera electronic imaging strategies could go into practical use.

Philo's knowledge of Einstein is well-known because his high school chemistry teacher, Justin Tolman, caught him giving a clear explanation of relativity in the supposedly silent study hall. Tolman spent many hours mentoring Philo and supplying him with books, including "Practical Electricity." This is an almost seven-hundred-page tome that includes detailed introductions to the physics, including equations, behind what is explained in practical terms. Despite hesitating to enroll Philo in his senior chemistry class, Tolman allowed the freshman to sit in, and Philo became his best student. Several months later, in the spring of 1922, Philo carefully prepared and divulged to his teacher what he knew about television and the details of his invention, with the photoelectric effect producing the electronic image from the camera lens focused light, all the magnets and sweeping, and how it would start a new age for humanity. Many blackboard sessions were needed to finish the details. Twelve years later, at a disposition for the patent interferences, Tolman drew forth a notebook sheet sketch by Farnsworth of the Image Dissector's essential features and shocked the RCA attorneys who argued that a fifteen-year-old could never have done this.

When the family moved away from the high school he was attending, Philo's education was limited to some home-schooling and a few classes at Brigham Young University before his father's death in 1924. In 1926 he moved to Salt Lake City to find employment. He was running a radio shop with his lifelong friend Cliff Gardner, when he was introduced to professional charity fundraisers Les Gorrell and George Everson by the University employment office. They recognized Philo's talents and hired him, Gardner, and both of their sisters for their campaign work. During a break, Everson asked Philo about his plans. Farsworth shared his confidential ideas. Impressed by Philo's expertise and knowledge of existing television research, Everson and Gorrell consulted some engineers and professors, and decided to invest $6,000.

With the windfall, Philo, currently nineteen, and his fiancée, Elma (Pem) Gardner (eighteen), arranged a wedding. They were married in the presence of their families in Provo Utah. Shortly after the wedding the couple moved to Hollywood and set up their apartment as a laboratory. Pem, played a vital role in their work, learning to spot-weld, taking technical notes, and doing complex drawings. A professional glass blower was replaced by Cliff Gardner, who learned the craft and invented a jig to weld an optically flat plate to a bottle-shaped tube. Financier, Everson also contributed by winding the electromagnetic wire coils for focusing the electrons. Throughout his life, Philo gave equal credit to his wife for their successes.

Their first prototype exploded the first time it was turned on, quickly depleting the $6,000 budget. However, Everson and Gorrell's connections helped begin raising money from capitalists associated with the Crocker Bank in 1926. By the late summer of 1928, the total funds raised had reached $60,000, allowing the new company to secure a one-floor loft at 202 Green Street in San Francisco's Crocker building. The personnel list initially included Farnsworth, Gardner, and Pem. The first four patent applications for the Farnsworth television system were filed in January 1927, with the first patent claim focused on the "electrical image," which referred to the pattern of electric charge produced by light hitting a photoelectric surface. This claim became pivotal in the patent office ruling in favor of Farnsworth's patents in 1938 despite RCA's persistent and costly challenges.

The research conducted by the Farnsworth team was meticulous, and they achieved a significant breakthrough in September 1927 when they televised a horizontal line, and soon after, geometric figures. They then experimented with two-dimensional pictures. Cliff Gardner set up the camera with dazzling arc lights, and Farnsworth saw the images displayed clearly. However, clouds suddenly appeared to cover the image. It turned out that Gardner had blown smoke from his cigarette into the view, inadvertently discovering that they could televise moving objects. In May 1928, the Crocker investors became impatient, and the team entertained them with a demonstration. When their leader asked when they would see financial returns,

Farnsworth displayed the image of a dollar sign followed by the moving smoke and more, convincing them to invest an additional $40,000. He also convinced them to give him more time to achieve continuous television from movie film.

During the 1926-1931 period, which included the Great Depression's first two years, Farnsworth's San Francisco Crocker partnership and then the 1929 Television Laboratories Corporation flourished on the invention side. According to Abramson, quoted by Godfrey, Farnsworth had "the only operating camera tubes in the world," and from January 1st, 1927, to July 22nd, 1931, he filed twenty-one different television system patent applications. The Television Laboratories Corporation's articles of incorporation stated that the company would "deal in discoveries, inventions, trade names, trademarks, labels, and brands...To apply for, obtain, hold, ...patents and patent rights in all countries of the world," operate the laboratory, experiment, "make discoveries and inventions of all kinds," and manufacture supplies for television and radio. However, the enterprise struggled to maintain funding, seeking agreements from all radio companies to license their patents for royalties and underwriters to invest in them. Meanwhile, Farnsworth's Laboratories and RCA's objectives entered a period of bitter conflict in the 1930s.

The Image Dissector method, unfortunately, is inherently inefficient, requiring sunlight or burning hot floodlights. This is because while one tiny spot of the electron image is at the receptor, all the light energy that went into the rest of the image is wasted. Farnsworth invented some improvements, including an electron multiplier in the receptor. Abramson wrote Farnsworth's most flattering footnote, noting that, besides being the first to demonstrate an all-electronic television system, "one of his greatest triumphs" was to patent in 1933 a non-image dissector tube. (That patent, 2,087,683, was misleadingly titled "image dissector.") This tube used charge storage and low-velocity electron scanning, as the patent reads: "by means of a pencil of cathode rays, as in the hypothetical systems described by Campbell-Swinton." Abramson wrote that while there is no proof Farnsworth ever built this tube, its ideas went into RCA's charge storage Iconoscope and Image Orthicon tubes, which made indoor television studios possible. Charge storage meant all the light energy, all the time, went into making a pattern of electric charge accumulate over a surface. An electron beam scanned the surface, produced an electrical signal according to the level of charge at successive spots. The beam also gently neutralized that charge to begin the next cycle of accumulation.

By the early 1940s, Image Dissectors were superseded by RCA-developed charge storage tubes, beginning with the clumsily shaped Iconoscope. It was not until 1946 that a "perfect" commercial camera tube called the Image Orthicon was created, achieved by RCA combining everything with extremely pure and controlled materials development, including thin semiconducting glass and microscopic metallic screens. The essential ideas were covered by Farnsworth's patents. However, RCA and its scientists, beginning with Zworykin, must be credited for perfecting the picture tubes and charge storage camera tubes that brought us the quality of television as we knew it before digital (as in smartphones and other cameras, introduced into broadcasting in 1984).

Until modern digital sensors, Image Dissectors, because of their sturdiness and high resolution, remained a camera of choice over other tubes for weather satellites, the Space Shuttle, and International Space Station, where the spacecraft's angle is controlled by star images. Farnsworth's related ideas behind image enhancers went into military night vision equipment and the color camera used to televise the Apollo moon landings, as well as the photomultiplier, which is the extremely sensitive light detector used widely in particle physics research. Late in life, he said that seeing the televised Apollo moon landing made all his work worthwhile.

Godfrey devotes a short chapter to "The Farnsworth Legacies" about Farnsworth's place as "father of television." The chapter surveys some views of writers cited in the bibliography at the end of this chapter. Examining the origin of major modern technologies and other forms of human creativity reveals different kinds of accomplishments achieved by various individuals and organizations. Disagreements among historians about priority of independent inventions aside, there are different meaningful forms of the question of "who is first?": Who dreamed first? Who imagined first? Who invented a theory that eventually became practical first? Who built the technology first? Who demonstrated it publicly or privately first? Who led a corporation that sold it to millions of people first? Godfrey interviewed and quoted the RCA historian and media pioneer M. Phyllis Smith, who said that she could accept that Farnsworth was first in system and experimental development for a while during the early years, but it was RCA that first developed the viable commercial operations, after it had settled its patent disputes with Farnsworth.

The story presented underscores the ongoing challenge of corporate dominance that can hinder the wider public from accessing the benefits of innovation, yet can also enable the use of innovation by the masses. In addition, the narrative highlights the outstanding individuals responsible for pioneering inventions. Philo Farnsworth, a visionary inventor and entrepreneur, sought advisors and investors to realize his ideas. He established a lab that employed talented specialists to work together towards a common goal, much like Thomas Edison and other great inventors before and after him. Similarly, notable inventors from the past like Charles P. Steinmetz and from today like Dean Kamen, who founded the Advanced Regenerative Manufacturing Institute (ARMI, https://www.

armiusa.org/), have left an indelible mark on history. Kamen, for example, earned millions by leasing his inventions to larger corporations. He is best known for creating the Segway after he invented the iBOT, an electric wheelchair that could climb stairs. He founded the FIRST robotics program to help high school students explore the world of science and technology.

Today, aspiring inventors and scientists have access to a wealth of resources, including traditional and online books, documentaries, Massive Open Online Courses (MOOC), community or school "maker" spaces (https://www. makerspaces.com/what-is-a makerspace/), and programs like the National Inventors Hall of Fame Youth programs. Scientists and technologists are especially active contributors to the internet, making complex software for AI, web servers, robotics, and simulation accessible to anyone with a computer and an internet connection. High schools offer pre-engineering programs like FIRST robotics (https://www.firstinspires.org/), enrichment opportunities like Math Circles (https://mathcircles. org/), and research participation programs with competitions and mentorship from scientists (https://jshs.org/).

The author's advice to aspiring inventors and scientists is to enjoy a life of curiosity, seek out mentors and information, and embrace the language of science and mathematics. Mathematics is a powerful tool for describing our experiences and helps us think more clearly. Since hard work and time are required to overcome new challenges, persistence is key.

Bibliography of Chapter 19

Abramson, Albert, *The History of Television, 1880-1941*. Jefferson NC:McFarland and Company, 1987. "Pioneers of Television --- Philo Taylor Farnsworth," *SMPTE Journal*, Nov. 1992, p 770-784, especially footnote 28. "Pioneers of Television — Vladimir Kosma Zworykin," *SMPTE Journal*, Jul. 1981, p 571-590.

Academy of Television Arts and Sciences, "Philo T. Farnsworth: Hall of Fame Tribute," https://www.emmys.com/news/hall-fame/philo-t-farnsworth-hall-fame-tribute. "Farnsworth Corporate Achievement Award" established in 2003 to honor "an agency, company or institution whose contributions over time have significantly impacted television technology and engineering," https://www.emmys.com/awards/engineering-emmys/winners#farnsworth. "The Interviews: An Oral History of Television, Talking about Philo T. Farnsworth," with Elma G. Farnsworth and others https://interviews.televisionacademy.com/people/philo-t-farnsworth.

Croft, Terrell, *Practical Electricity*. New York:McGraw Hill, 1917. https://archive.org/details/practicalelectr01crofgoog

Everson, George, *The Story of Television, The Life of Philo T. Farnsworth*. NY: W. W. Norton, 1949. Account of Farnsworth's longtime supporter, friend and business partner.

Farnsworth, Elma G., *Distant Vision; Romance & Discovery on an Invisible Frontier*. Salt Lake City:PemberlyKent, 1990. Memoir by Farnsworth's wife "Pem."

Farnsworth, Philo T., journal articles: Farnsworth and his associates published very few journal papers compared to RCA's scientists and engineers. "Television by Electron

Image Scanning," *Journal of the Franklin Institute*, Vol 218, Issue 4, October 1934, p 411-444. The physics of the Image Dissector is clearly detailed in a 1961 research memo from ITT Industrial Laboratories, Ft. Wayne, Indiana available at https://frank.pocnet.net/other/ITT/ITT_ImgDis.pdf. Philo T. Farnsworth, "Scanning with an electric pencil," *Television News*. NY:H. Gernsback, Mar.-Apr. 1931, p 48-51, 74. https://worldradiohistory.com/Archive-Television-News/Television-News-1931-Mar-Apr.pdf

Godfrey, Donald G., *Philo T. Farnsworth: The Father of Television*. Salt Lake City:University of Utah Press, 2001. This is probably our most scholarly and objective source. The "false dawn" subsection is p 130-134.

Haussler, William, "Television I: A $13,000,000 'If'," *Fortune Magazine*, April 1939 Vol 19 Issue 4 p 52-59, 168, 172, 174, 176, 178, 180, 182. "Television II: 'Fade In Camera One'," May 1939 Vol. 19 Issue 5, p 69-74, 154, 157-158, 160, 162, 164.

Kalan, Elliot, essay "(Tele)Visions of Tomorrow in section Enter the World of Tomorrow: To Futurama, and Beyond", *World's Fair, Biblion*. New York Public Library, archived 2020. https://wayback.archive-it.org/11788/20200108143911/http://exhibitions.nypl.org/biblion/worldsfair/enter-world-tomorrow-futurama-and-beyond/essay/essay-kalan-television

Kemper, Steve, *Code name Ginger: the story behind Segway and Dean Kamen's quest to invent a new world*. Boston: Harvard Business School Press, 2003. Kamen's company website http://www.dekaresearch.com/

Krull, Kathleen, *The boy who invented TV: the story of Philo Farnsworth*. Alfred A. Knopf, 2009. Nicely illustrated children's book.

Donald K. Lipponcott et. al., Brief on Behalf of Philo T. Farnsworth, US Patent Office, Philo T. Farnsworth vs. Vladimir K. Zworykin, Interference No. 64,027, about Farnsworth's and Tolman's testimony, also "Television Ruling Won by Farnsworth" clipping from Examiner, 5/24/38. Arizona State University Library Special Collections, Philo T. Farnsworth and George Everson Papers, MS SC FA, Box 6, folder 2. Lippincott was Farnsworth's long time engineering trained patent attorney and friend who wrote and defended most of his patents.

New York Times, "Gain in Television Laid to Patenting," 4:5, Jan. 20, 1939.

Roberts, Russell, *Philo T. Farnsworth: The Life of Television's Forgotten Inventor*. Bear Delaware: Mitchell Lane, 2004, in juvenile series "Unlocking the secrets of science." This is one of several other juvenile biographies.

Savenick, Phil, web publication on Farnsworth, 2006 https://www.thehistoryoftv.com/ . The Television Academy presents Savenick's work: https://www.emmys.com/news/online-originals/shooting-moon. Writer and producer of "Farnsworth, Jessica, *PHILO FARNSWORTH: the most famous man you never heard of*" narrated by Farnsworth's great granddaughter, 2013, https://www.youtube.com/watch?v=HHy04aN0jfI. See also Youtube search for Philo Farnsworth.

Schatzkin, Paul, *The Boy Who Invented Television: A Story of Inspiration, Persistence and Quiet Passion*. Silver Spring, MD:TeamCom Books, 2002. This rich, personal history results from 25 years of research, interviews, friendship and advocacy with Farnsworth family members and associates, including George Everson. https://farnovision.com

Schwartz, Evan I., *The Last Lone Inventor: A Tale of Genius, Deceit, and the Birth of Television*. NY: Harper Collins, 2002.

Stashower, Daniel, *The Boy Genius and the Mogul*. NY: Broadway Books, Random House, 2002. Emphasizes Farnsworth's personal difficulties.

Tolman, Justin, Letter to Mr. and Mrs. Farnsworth, September 5, 1940 with 4 page typescript "The Cradle of Television" written for a University of Utah publication, apparently unpublished. Tolman describes his interactions with Farnsworth. Special Collections, J. Willard Marriott Library, The University of Utah Collection Philo T. and Elma G. Farnsworth papers, 1924-1992, Collection MS 0648, Box 3, Folder 2. https://archiveswest.orbiscascade.org/ark:/80444/xv98312#dscID

Udelson, Joseph H., *The Great Television Race*. University Alabama: University of Alabama Press, 1982. Surveys technology over a long period of history.

Waldrop, Frank C. and Borkin, Joseph, *Television, A Struggle for Power*. NY: William Morrow, 1938. Introduction by George Henry Payne, member of the Federal Communications Commission. This contemporary account covers RCA's radio monopoly and epitomizes our continuing corporate use and abuse of the patent system. Its quotations include Farnsworth's and Zworykin's testimonies at the 1935 patent interference, and Philco's 1936 suit claiming RCA "radio men took the Philco girls" and "did provide ... expensive and lavish entertainment ... liquors ... compromising situations ... to bribe ... to furnish ... confidential information." This book relates the evolution of patenting and inventions simple enough for anyone to build to become so complex that inventive insight is just the beginning of an expensive investor funded development project. The dissolution of RCA's radio trust in 1932 (p199-209) is described and then related to this patent interference (p210-215). There, fragments of Farnsworth's and Zworykin's testimonies about their youthful accomplishments are compared.

CHAPTER 20

Brooklyn, New York:
Glimpses of a Hometown

I was born shortly before the Second World War in a Jewish hospital in the Bedford-Stuyvesant section of Brooklyn, New York. Though destined to become the nation's second largest black ghetto (behind Harlem), there remained numerous Irish, Germans, and Jews still clinging to bourgeois respectability. Solidity emanated from the architecture itself: block after block of sturdy brownstones, and enough Victorian Gothic churches to confirm the old image of Brooklyn as a city of churches. My first childhood home, 260 Stuyvesant Avenue, was a brownstone. Brownstone neighborhoods still move me, I assume, because I absorbed the ambience of those early years. I recall strolling with my parents on bright Sunday mornings, examining the wrought iron ornamentation and observing the church-goers. To my horror, many of them were powdered matrons decked out in ghastly fox pelts (with the heads still attached).

My father's business was a grocery on the corner of Gates Avenue and Stuyvesant. Gates Avenue was already somewhat blighted when I first came to know it. Its sidewalks were in disrepair and its roadways consisted of antiquated cobblestone or, more accurately, Belgian brick. Yet it had an

*element of romance too, a trolley car line that ran the length
of the borough from Ridgewood to Borough Hall. My aunts
sometimes took me on that line to accompany them while
they shopped at Abraham and Strauss and other downtown
emporia. I loathed the shopping part, but the trip was more
than tolerable because I got to ride the trolley. Objectively
trolleys were slow-moving at best. They easily got caught up
in traffic, particularly if they became detached from their
overhead wires. Their bench seats were definitely tough on
posteriors. Passengers also faced the danger of auto traffic as
they boarded or exited the trolleys. Even worse was the danger
to kids when they tried to steal a ride on the rear outdoor
metalwork. Trolleys nevertheless had their distinctive charm,
and Brooklyn lost some of its own when this form of transit
was replaced by buses in the early 1950s.*

*The Gates Avenue grocery supported not only my
immediate family but my grandmother, my two aunts, and
my uncle. They lived above the premises so that a visit to the
store was a family occasion. I was there often as a young
child since we lived within easy walking distance. Because of
its mostly southern black clientele, Spear's could have been an
establishment in Decatur, Georgia or most other Dixie towns.
There were barrels of yams, hominy grits, rice and beans and,
in the meat department, ham hocks, fat back, pigs' knuckles,
hogshead cheese, and other "soul" food that, it was made clear,
was off limits to Jewish folk, even if they ate bacon. Beer also
sold briskly, with Rheingold outselling products of other local
breweries. The Rheingold Company advertised a great deal,
but even my little kid's mind could grasp the incongruity
of the posters of the Miss Rheingold contestants in a setting
where, besides our family, they constituted the only white
faces much of the time. Incidentally, white faces occasionally
included a red-faced cop who secluded himself in the back
room to imbibe a refreshment forbidden to him while on duty.*

I became accustomed to black faces of all hues and shapes but never achieved fluency in the English spoken by recent migrants from the South. Years later, as an adolescent working in the store during school breaks, I would sometimes stare blankly in response to a customer's requests, until extricated from this embarrassment by my father's or grandmother's interpretation assistance.

Physically Albina, my grandma, was much like other immigrant women of her generation. She was under five feet tall, tiny except for her conspicuously large feet. A widow since before my birth, she spoke heavily-accented English, wore her long, still mostly dark hair in a turn-of-the-century bun, and drank tea from a glass, Eastern European style. Though not much of a homebody – her life was the store – she did make delicious Jewish potato pancakes (latkes).

It was as a businesswoman that Grandma showed her mettle, gossiping politely with customers, never forgetting a name, eschewing the adding machine to calculate sums rapidly on the side of a brown paper bag. When provoked she could retaliate aggressively, for example, using her broom to disperse teenage delinquents creating havoc on the front stoop.

Grandma was part of the tough generation that had survived the rude "world of our fathers." Like many others, she had left her parents in Europe, never to see them again (unfortunately they lived long enough to die in the Holocaust). After working briefly as a domestic, she married my grandfather, a sweet, intelligent man but a dreamer with little aptitude for business. It was up to her to hold things together, and this she accomplished even during the brutal years of the Great Depression.

By the late thirties, however, my father was the heart and soul of the family business. He worked at least twelve hours a day, six days a week, and sometimes even three hours on

Sunday mornings. Yet he and I managed to spend a bit of time together, perhaps at a neighborhood playground, the Prospect Park Zoo, or viewing a "Tarzan" or Walt Disney movie. I especially loved our excursions on the Myrtle or Lexington Avenue elevated lines (Brooklyn's Lexington Avenue line), ancient structures that swayed with the rumble of the trains and provided a peeping Tom's perspective into the lives of people unlucky enough to live along their noisy routes.[1]

◆

As should be apparent from the preceding reminiscences, post-World War I Brooklyn had a host of recent immigrants (and their offspring) seeking a better life. Still, the borough also had many reminders of a modern American city. These included department stores, lavish theaters, reasonably tall office buildings, luxurious hotels, belts of industry and commerce, its own newspaper (the *Brooklyn Eagle*), a great park and zoo (Prospect Park), the Botanic Gardens, the Brooklyn Museum, numerous public libraries, a huge and stately cemetery (Greenwood), Coney Island, Brighton Beach, a major league baseball team (the Dodgers) and, as noted above, thousands of well-preserved brownstones. The overwhelmingly (non-Chinese population) ate out at "the Chinks" and various other restaurants and had their clothes laundered and pressed at dry cleaners (and at incredibly inexpensive Chinese laundries). Brooklyn even had its own holiday, called Brooklyn Day or sometimes Anniversary Day. Few people knew anything about its origins, especially not school children who nonetheless loved the respite it provided from their un-airconditioned classrooms in June.[2]

The part of the seventeenth century Dutch colony of New Amsterdam, across the East River and into southwestern Long Island, received the name Breukelen. Its namesake was a small town in the Netherlands not far from Amsterdam. The near future would bring an English conquest and eventually an anglicized name. Population growth was slow into the nineteenth century, but by 1834 the community had merited the status of a city. In fact, by the 1890s, Brooklyn had become the third largest city in the United States (second only to New York and Chicago). In the process of growth, the city had absorbed all the various towns, villages, and farmland that constituted King's County. But then, in 1898, something happened that was perceived by many residents as a reversal of fortunes. Brooklyn's city fathers joined those of Manhattan, Queens, the Bronx, and Staten Island in creating the New York City of the five boroughs.

By the late 1930s, Brooklyn clearly had become an entity of neighborhoods, most of them dominated by one or more ethnic groups. At times, however, there would be significant population shifts. As noted above, for instance, the predominantly Irish, German, and Jewish character of Bedford-Stuyvesant was being transformed into an African American enclave, for reasons that were not difficult to discern.

The southern edge of Bed-Stuy had two parallel, and unsightly, modes of transit: the Fulton Street El and the Long Island Railroad's Atlantic Avenue line. In this, the least desirable part of the neighborhood, the number of blacks began to grow, having been attracted by low housing costs and, perhaps even more so, by landlords willing to rent to them. And, just as Jews from Manhattan's Lower East Side tenements were drawn to Brooklyn's Williamsburg section in part by the convenience of the Broadway line, so in the late thirties blacks in Harlem could take the new IND subway line all the way to Bed-Stuy (the old Fulton Street El was torn down). This new connection inspired the Duke Ellington jazz number *Take the A Train*. [3]

Many other Brooklyn ethnic neighborhoods were also highly identifiable. For example, Scandinavians had settled in Sunset Park and Bay Ridge, drawn by nearness to the port of Brooklyn and the seafaring and ship-building jobs it stimulated.

The names of local institutions were often indicative of their Scandinavian origins: the Norwegian Hospital, the Lutheran Hospital, *Imatra* (a Finnish social and benevolent society), and more.

Red Hook was a tough, predominantly Irish working-class district, its nicer parts later renamed Cobble Hill and Carroll Gardens by real estate companies. The notorious Al Capone lived there as a youth and, in fact, that is where "Scarface" acquired his appropriate nickname. The Greenpoint section had four dominant ethnicities: Irish, Italian, Polish, and Ukrainian, while neighboring Williamsburg was a mixture of Orthodox and Hasidic Jews, Neapolitan and Sicilian Italians, and Poles and Ukrainians. Near the Brooklyn-Queens border, Bushwick was mostly German. Bushwick Avenue, the main street, featured numerous breweries and *Hausfraus* often seen sweeping the sidewalks and gutters in front of their homes.

Jews constituted over one-third of all foreign-born people moving to Brooklyn in the twentieth century. Many of them settled in Brownsville, although the more adventurous ones chose homes in Crown Heights, Flatbush, Borough Park, and Brighton Beach. Still, Brownsville was ninety-five percent Jewish, and Pitkin Avenue was its "main drag." It had the restaurants, cafeterias, clothing shops of every description, and the Loew's Pitkin Movie Theater. Brownsville was also home to Hymie Schorenstein, one of the most colorful, and powerful, of the borough's Democratic Party leadership. One of his achievements was convincing a lot of Jews to forsake Socialism for the Democrats. A more nefarious character with headquarters in Brownsville was Louis "Lepke" Buchalter, a leader of one of America's most brutal gangs. He and his cohorts specialized in industrial and labor racketeering and ran "Murder Incorporated," a nationwide elimination service that did away with persons the "Mob" identified as troublemakers.[5]

In the thirties Jews and Italians found themselves living in two adjacent sections of what local historians call "the new Brooklyn," which was mostly in the southern part of the borough. Not that they lived together. Jews were mostly in East Flatbush, Italians in Canarsie, with the Long Island Railroad's tracks a virtual border. Although there was a bit of truth to the assertion that Jews and Italians "looked alike," the two neighborhoods did not. East Flatbush consisted of mainly brick or stucco row houses, while Canarsie had a more agrarian flavor, sometimes with homes bordered by rows of vegetable gardens.[6]

Ethnic comity in pre-World War Brooklyn existed but was not always the case. British scholar Julius Stewart, for his part, reminds us that black migrants to Bedford-Stuyvesant and the Hasidic Jews moving into nearby Williamsburg had nothing to do with each other. Perhaps more startling was the enmity in Williamsburg itself between the Hasids and the so-called Modern Orthodox Jews.[7]

Brooklyn-born historian Elliot Willensky was more blunt:

The idea that the people in this melting pot lived happily with one another in a pastel fairy land was hardly borne out by the bloody noses of kids who voyaged into somebody else's turf, or by walls chalked with ethnic slurs ... For every Abie's Irish Rose you could name, there were at least two houses that were in mourning for sons and daughters who had married out of the faith ...."[8]

Like Manhattan and the Bronx, Brooklyn was a noisy place. The noise emanated from numerous sources: els, police cars, ambulances, fire engines, pneumatic drills and, in winter, from the early morning sound of a coal truck unloading its cargo down a metal chute into a cellar bin.

Early morning and into the day brought less annoying sounds. The milkman and his horse delivered bottles of milk (with toppings of heavy cream). Other horse-drawn vehicles unloaded baked products, freshly laundered diapers, fruits and vegetables, seltzer, and cakes of ice for the still common ice boxes. These services saved housewives countless trips to regular stores. But going shopping was sometimes a pleasurable experience. The chain of Ebinger's German Bakery was a case in point, as many of its former customers later testified:

Throughout the Bedford and Snyder Avenue area, the aromas from Ebinger's Baking plant filled the air. It supplied all the Ebinger bakeries in Brooklyn. My favorites were Othellos: little mounds of buttercream smothered with chocolate …

Ebinger's goods were so nicely presented, with extreme cleanliness and fine taste. By two o'clock in the afternoon the Eighteenth Avenue store would not have anything to sell …

Every Saturday morning, I'd walk down King's Highway and try the Ebinger's near Coney Island Avenue. If it was too crowded or out of what I wanted, I'd go to the Ebinger's on East Seventeenth Street. From there, to the one on Avenue M and then on to the one on Avenue J. If need be, I'd go to all four in order to get the "blackout" cake ….[9]

Getting back briefly to Brooklyn's housing, its variety rivaled that found at Ebinger's. There were a lot of slums but, at the same time, surviving mansions and what might be termed upper middle class apartment buildings. Prospect Park West, Ocean Avenue, and Eastern Parkway featured many of them, and they were mostly populated even during the worst years of the Depression.[10]

Brooklyn produced not only a huge variety of mouth-watering foods but a veritable brigade of successful show business personalities. A partial list includes the following: Leonard Bernstein, Jackie Gleason, George Gershwin, Mickey Rooney, Lena Horne, Moss Hart, Danny Kaye, Buddy Hackett, Woody Allen, Mel Brooks, Mary Tyler Moore, Shelley Winters, Sam Levinson, Phil Silvers, Mae West, Barbara Stanwyck, and Barbra Streisand.

Brooklyn was also fertile soil for literary figures, whether native born or domiciled there. The former included Henry

Roth, Irving Shulman, Norman Podhoretz, Irwin Shaw, Alfred Kazin, and Arthur Miller. Among the outsiders were Carson McCullers, W. H. Auden, Thomas Wolfe, Richard Wright, and Marianne Moore.[11]

The founding of Brooklyn College also enhanced the borough's intellectual life. It had a modest start in the 1920s – in Manhattan – as part of City College's extension program, before moving in 1930 to rented quarters in downtown Brooklyn. Federal funds made available in 1935 allowed ground to be broken for a forty-three-acre campus on a former golf course in Midwood. The third city-owned college, it was the first one to be co-educational (City College was all male, Hunter all female).

On October 28, 1936 President Roosevelt arrived at the site to help lay the cornerstone for the projected gymnasium that ultimately was named after him. This was part of his campaign for a second term, and Brooklyn was home to a lot of registered Democrats. The new campus emerged over time. It consisted of what were supposed to be Georgian-style buildings patterned after those at Harvard (though the resemblance was far from perfect). [12]

Brooklyn College may not have been a totally mature institution, but by the late thirties it had already acquired a recognizable image. Many of its students adopted a distinctive left-wing outlook, which motivated conservatives to adopt the following nickname for the school: *The Little Red Schoolhouse*. Faculty were also suspect. For example, the House Un-American Activities Committee subpoenaed three professors to testify about radical activities and Communist propaganda on campus. One of these events, on March 24, 1938, was what participants termed an "Anti-fascist Peace Demonstration." Many students also demonstrated in support of the Czechs during the Munich Conference in September of that year.[13]

Irwin Shaw, author of the highly successful novel *The Young Lions*, later summed up the impact of his *alma mater*, while derogating his hometown. Brooklyn College, he wrote, was "a wonderful school … It was free and it taught me all I needed to know to get out of Brooklyn."[14]

But James Agee, a native of Knoxville, Tennessee – a brilliant novelist, journalist, and film and television writer – took a far more positive view of his sometime residence. These sentiments would have appeared in *Fortune* magazine, except that its editor found them "too strong to print." The piece, including this excerpt, later appeared posthumously in a small book edited by Jonathan Lethem, a novelist born and raised in Brooklyn:

A few American cities, Manhattan chief among them, have some mad magnetic energy which sucks all others into "provincialism;" and Brooklyn of all great cities is nearest the magnet and is indeed "provincial." It is provincial as a land of rich earth and of this earth is an enormous farm, whose crop is far less "industrial" or "financial" or "notable" or in any way "distinguished" or "definable" than it is of human flesh and being. And this fact alone, which of itself makes Brooklyn so featureless, so little known, to many so laughable … that two million human beings are alive and living there, invest the city in an extraordinarily high, piteous and invaluable dignity, well beyond a touch of laughter, defense, or need of notice ….[15]

Notes: Chapter 20

1 Sheldon Spear, *Growing Up Shy in Brooklyn*. Wilkes-Barre, PA.: Jemags & Co., 1982, 1-7.

2 Elliot Willensky, *When Brooklyn was the World. 1920-1957.* New York: Harmony Books, 1986, 24-25, 27-28, 32. Brooklyn Day marked the creation in 1829 of the Brooklyn Sunday School Union, a Protestant religious organization.

3 *Ibid.*, This ghetto steadily extended northward until one day it would surpass Harlem in its African American population. The Crown Heights section also had an earlier, smaller black population. During the worst days of the Depression, a so-called "slave market" developed near the Bedford Avenue-Eastern Parkway intersection where well-off whites drove by to hire black female domestic help at rates of 20-35 cents an hour.

4 *Ibid.*, 58-64.

5 *Ibid.*, 104, 107, 165-166.

6 *Ibid.*, 101-102.

7 Jules Stewart, *Gotham Rising. New York in the 1930s.* London, New York: I. B. Taurus, 2016, 225.

8 Willensky, *op. cit.*, 103-104.

9 Quoted in Myrna Katz Frommer and Harvey Frommer, *It Happened in Brooklyn*. New York, San Diego, London: Harcourt Brace and Company, 1993, 92-93.

10 Willensky, *op. cit.*, "Hoovervilles" were also to be seen.

11 *Ibid.*, 21.

12 *Ibid.*, 126-127.

13 *NYT*, Mar. 25, 1938, 7; Apr. 16, 1938, 4; Sept. 24, 1938, 3.

14 Quoted in Willensky, *op. cit.*, 139.

15 James Agee, *Brooklyn Is. Southeast of the Island: Travel Notes.* Preface by Jonathan Lethem: Fordham University Press, 2005, 5-6.

ABOUT THE AUTHOR

A native of Brooklyn, New York, Sheldon Spear earned a BA in political science from Brooklyn College, an MA in history from Syracuse University, and a PhD in history from New York University. Now retired, he taught history at the college level for more than thirty-five years. Spear is the author of journal articles on a variety of subjects. His full-length works include studies of northeastern Pennsylvania, of Pennsylvania from 1750 to 1950, and a biography of prominent Pennsylvania congressman Daniel J. Flood. He has also written numerous guest columns for the *Wilkes-Barre Citizens Voice*, lectured frequently to community gatherings, and entertained listeners on local radio.

Spear's awards include the New York Regents College Scholarship and National Endowment for the Humanities grants on Russian Literature and Society (at the University of Illinois) and on New World Slavery (at Johns Hopkins University).

New Yorkers by birth, Sheldon and his wife Marsha have resided in northeastern Pennsylvania for the last fifty-five years. They are the parents of Jennifer, Geoffrey, and Eric and the grandparents of Erin, Paige, Zoe, Cora, Miriam, and Ruth.

Printed in the United States
by Baker & Taylor Publisher Services